This Moment on Earth

John Kerry
Teresa Heinz Kerry

THIS MOMENT ON EARTH

TODAY'S NEW ENVIRONMENTALISTS
AND THEIR VISION FOR THE FUTURE

PublicAffairs

NEW YORK

The text is printed on ancient forest friendly Enviro Edition 100 55# cream white smooth vellum. The paper is made of 100 percent postconsumer recycled content, was processed chlorine free, and has been certified by the Forest Stewardship Council, Environmental Choice Ecologo, and Biogas.

TEXT DESIGN AND COMPOSITION BY JENNY DOSSIN. TEXT SET IN ITC NEW BASKERVILLE.

Cataloging-in-Publication data is available from the Library of Congress.
ISBN–13: 978–1–58648–431–6
ISBN–10: 1–58648–431–1

FIRST EDITION
10 9 8 7 6 5 4 3 2 1

In memory of my mother, who first taught me to cherish the Earth.
For Teresa's and my children, and future generations.

JK

To my grandchild and all the grandchildren in the world,
with a heart full of resolute hope.

THK

CONTENTS

INTRODUCTION

We were inspired to write this book during the 2004 presidential campaign. In community after community, state after state, we encountered Americans who were concerned about the environment and hopeful that together we could reverse our downward course. This book is a reflection of that grassroots enthusiasm as well as our own long-term commitment to these issues.

When we first started our research for the book, the environmental movement was reeling. A lot of pundits in Washington were writing the movement off, even going so far as to declare it dead. The science of global climate change, though already certain, was under attack, and Al Gore's *An Inconvenient Truth* had not yet been released. But since then, thankfully, there has been a significant awakening. *An Inconvenient Truth,* a brilliant book and film, has reached people globally, expanding the sense of urgency about climate change and significantly moving the debate forward. Former Vice President Gore deserves all of the credit he has received for his most recent contribution in a life of public service.

In this book we reconfirm the urgent threat of global climate change, while celebrating the efforts of citizens across the nation who are taking steps to combat this problem and elude catastrophe. We also examine other environmental challenges, such as toxins in the environment, environmental justice, the health of our waterways, and energy policy: issues that are attracting a new breed of activists to the grassroots movement for change. In describing the scale of the danger, we hope this book reveals the breadth of opportunity for those whose innovation and creativity can rise to meet the threat. Exciting new market opportunities are staring us in the face. There is enormous potential for us to create jobs, enhance security, improve the health of all Americans, and even make money, if only we seize the moment.

We explore the reasons for the heightened crisis as well as the ways we believe Americans can and must respond, both as individuals and as a nation. The past 150 years of industrial progress have stretched the capacity of human beings and the planet beyond anything our great-great-grandparents could have imagined. We have harnessed natural resources in positive ways—not just to feed, clothe, and house rapidly growing populations, but to increase the length and quality of life for hundreds of millions of people. But there's also no question that the careless exploitation of these same resources has begun to threaten the very foundations of life. Science and technology brought about tremendous progress, making our modern society possible; but now, science and technology can enable us to accurately measure the unintended downside to that progress as well as to assess the threats that environmental problems pose to the quality of life that we often take for granted.

We devote considerable space in this book to a sober narration of those measurements, their implications, and their management. After all, the contemporary American debate over the environment has become so politicized that the basic facts have often been lost in the noise of partisan and ideological conflict, particularly over the past six years. But aside from presenting the facts, this book has one principal objective. Langston Hughes wrote a famous poem in which he talked of the need to "make America America again." Though he was writing more than half a century ago, his poem still challenges us to live up to our values. The people you will encounter in this book seek to restore a very traditional sense of responsibility for environmental stewardship to our way of life today. The status quo poses enormous dangers to the Earth, to our lives and the lives of our fellow citizens, and most of all, to our children and grandchildren. This book will introduce you to Americans with innovative, pioneering spirits who are already discovering solutions for our environmental problems.

Why is their work so important? Because they are proving we don't have to sit quietly by while doomsday environmental scenarios play out. Their initiative is living testimony that no one has to surrender to pessimism or scare tactics. They tell us that instead of empty slogans and long laundry lists of bite-sized ideas tinkering at the edges of outdated debates, we can embark on a revolution that will put our future back into our own hands. All of this—a whole world of opportunity—is possible if we face facts, innovate, adapt, and lead, just as Americans have again and again in moments of great challenge.

No one is saying that it will be easy. Change will not come overnight. One big obstacle to mobilizing Americans to meet this challenge is that so much of the modern conservative movement, and so much of the leadership of today's Republican Party, have chosen to make any and every environmental cause "enemy territory." Given the rich environmentalist tradition in the GOP, from Teddy Roosevelt to Richard Nixon (who signed the Clean Air Act and the Clean Water Act), this sea change has been very damaging, especially when echoed in a right-wing political culture that has demonized every conceivable environmental proposal. The decline of bipartisan support for environmental issues has also stemmed from broader attacks on environmentalism as a special-interest cause: as elitist, alarmist, antigrowth, impractical, overwhelmingly white, costly, and irrationally uncompromising.

In truth, environmentalism isn't dead, it's just being reborn—the very idea of what it means to be an "environmentalist" is being revolutionized. People from all walks of life, without concern for party or ideological lines, are coming together in unprecedented numbers across the globe. They are doing so with greater urgency and on a bigger scale than ever before. There is an acceleration of grassroots energy driven by a new shared acknowledgment—we are running out of time on a host of issues. People not only see a potential tipping point on global climate change, they also fear tipping points elsewhere—in air pollution, deforestation, fisheries depletion, and ocean pollution to mention a few. Not only has this awakened a new cross-cultural, cross-generational level of activism, it has attracted a record amount of investment—hundreds of millions of dollars—and major corporate leaders who are committed to a new course.

The new environmentalist knows that caring about the environment can no longer be mislabeled as caring *less* about national security, the economy, health care, family, education, profit, or community. Rather, the leaders of today's new environmental movement understand these issues are all connected: that the damage we are doing to our environment injures everything important to us as well as each of us individually. "The environment" is no longer to be dismissed as some sort of nonhuman world of snail darters and lab rats and abstract measurements of our water or atmospheric quality. It is much, much more—it is what we put into our bodies, and it is what we put into the very things that make our lives possible.

This new environmentalism is a cause in which Washington is but one part of the solution. Progress can only occur through partnerships between and among states, local governments, communities, and businesses, and most importantly, it can only occur with the leadership of visionary and gutsy individuals.

Above all, we want this book to expose the false choices—the straw men—put forward to purposefully slow or reverse progress in environmentalism and politicize the debate. Today, many Americans who care about the environment don't think of themselves as environmentalists simply because a lot of money has been spent by the other side to brand the word as a negative and define them as "unrealistic extremists," zealots who put narrow interests above common sense. No more: The new environmentalists are farmers, ranchers, mothers, fathers, evangelical Christians, and bottom-line businesspeople, all of whom are unrestricted by party label. In fact, the premise that addressing environmental challenges is "liberal," whereas denying those challenges is "conservative," is refuted by the whole history of the conservation movement, by the growing ranks of conservative religious leaders demanding an agenda of "creation care," and by traditional green activists who are adopting increasingly business-friendly and politically practical choices.

The idea that America must choose between environmental progress and economic growth is refuted by the "green innovations" already on display by entrepreneurial pioneers and reflected in the vast new markets developing for clean energy technologies. For example, in 2006, the founder and chairman of Dell computers, Michael Dell, a Republican, explained to *Time* magazine that he was encouraging every one of Dell's customers to pay a little more for their purchases so the surplus could be spent planting trees to create what some would call a "carbon neutral" transaction. Michael Dell cited the importance to him of his company's Greenpeace ranking—he saw it as a business asset as well as a moral choice. When asked whether he saw himself as an environmentalist, his answer was telling: "I don't like to consider myself very often. . . . But I do have a lot of trees."

When the founder of a highly successful company suggests he will build the company's customer base by offering them the chance to pay the equivalent of a voluntary tax, to be devoted to a positive environmental contribution, it's clear that a substantial change of attitude has taken place in a few short years. Dell is not alone. In January 2007, the *New York Times* reported that ten major companies had banded together with environmental groups to form the United States Climate Action Partnership, an alliance that plans to call for firm nationwide limits on carbon dioxide emissions. The companies include some household names—Alcoa, BP, Caterpillar, Duke Energy, DuPont, FPL Group, General Electric, Lehman Brothers, PG&E, PNM Resources—and are based all over the country, in Florida, New Mexico, California, North Carolina, and beyond.

Our book also refutes the myth that something in the American character makes a response to these challenges impossible. The idea that Americans aren't willing to embrace change is just plain wrong. Throughout our history, Americans have always demonstrated an enormous sense of moral obligation. America's standing as the most religiously observant advanced democracy means that our citizens acknowledge priorities reaching beyond the current generation. We readily accept responsibilities transcending the interests of any one individual, family, community, or nation. The current interest that evangelical Protestants have shown in taking action on global climate change is just one example of this persistent sense of responsibility.

And America's well-earned status as the world's great laboratory of individual initiative and innovation makes this country the best hope for the civic and technological breakthroughs necessary to turn problems into profits. We hope that, if nothing else, the readers of this book will learn this: Environmental problems now perceived as "lose-lose" or "win-lose" propositions can be "win-win." But for that to happen, we will have to call upon some of the strengths we have shown in the past in America: our sense of responsibility, our openness to innovation, and our determination to succeed. With these strengths, we can create the kind of solutions our country has produced before as we faced challenges ranging from the rise of industrialization to the Great Depression, from the Manhattan Project to the Apollo Project.

As it happens, the whole history, past and present, of American environmental progress has largely been inspired by pioneers who didn't think of themselves as "environmentalists," who never spent much time in Washington, and who rarely imagined that they were advancing any ideology other than commonsense realism. Most of this book is organized to emphasize the stories of these pioneers, from historical giants who framed the movement, like Rachel Carson, to people most Americans have never heard of, like Helen Reddout and Janine Fitzgerald. They are joined by better-known activists, people like Denis Hayes, Amory Lovins, Deirdre Imus, and Robert Kennedy, Jr., as well as scientists like Dr. John Holdren and Dr. Daniel Fagre.

On every issue addressed in this book, our purpose is to inform, warn, and inspire. We do so with the conviction that once we are put to the task, there is nothing American ingenuity cannot accomplish. If we have any bias, it's against the sort of top-down reliance on Washington that has characterized environmentalism in the past. True, national leadership remains critical, as evidenced by the losses incurred during the current administration, which has intentionally built numerous barriers to environmental progress. But it's also increasingly apparent that bottom-up, citizen-based environmentalism, backed up by laws with teeth, is, in the long run, the most effective approach.

One of the central challenges we faced in writing this book was how to accurately describe the predicament human beings have created, while still conveying our bedrock faith in the possibility of change. Some of the environmental problems now facing our planet seem so dire and extreme that it would be easy for people to just throw up their hands in despair or to deny those problems entirely— as some have. But we choose to believe in the art of the possible. We are convinced that in these challenges there are great opportunities, despite the severity of the crisis. Knowledge is power. Armed with the facts, Americans have all the opportunity in the world to act. There are many reasons to be hopeful as our society confronts the environmental realities of our time. Those realities may be complicated and

difficult to change, butwith individual and collective action—yours included—they are ours to meet and master.

In the end, we intend this to be a rigorously "reality-based" account
of the environmental challenge, and above all, a realistic account of
what Americans, from a mother on Cape Cod to our leaders in Washington, can do to make this moment, this hour of Earth's history, a testament to the human race's ability to preserve and nourish Creation.

After you have read this book, if you want to join the activists making a difference in their communities, please join the campaign at
www.thismomentonearth.com.

CHAPTER ONE

The Art of the Possible

The people you will meet in this book do not all know each other. They did not meet on an environmental Web site. They do not necessarily buy organic vegetables or fair trade coffee. They are not even all members of the same political party. In fact, many of them do not consider themselves part of a "movement," or, for that matter, even want to be called "environmentalists." They are down to earth pragmatic people who have set out to solve a problem, often in the face of great opposition from vested interests, and largely unsupported by government. But the odds have not deterred them.

What they have in common is that the changes they have brought about all began as spirited, individual crusades backed by nothing more than a sense that they were doing the right thing. It was right to want to stop a neighborhood from being turned into a toxic dump; it was right to want the fish in the river to be healthy and free from open sores; it was right to want to halt short-term drilling for gas that would ruin an otherwise pristine forest; it was right to insist that there is no law of nature requiring that we surround ourselves with toxic chemicals. Then, having arrived at that decision, they each found others to band with locally, determined the best course of action and stirred up their neighbors and friends, knowing that one of the privileges of living in a democracy is that if enough people want to change the way things are done, change is bound to happen.

Driven by concern for their surroundings, they have set an example for the rest of us. Their stories show us change pursued brilliantly and bravely, and their endeavors—and the many other examples of individual and collective action taking place across the country—represent the potential for a sea change in our national philosophy. "Politics," it was said by the Prussian statesman Carl von Bismarck, "is the art of the possible." These individuals, like so many other people we have met throughout our lives—particularly in our work to protect America's natural resources—have embraced the art of the possible. Together they expand our sense of what can be accomplished, providing tangible hope that real achievements are within our reach. If the journey of a thousand miles begins with a single step, then the men and women described here have shown us how to take the first steps in the thousand-mile journey to achieve a healthy, sustainable planet for our families and for our future.

One person in modern times who embodied the art of the possible, perhaps more than anyone else, we were unfortunately not able to meet. She grew up in a small town just outside Pittsburgh, Pennsylvania, along the shores of the Allegheny River. Having inherited a love of nature from her mother, she studied biology and later worked writing radio ads for the U.S. Bureau of Fisheries. Those who knew her often spoke of her shyness and quiet reserve. But she exhibited a stubborn perseverance that showed generations of Americans what was possible, achieving things that literally seemed beyond the capacity of any one individual.

That person was Rachel Carson.

.   .   .

In the summer of 1957, Rachel Carson received a letter from a friend on Cape Cod—a letter that would come to alter the course of American social history. Carson had once worked for the U.S. Fish and Wildlife Service in Washington, D.C., and her friend Olga Owens Huckins was writing to ask for her help. Huckins had recently observed an airplane flying over her property that was spraying a chemical to control mosquitoes in the nearby woods. The following day, she came outside to find songbirds, grasshoppers, and other insects dead on her lawn. She contacted state officials, and they assured her that the chemical being sprayed—a pesticide called DDT—was harmless. Reluctant to accept what appeared to be, at best, faulty information, and at worst, utter deceit, she contacted Carson to inquire if she knew of anyone in Washington who could help prevent future sprayings.

This was a topic in which Carson had great interest. She had written two popular books about nature and the environment, and thirteen years earlier had proposed an article to *Reader's Digest* exploring the biological and ecological hazards posed by DDT, which, at the time, was just coming into wide commercial use. The magazine had rejected the idea, and Carson had put her research aside, though not her concern. After receiving her friend's letter, she again tried to interest the magazine, but once again, the editors turned her down. Unwilling—or perhaps unable—to let the issue die, Carson decided to write a book. With that began one of the iconic successes of the environmental movement, as Rachel Carson, through her own strength and perseverance, set about transforming the nation's awareness of the perils of DDT.

DDT, short for dichlorodiphenyltrichloroethane, was developed as the first modern pesticide in 1939. During World War II, Allied troops used it with great effect in the South Pacific islands to eradicate insects that were known to cause malaria and other diseases, and also to protect soldiers against lice. It was cheap to produce and quickly came to be considered the strongest and most effective pesticide available, able to kill hundreds of different insects at once. In 1945, to the delight of farmers struggling against crop-killing insects, it entered the American market, and three years later, for discovering DDT's insecticidal properties, Paul Müller, a Swiss scientist, was awarded a Nobel Prize.

When Rachel Carson started her research into DDT, it had already been in wide use in the United States for more than a decade. Industry officials claimed that, despite the fact that the pesticide was the most powerful agent yet developed against a wide variety of insects, it had no impact on other life forms, including humans. Carson had long questioned that assertion, and after conducting meticulous and exhaustive research, including interviews with the nation's preeminent scientists and a careful review of thousands of scientific documents, she discovered that she had been right to do so. Her book *Silent Spring,* released in 1962, documented the extent to which DDT wreaked havoc on the environment, eliminating species in sprayed areas and disrupting the delicate balance of the ecosystem. "These sprays, dusts, and aerosols are now applied almost universally to farms, gardens, forests, and homes," she wrote, "non-selective chemicals that have the power to kill every insect, the 'good' and the 'bad,' to still the song of birds and the leaping of fish in the streams, to coat the leaves with a deadly film, and to linger on in soil—all this though the intended target may be only a few weeds or insects."

She found that once the spray entered the environment, it was passed from one organism to another through the food chain, as were its harmful properties: "We poison the caddis flies in a stream and the salmon runs dwindle and die. We poison the gnats in a lake and the poison ravels from link to link of the food chain and soon the birds of the lake margins become its victims." Once inside the human body, she learned, the chemical did not dilute or break down; instead, it accumulated in fat and tissues, becoming more and more concentrated with every new exposure. She explained that if a human were to take in, regularly over time, as little as one-tenth of one part per million from, say, eggs laid by hens that had been fed alfalfa from fields dusted by DDT, the concentration of the chemicals could eventually reach ten to fifteen parts per million in the individual's body. In chilling and eloquent language, she described what could happen if the indiscriminate use of harmful pesticides continued unabated, depicting a town where all forms of life, including children, had been poisoned, and the "voices of spring" had become silent.

The book, which first appeared as a series of three articles in the *New Yorker* in 1962, shocked readers and enraged the chemical industry. Industry leaders launched an immediate campaign against Carson, questioning her research, her findings, and her sanity. She was even called a Communist. Not long after the publication of *Silent Spring*, an industry spokesman said of her work: "The major claims of Miss Rachel Carson's book, *Silent Spring*, are gross distortions of the actual facts, completely unsupported by scientific, experimental evidence, and general practical experience in the field."

But Rachel Carson was not easily intimidated. Her research was exact, and her approach precise. A quiet woman, she defended her work on national television and to reporters from newspapers across the United States—advocating not for the abandonment of pesticides, but for a wiser use of them. She told a CBS reporter, "It is the public that is being asked to assume the risks that the insect controllers calculate. The public must decide whether it wishes to continue on the present road, and it can do so only when in full possession of the facts. . . . We still haven't become mature enough to think of ourselves as only a tiny part of a vast and incredible universe. Man's attitude toward nature is today critically important simply because we have now acquired a fateful power to alter and destroy nature."

Readers flocked to her cause, and *Silent Spring* reached the top of the *New York Times* bestseller list. Her critics were ultimately silenced when President John F. Kennedy ordered his Science Advisory Committee to look into her findings and propose recommendations for the use and regulation of pesticides. Their report was issued on May 15, 1963, and it cautioned against the blanket use of toxic chemicals, calling for research into the potential health hazards they posed. DDT was eventually banned with the passage of the 1972 Federal Insecticide, Fungicide and Rodenticide Act (FIFRA) requiring health and safety testing of all pesticides.

More than forty years later, it is difficult to encapsulate the full extent of Rachel Carson's legacy. A public made aware of the harms of pesticides began to consider how fragile the relationship can be between technology and biology, and how, left unchecked, or implemented with insufficient foresight, "progress" can have harmful, often unintended consequences for our land, our water, our air, and our health. It was this public concern, and a broadening of the idea of what "conservation" meant, that led to a groundswell of involvement and the modern environmental movement—a movement that eventually culminated in the first Earth Day in 1970, the formation of the Environmental Protection Agency and the passage of the Clean Air Act that same year, and enactment of the Clean Water Act in 1972.

GOOD INTENTIONS

Rachel Carson's basic message was revolutionary, but her prescriptions were reasonable. By linking environmental degradation to human health, she brought to light the great need for us to take precautions before further harm was unleashed. She showed us that short-term gains may only create long-term problems. She offered leadership because she was willing to focus on solving a problem.

She defined the art of the possible, prompting us now to take more seriously our responsibility as stewards of this planet. Perhaps, there has never been a time, since the publication of *Silent Spring*, when we have needed to be reminded of this obligation more than at this very moment.

The planet is in crisis. In all industrialized nations, and particularly here in the United States, evidence shows that we live in a world so infused with toxins that they have made their way into the soil, the air and water, and our bodies, from conception to the end of life. This stark reality was bluntly confirmed in March 2005 with the release of the United Nations' global Millennium Ecosystem Assessment, a four-year study involving more than 1,350 scientists and other experts from ninety-five countries. It was the most comprehensive look at the health of the world's oceans, land, forests, species, and atmosphere to date, and its conclusion was bleak: Many of the world's ecosystems are headed for collapse unless radical measures are implemented to revive them.

According to the report, over the past fifty years human actions have depleted the Earth's natural resources on an unprecedented scale to satisfy growing demands for food, fresh water, timber, fiber, and fuel. The report's authors warned about the calamitous state of many of the world's fish stocks; the intense vulnerability of the 2 billion people living in dry regions to the loss of ecosystem services, including water supply; and the growing threat to ecosystems from climate change and nutrient pollution.

"Human activities have taken the planet to the edge of a massive wave of species extinctions, further threatening our own well-being," the report stated. "Today's technology and knowledge can reduce considerably the human impact on ecosystems. They are unlikely to be deployed fully, however, until ecosystem services cease to be perceived as free and limitless, and their full value is taken into account."

The planet is, of course, resilient and bountiful, and humans have long adapted to its natural cycles of change. But, as this report reminds us, that does not mean we can simply ignore reality or fail to consider the damage we are doing. The tragic, and indeed, inconvenient truth is that many of our habitual activities leave behind pollution that threatens later generations and our own way of life. We barely give a second thought to many of them—from harvesting and burning fossil fuels, to employing chemicals in the manufacture of products we use in our homes, to driving cars that use large amounts of gasoline. At best, succeeding generations will be forced to dedicate their time, their resources, and a vast effort to dealing with the consequences of our choices. At worst, their very survival is at risk.

The most ordinary items of our daily life—perhaps especially these items—are worth reevaluating in light of our precarious relationship with the Earth. Even something as simple as, say, a baby's diaper.

Since ancient times, parents have sought to find convenient and reliable means of keeping their infants nourished and clean. Native American mothers used milkweed to protect their children, Inuits used moss wrapped in animal skins, and pioneers of the American West used hand-stitched cotton. During World War II, when many women were called to work in the factories, diaper services sprang up, delivering clean cloth diapers to American homes.

Today, the vast majority of American families use plastic disposable diapers, which first entered the U.S. market in the 1940s. In many ways, the story of the disposable diaper is a quintessential story of American inventiveness and ingenuity. A former magazine editor and Connecticut mother named Marion Donovan, frustrated with wet diapers and soiled baby clothes, decided to cut plastic from her shower curtain and sew it to cloth. A few years later, after experimenting with several prototypes, her invention, which she dubbed the "Boater" diaper, was selling at Saks Fifth Avenue in New York. It was made of parachute nylon that protected the cloth diaper, a design that made it possible for larger companies to eventually develop the diapers used in so many American homes today.

The disposable diaper was convenient and gave millions of American parents—especially mothers—a new sense of freedom. But what did the introduction of the disposable diaper mean for the planet? Sixty years or so after the "Boater" hit Saks, it is estimated that more than 18 billion disposable diapers are used in this country each year. The manufacture of these diapers requires 82,000 tons of plastic, which is made, in part, with crude oil. The absorbent inner layer is manufactured from wood pulp, derived from more than a quarter of a million trees cut down each year solely for this purpose. To make the diapers a crisp white color, a sign of cleanliness and sterility, the wood pulp is bleached with chlorine gas, a process that emits some of the most toxic chemicals ever made by humans, including dioxins, which are associated with birth defects, miscarriages, and cancer. Additionally, 18 billion diapers each year translate into a lot of trash. Diapers are now the third-largest single contributor to solid waste at landfills, where they may take as long as *500 years* to biodegrade. Furthermore, the waste that goes to the landfill with the diaper, should parents not first flush it, brings with it viruses and bacteria that can end up in our waterways, posing serious health risks.

Certainly, this was not the intention of Marion Donovan or others like her who were seeking simply to make life more convenient for families. The same can be said of most of the products we make and use today. When Henry Ford founded the Ford Motor Company in 1903, he truly revolutionized American transportation. Making use of the assembly line, he brought a streamlined efficiency to the factory floor making what was once a luxury item available to thousands of American families for the first time.

But efficiency for Ford meant achieving the highest level of production at the lowest cost—it did not take into consideration what would happen at the end of the useful life of the car. Even today, few manufacturers or consumers are concerned about what happens to something once they have thrown it away. When our cars break down, we haul them to a junkyard, where they will may sit and rot for decades. When a laptop computer, cell phone, or iPod is out of date or broken, consumers simply throw away the old one and replace it. The casual discarding of manufactured products—their built-in obsolescence—is a relatively new phenomenon. Only recently people were accustomed to taking items such as their television sets to be repaired and their shoes to the cobbler to be resoled. Companies now spend a lot of money attempting to update products that barely need updating. The idea of "single use" has spread to everything from dusting cloths to cameras.

The manufacturers of these products did not set out to create vast amounts of waste, fill our landfills, or poison our land. And when consumers purchase the products, use them up, and toss them into the trash, that is not their intention either. But, nevertheless, the planet has paid the price for our convenience. Now is the time when we have to confront a crucial question: If that is not our intention, then what is?

That is the question addressed by Bill McDonough, one of the nation's most visionary thinkers. As the principal of William McDonough + Partners Architects, and founder, with Dr. Michael Braungart, of MBDC, a product, process, and materials design firm dedicated to revolutionizing the design of products and services, he invites us to think differently about what is possible in tending to the planet. He has noted with irony that "if our intention was to create climate change and global warming, destroy the ecosystems of places like Alaska and Colorado, poison the places where we live, disrupt our cultural and natural resources, leave behind chemicals that will require regulation by future generations, then we're doing a great job."

In the many conversations we three have had over the years, McDonough often returns to one principal idea: Many of the systems we use today—systems conceived largely during the Industrial Revolution that rely heavily on nonrenewable energy sources, create vast amounts of pollution, and introduce new human-made chemicals into the environment each day—were not born of necessity: "We are not victims of an unfortunate physics," he says. "Neither physical nor economic laws require that we lock ourselves up in buildings that don't breathe, or that we fill our surroundings with chemicals that poison our bodies, or that we be made to use tools that hurt us physically. Those outcomes are dictated not by laws of nature, but by our failure to remember a cardinal principle of design: products do what you ask of them." The systems now in place came to be, rather, simply because environmental considerations were not factored into the equation at the design stage.

After spending just a few minutes listening to McDonough, it's hard *not* to imagine another way. Imagine if the basic materials we used were not designed simply to be used up and thrown away, but rather, could be removed and reused easily to manufacture the next generation of products. Imagine if, at the end of a car's life, for instance, the automobile was not taken to a junkyard to rot, its chemical toxins seeping into the Earth, but was easily disassembled and its parts upgraded to become another car. What if books were not made of paper—formed from trees, one of our most precious resources— but of materials that were so clean they could be thrown into the garden to feed the plants? Imagine a highway system lined with a ribbon of solar panels to capture energy and provide electricity to homes, offices, and factories from Bangor to Berkeley.

Bill McDonough is leading the way not just in asking these questions but in making his ideas a reality, as he explained in 2000, in a book written with his colleague Michael Braungart: *Cradle to Cradle: Remaking the Way We Make Things*. At the core of their "cradle to cradle" philosophy is a simple truth: Human health, the strength of our economy, and the well-being of our environment are all connected. Rather

11

than maintaining today's industrial system that "takes, makes and wastes," we have the ability to create goods and services that generate ecological, social, and economic value. McDonough and Braungart argue that the conflict between industry and the environment is not an indictment of commerce, but an outgrowth of short-sighted design. The design of products and manufacturing systems growing out of the Industrial Revolution reflected the spirit of the day—and yielded a host of unintended yet tragic consequences.

Today, with our growing knowledge of the living earth, design can reflect a new spirit. In fact, as the authors of *Cradle to Cradle* point out, when designers employ the intelligence of natural systems—like the abundance of the sun's energy—they can create products, industrial systems, buildings, even regional plans that allow nature and commerce to fruitfully coexist. Changing over to a cradle-to-cradle system would require a fundamental rethinking of product design and our relationship to the planet. Rather than using products once and sending them to the landfill, we would design materials that, at the end of their useful life, could be safely returned to the Earth or reused to make other products. Simply put, a cradle-to-cradle system would eliminate the concept of toxic waste inherent in the current cradle-to-grave way we do things, resolving the conflict between nature and commerce.

McDonough and Braungart's book itself is a symbol of what is possible. The "paper" used in the book does not come from trees, but from plastic resins and inorganic fillers. It has the look and feel of high-quality paper, but it's even better. It's rugged and waterproof. "This 'treeless' book," McDonough explained, "points the way toward the day when books, like many other products, can be used, recycled, and used again without losing any material quality—in cradle-to-cradle cycles." It would be easy to label their way of thinking as spirited but impossible optimism if, in fact, they hadn't already made the leap from theory to practice. McDonough and Braungart have developed a Cradle-to-Cradle certification process, providing companies with a means of indicating their achievement in sustainable design and customers the ability to choose products they know are safe.

One product that's been redesigned with the cradle-to-cradle philosophy is, in fact, the diaper. The "gDiaper," developed by Portland residents Jason and Kim Graham-Nye, is the first completely new diaper developed in the United States in more than forty years. It includes a washable outer pant and an absorbent inner liner. Rather than throwing away the entire diaper after one use, parents can safely flush the inner liner down the toilet and wash and reuse the outer part. gDiapers are made with no chlorine or perfumes, and the flushable inner liners are so safe for the environment that they can even be composted in a garden, where they would biodegrade in less than 150 days.

Bill McDonough is also working with many Fortune 500 companies to implement cradle-to-cradle design. In partnership with clients ranging from the Swiss textile mill Rohner to the dye- and chemical-manufactuer Ciby-Geigy to global megacorporations like the Ford Motor Company, he has shown that designers attuned to this cradle-to-cradle philosophy can replicate nature's benign closed-loop systems in the worlds of commerce and community. The result: safe, beneficial materials that either naturally biodegrade or provide high-quality resources for the next generation of products; buildings designed to produce more energy than they consume; cities and towns tapped into local energy flows; places in every human realm that renew a sense of participation in the landscape.

REINVENTING A CITY

Teresa: Bill McDonough's example presents a challenge. If it is possible to reimagine a product, a process, and ultimately a corporation, what is the limit to the potential for reconceptualizing our industrial cities? Can an entire city, one with a history of industrial corrosion and decay, be revived? That question has been put to the test in Rachel Carson's hometown, as well as my own since 1966, Pittsburgh—a place that embodies the art of what is possible more than any other that I know.

If you haven't visited Pittsburgh in recent years, I have a good idea of the impression you may have of it—the images of dirty Pittsburgh in the 1960s and 1970s were stark enough to become seared into the minds of generations of Americans. Factories along the Allegheny, Ohio, and Monongahela rivers spewed darkened clouds of smoky death. The rivers themselves ran brown and bubbly from toxins, and the buildings of downtown—many of them decrepit or abandoned after the collapse of the steel industry—were blackened with soot.

There was, in fact, rarely a time in the city's long history that people did not hold such a bleak opinion of our city. In 1866, prominent American biographer James Parton described Pittsburgh during a visit to the city as "Hell with the Lid off." Some twenty years later, noted English philosopher Herbert Spencer wrote, "Six months residence here would justify suicide." And the iconic architect Frank Lloyd Wright told a journalist in 1939: "An interesting city—interesting in the same way as a collision involving a truck, a school bus and five cars would be interesting."

Residents of Pittsburgh have learned to avoid offense at such sentiments. We've all grown up aware of the city's history. One thing was clear from the beginning of Pittsburgh's ride on the wave of the Industrial Revolution in the mid–1800s: The manufacturing muscle that would make it stand out on the international map well into the twentieth century was also its curse. For years, Pittsburgh's air was full of particulates, its rivers were rife with industrial wastes, and its people labored in some of the least healthy conditions in the country in the factories and smelting works. These conditions made sense only because Pittsburgh was so productive that most business leaders, public officials, and even front-line workers believed that environmental degradation was one of the necessary costs of doing robust business, of ensuring that the city remained the gateway to the West, the supplier to the growing nation. Like many industrial cities, Pittsburgh had forsaken its land, abused its rivers, and turned away from its waterfront for decades. So ingrained was that mentality that "Stay away from the rivers!" had become a mantra for generations of Pittsburgh moms sending their children out to play.

In the 1970s, the city began a quick and steady economic decline. It had been eclipsed by other manufacturing centers, the steel industry was collapsing, and the city practically perished. With its industrial base defunct, people left by the thousands. (In the mid-1990s, still down on its luck, desperate for development, and convinced that no one could really value living on its rivers, the city gave away the development rights for a prime piece of downtown riverfront property for a dollar.)

But then, in the ensuing years, something else started to happen—some people and businesses embraced a new vision for the city. Perhaps it was because things had gotten so bad that there was nowhere to go but up. Whatever the reasons, the collective consciousness of the city shifted from an acceptance of Pittsburgh as an industrial dumping ground to a determination that no community has to settle for pollution and waste, no matter how deep-seated the industrial heritage—that there is nothing inevitable about a city's environmental decline. People decided that the decline could, in fact, not only be stopped, but reversed. Carrying through on the promise of this idea would require the same persistence, ingenuity, and willingness to see a better alternative that Rachel Carson saw on Cape Cod, but the people of Pittsburgh proved equal to the task.

The spirit of possibility was in fact part of Pittsburgh's heritage quite as much as its industrial blemishes were. The city had a continuous history of individual activists working on behalf of the environment, including pioneering women's health groups, the businessmen-philanthropists Henry John Heinz II and Richard King Mellon,

Senator John Heinz, and brave local elected officials, none more than David L. Lawrence, the city's mayor in 1946–1959 and then Governor of Pennsylvania. These prominent individuals gave public face to the idea of Pittsburgh's improvements so that it could take root at the highest levels of city government and be driven and sustained by a unique coalition of elected officials; representatives of foundations, including the Heinz Foundations; and, most importantly, talented and dedicated city residents. The result has been nearly beyond our imagination.

In many ways, the city is helping to define the next Industrial Revolution—a revolution in green design and sustainability. Pittsburgh is today considered among the "greenest" cities in the nation, alongside places like Portland and Chicago. Until recently, our city had more "green buildings"—meaning they are highly efficient and ecologically beneficial—than any other American city.

The first green office-design project in Pittsburgh was, in fact, Bill McDonough's redesign of the Heinz Family Offices on the thirty-second floor of a downtown office tower. The redesign, which employed innovative heating and cooling methods and environmentally friendly materials, served as a laboratory and model for others to learn from, and not just locally. The Discovery Channel has reported on it; architectural magazines have written about it; and builders, designers, and architects from across the country have come to study its features. Importantly for Pittsburgh, the developer, who had never before been exposed to environmental engineering, has become a dedicated green builder and has funded a chair of environmental engineering at the University of Pittsburgh.

The redesign of the Heinz Family Offices revealed to many in the city that good design must mean green design. Now, green buildings dot the city landscape—there are seventy in all. The crowning achievement for us has been the David L. Lawrence Convention Center. Opened in 2003 on an eight-acre site along the Allegheny River, and designed by the celebrated architect Rafael Viñoly, the building is not just the only green convention center in the world, but the largest green building in the world. No other building incorporates so many sustainable systems. A water reclamation system was put in place to reduce potable water use by nearly 60 percent. The building processes all of its waste. It maximizes the use of nontoxic materials, including paint and carpets that do not emit harmful fumes. It makes the greatest possible use of natural ventilation, and it includes skylights on the roof and a glass wall to bring natural light into the exhibition space. It also includes energy-saving technologies such as daylight sensors, which has led to an annual estimated savings in energy costs of nearly 35 percent.

The green building movement in Pittsburgh has not only helped to bring a renewed sense of beauty and activity to the city; it has also been an economic windfall, encouraging the development of a robust sector of the next Industrial Revolution. The city, we believe, is slated to become the center of "green chemistry," leading the way in the design of chemical products and processes that reduce or eliminate the use and generation of hazardous substances.

The same thinking of what is possible has been applied to the city's riverfront by the River Life Task-force, comprised of representatives from all city sectors. The resulting Three Rivers Park is an ambitious undertaking that will ultimately encompass 13 miles of open space along the waterfront and establish important connections to adjacent neighborhoods.

Sustainable-development principles define not only the way that buildings are now constructed in Pittsburgh, but also the things occurring inside of them. Pittsburgh is home to several world-class universities and research centers that have achieved excellence in environmental research. The Center for Environmental Oncology at the University of Pittsburgh's Cancer Institute embodies an integrated approach to environmental health. It is the locus of greening activities for the entire medical system and sponsors cutting-edge research on the link between the environment and disease. The preventive medicine program at the Magee Women's Hospital trains professionals in how to recognize the possible environmental causes of both symptoms and disease.

And best of all, the city is now becoming a dynamic urban center and increasingly recognized for the high quality of life enjoyed by its residents. In 2005, *The Economist* ranked Pittsburgh the most livable city in the United States, along with Cleveland, Ohio. Of course, nobody would argue that Pittsburgh is not without its problems—the region is burdened by an aging sewer infrastructure that allows polluted water to pour into rivers after storms, and coal-fueled power plants, as well as diesel emissions, still drag down air quality. But we know that we can create a better future for our great cities; we just have to decide on that as our goal and start chipping away at it, one solution at a time. If a city like Pittsburgh can gain recognition as a leader in green development, success is achievable in all our cities.

All of the stories that follow are about people who have embraced the art of the possible. They took on what at first seemed to be insurmountable problems. Solutions, if they existed at all, seemed quite out of reach. Can one man clean up an entire river? Could one woman save a mountain forest? On their own, probably not. But through their example, and by inspiring others to help them, absolutely. And that is the pattern observed again and again: American ingenuity and individual will have led to entire communities taking up a cause, because sometimes, right makes might. Pittsburgh is a perfect example. Its recovery was a task quite beyond any one person. But once individuals with imagination begin to envision a better future and become determined enough to convince others and lead the way, the art of the possible is vastly expanded. In the end, a city can indeed be transformed. And if a city, why not a nation, or a world?

CHAPTER TWO

A Body of Evidence

Teresa: Long before Pittsburgh became my American home, I had a home in Africa. My family's residence in Mozambique was a remarkable place to grow up. On some weekends and holidays, my playground was the African savanna, with its starry skies and its grassy arid wilderness, populated by eerily shaped trees. I remember, too, the bright orangey-red flamboyants and the softness of the jacarandas flanking the streets of my hometown. There were birds of all kinds, and the animals—plain, dotted, and striped, tiny and large—seemed a brilliant splash of creation.

My free time as a child ranged from the dreamy to the adventurous. I played the piano, and I played make-believe. I loved to climb trees and collect avocadoes, mangoes, citrus fruits, and other delectables. I made medical rounds with my dad, Dr. José Simões-Ferreira, and saw him talk to his patients and care for them. I also did "rounds" in the garden with my loving mother, Balú, and began to learn about flowers, especially roses, as well as trees and shrubs. My parents both taught me to nurture life and enjoy it.

Nature was also my earliest classroom. Almost daily, my cousin and I would search for beetles, or anything that crawled. One day, we found a strange one, picked it up, and took it to "the men" at the Museum of Natural History, then called Museum of Alvaro de Castro, a very beautiful colonial structure with a great collection of African species, located right next to my granny's house. Imagine our delight in finding a beetle never before identified, bringing it to the museum, and having it named for us, a pair of curious children. We visited that museum often, and every now and then we saw some extraordinary things. I will never forget the day a giant crocodile was brought in. In the middle of its opened stomach, there was the unmistakable small arm of a child it had killed—an awesome sign of the harsh reality of the savanna.

Such a gruesome sight frightened us, but in the East Africa of my youth, it was just a sign of how vulnerable life was. The interplay of nature, health, and survival was a given, something that people who lived close to the natural world intuitively understood. One learned to respect the rules—like the fact that one should not swim at dawn or dusk, when the only things moving are those looking for food—because they had such obvious implications for one's personal well-being. Nature also taught us the virtue of prevention—of solving problems by not creating them in the first place. Africa gave us a powerful sense of our place in the larger world, and that was a great source of strength for us. We learned to find joy, humility, and a healthy sense of self on the savanna.

That understanding was reinforced by my father. He came to

Mozambique from Portugal as a young doctor to work in the bush, mostly on tropical diseases, and fell in love with the land and its people. My father was a very well-regarded physician, adored by his patients. He worked at prominent hospitals in Lisbon and Paris and at the Mayo Clinic. After those experiences, he founded the cancer clinic at the hospital in the capital of Mozambique. He was an avid student of both the science and the art of medicine. On weekends, which we often spent at a little cottage in the bush, he would devote hours to treating the people, mostly children, who would start gathering in our garden before sunrise. I was always struck by how engaged he was and how closely he listened to them as he asked about their lives. Observing him in these moments, and listening to the questions he asked, provided a great lesson for me in how illness and survival can be related to one's environment and the practices of daily life.

In many ways, the sense of connectedness I learned from growing up in Africa, and from my parents' example, shaped not only how I sought to tend to the environment, but also how I have come to define it. As Bill McDonough and Rachel Carson show us, the modern definition of the "environment," the idea that it is external to ourselves, does not work now, if it ever did, because it is neither accurate nor meaningful. The environment is not just the context in which people exist, or a passive backdrop to our lives; the environment, as the term has value to our survival, is the conditioner of life itself—our skin that is neatly woven into every facet of our lives. The decisions we make throughout the day are all part of this, from the cars we drive, to the food we eat, to the products we use. In other words, the environment is not something outside of ourselves. The environment is our homes, our bodies, and ultimately, our health and the choices we make.

It is all connected. And therein lies the beauty. Let me share with you a true story about good intentions and unintended consequences. It is a story about cats.

A few decades ago, the World Health Organization (WHO) tried to end a malaria epidemic in Borneo by using DDT to wipe out the local mosquito population. Unfortunately, there were unintended consequences, just as Rachel Carson had described in *Silent Spring*. In the case of Borneo, the DDT also wiped out the wasps that controlled the local thatch-eating insects, with the result that many of the roofs on the Bornean homes started to cave in. Meanwhile, the DDT accumulated in the local lizard population, which caused the cats that ate the lizards to die, thereby unleashing a ferocious infestation of rats. Ultimately, WHO was forced to parachute in 14,000 new cats to control the rats in what was known officially as Operation Cat Drop.

The story illustrates the high price of linear thinking. The simple fact is that problems never exist in isolation—nor do solutions. Assuming otherwise invites a host of unintended consequences and leads us where we never intended to go. A lot of what we do in life is like that. We make simple assumptions, we act in a hurry, we forget to worry about the details. And one day we wake up and all the cats are dead.

As we re-define our understanding of environmental responsibility we'd like to ask you to think about the products that you use on a daily basis. Because just as the chemicals used to manufacture a child's diaper have unintended but far-reaching consequences on the planet, we must consider if the chemicals we come into contact with each day have similar consequences on our environment—and our bodies. How many of the products we use each day, even before ever leaving the house, have ingredients we cannot name (let alone pronounce) with chemical properties we do not understand? Many of us take our showers behind vinyl shower curtains and use shampoos and lotions with added fragrance and other chemical ingredients. We may scrub down a cutting board with a disinfectant, vacuum the stain-proof carpet, put on clothes labeled "wrinkle-free," and do laundry with "ocean"-scented detergent. Perhaps we drink milk that originated at a factory farm, where the animals were pumped full of antibiotics and growth hormones, or we eat a peach that was grown with a number of pesticides.

Surely many modern products, like wrinkle-free clothing and stain-proof carpeting, bring a sense of convenience to our lives, but are we unwittingly paying a price for that convenience? The truth of the matter is that we are coming into contact with hundreds, if not thousands, of chemicals every day, just in the products we use. When *Silent Spring* was first published in 1962, there were approximately 500 new industrial chemicals being introduced to the market each year. "The figure is staggering and its implications are not easily grasped," Carson wrote. "Five hundred new chemicals to which the bodies of men and animals are required somehow to adapt each year, chemicals totally outside the limits of biologic experience."

Since that time, the number of chemicals on the consumer market has multiplied dramatically. According to the Environmental Protection Agency (EPA), pesticide use alone has increased by about 50 percent over the past thirty-six years. In fact, there are now *more than 80,000 chemicals* in widespread use in commerce. This year we will manufacture or import more than 1 million pounds each of about 3,000 of these chemicals.

Rachel Carson asked the right question: What impact do these chemicals have on the ecosystem, including our own bodies? Unfortunately, that is a question we really cannot answer. Many consumers assume that because the government requires tough testing of medications before they enter the market, it would be equally tough with all the products we use on our bodies and in our homes. Sadly, that's just not true. Outside of drugs and pesticides, the chemicals used to manufacture many of the products we use each day—cosmetics, personal-care products, cleaning agents—are never tested to determine if they are harmful to human health. The current law requires only that new chemicals—1,700 of which enter the market each year, according to government figures—be tested for toxicity *only* if, based on the profile of similar chemicals, there are some scientific grounds for believing they could prove to be harmful. This is no more effective than closing the barn door after the horses have bolted. And, to ban or restrict the use of a chemical, the EPA must find that the chemical poses an "unreasonable risk," but the definition of unreasonable risk is so limited that in the thirty years that the laws have been on the books, the EPA has only banned or limited the use of five existing chemicals or groups of chemicals. What's more, our laws do not even require manufacturers to label many of the chemicals that we encounter on a regular basis.

This is of particular concern because we know without doubt from biomonitoring tests—which test people's blood, urine, serum, saliva, hair, and body tissue for synthetic chemicals—that the chemicals we come into contact with are seeping inside of us, a factor known as the body burden. In fact, every one of us—women and men, young and old, whether we work in factories or offices—is carrying almost 200 different synthetic or toxic chemicals in our fatty tissues.

Since 2001, the Centers for Disease Control and Prevention (CDC) has been conducting studies every two years to track levels of certain chemicals in people's bodies. The most recent report of this biomonitoring, issued in 2005, tested for levels of 148 chemicals in the blood of several thousand participants. All of the chemicals tested, some of which have been banned for decades, were found in at least some of the participants. Similar results were found through biomonitoring tests conducted by the Environmental Working Group (EWG), a D.C.-based environmental organization. Since 2000, EWG has spearheaded six studies finding 455 industrial pollutants, pesticides, and other chemicals in the blood, urine, and breast milk of 72 people altogether, from newborns and grandparents to mothers and teens. Their testing of nine adults from five different states found a total of 171 pollutants to be present, and each person had an average of 56 carcinogens in his or her body.

In my case, I have learned that my body contains particularly high levels of lead and mercury, two metals that are known to be toxic to the nervous system. The presence of lead, I believe, is partly due to the old lead service lines that carry water to my home in Washington, D.C., where I have lived for three decades. The mercury comes from eating seafood contaminated by mercury from polluting power plants.

Knowing there are 80,000 chemicals on the market today, and that many of them can enter our bodies, we must ask if there is a connection between disease and the chemicals we use so indiscriminately. Here are some unsettling facts: One woman in three will develop cancer over the course of her life. One in four will suffer from depression. Some 5 to 10 percent of all couples are infertile. Autoimmune diseases like lupus and multiple sclerosis, in which one's immune system attacks itself by mistake, are on the rise. Seventy-five percent of those who suffer from these diseases are women.

Since the 1960s, we've seen a particularly disturbing trend in the number of women being diagnosed with breast cancer, especially young women. In the 1960s, one in twenty women nationally was diagnosed with breast cancer. By 1993, it was one in nine. Today, it is closer to one in seven. Some of this increase may be due to advances in detection, and a fraction is attributable to hormones prescribed to women, but the causes of most cases of breast cancer cannot be explained. According to the Breast Cancer Fund and Breast Cancer Action, *fewer than 10 percent* of women diagnosed with breast cancer are born with a genetic susceptibility to the disease, and as many as half of the women who are diagnosed today have no known risk factors associated with breast cancer, such as family history, race, socioeconomic status, and childbearing experience.

Why are so many women getting breast cancer? And why do so many who get the disease have few known risk factors for it? With news of breast-cancer clusters—places like Marin County in the Bay Area of California and the Northeast corridor from Philadelphia to New York City, where rates are higher than the national average—shouldn't we be asking whether environmental factors could be having an influence?

Fortunately for all of us, a group of pioneering women have not only asked these questions, they are working tirelessly for the answers.

REFUSING TO REMAIN SILENT

In 1993, the Massachusetts Department of Public Health announced some alarming news: Women on Cape Cod were being diagnosed with breast cancer at a significantly higher rate than those who lived elsewhere in the state. The news concerned many area residents, including Ellen Parker. Through the years, Ellen, an oncology social worker, had counseled many women who had become gravely ill with the disease, many of whom eventually died from it. "When I was a child, my mother had one friend who had breast cancer, but it was very different for me as an adult," Ellen remembers. "So many women I knew—even women in their twenties and thirties—were getting diagnosed, and becoming quite ill."

Two years earlier, in 1991, Ellen and a number of her friends and colleagues had helped found the Massachusetts Breast Cancer Coalition (MBCC) to increase public awareness about the disease and advocate for a cure. In the organization's first two years, they had successfully lobbied the state legislature to declare breast cancer an epidemic, making our state the first to take this important step. Then, when news of the Cape Cod rates were made public in 1993, Ellen and other members of the MBCC began to consider something else. Advocating for a cure was certainly necessary, but, they wondered, why was the research not also focused on finding out why women were being diagnosed in the first place? This was a question that none of these women had the training to answer. But they put aside reservations about their own limitations and decided to gather at Ellen's house to talk about the possibilities.

Cheryl Osimo, a resident of Cape Cod, was eager to join that discussion. A former elementary school teacher and mother of two, Cheryl had been diagnosed with breast cancer two years earlier, at the age of forty. Thankfully, after treatment, she beat the disease and got a clean bill of health, but she continued to struggle with the question of what had led her to develop breast cancer in the first place—she had no family history of the disease and no known risk factors. She often thought about an experience she'd had after moving into her house on the Cape in 1978, near where she had come in the summers as a child. One afternoon, men arrived to spray a pond near her property for pests. In their protective gear, they had reminded Cheryl of astronauts walking on the moon. At the time, she had thought little of it.

"To this day, I am dismayed by my own ignorance," she recently explained from her pretty, comfortable home in the quaint Cape town of Barnstable. "Why didn't I think about how his spraying would affect us downwind? Why didn't I realize that if he wore all that protective gear, I should be worried about my children playing in the sandbox? And why wasn't I concerned about those chemicals drifting into our home?" After her diagnosis, she had volunteered with the Massachusetts Breast Cancer Coalition, where she met Ellen, and she arrived at Ellen's house that afternoon in 1993 ready to do whatever she could to get answers to the many questions she had about the causes of her cancer. As the discussion turned to the Cape Cod study, it didn't take long for someone to ask the question so many of those present had already asked themselves: Was something in the environment—namely, the chemicals being used on their lawns and in their homes, and ending up in their water—contributing to the increased incidence of breast cancer?

"The idea that the environment may be part of the problem wasn't even part of the common mind-set," Ellen remembers. "But we knew if we were going to really take on this disease we needed to look at something different. The group felt they needed to take a leap not unlike the one that Rachel Carson had, when she began to look at DDT." That leap was a considerable one, but before too long, the women had established a new organization, which they named the Silent Spring Institute in honor of Rachel Carson. This name was particularly fitting, not just because the women were carrying on her legacy, but because Carson had herself been diagnosed with breast cancer. Though she never spoke of it publicly, her diagnosis came at the time she was writing *Silent Spring*, and in 1964, just two years after the book's release, she died. She was just fifty-seven years old.

Soon after its establishment, the Silent Spring Institute was awarded $3 million from the Massachusetts Department of Public Health to launch the Cape Cod Breast Cancer and Environment Study. The researchers at Silent Spring were particularly interested in studying the link between breast cancer and a woman's exposure to chemicals, especially one type of chemical called endocrine disruptors. These chemicals, which are used in the manufacture of so many household and personal-care products, including cosmetics, detergents, cleaning products, and some building materials, can disrupt our fragile and complex hormonal system. Some endocrine disruptors mimic estrogen, which we now know plays a role in a woman's chances of developing breast cancer. One of the most compelling and comprehensive studies written on the topic of endocrine disruptors is *Our Stolen Future*, a book by Theo Colborn, Dianne Dumanoski, and John Peterson Myers. First published in 1996, this book brought the issue of endocrine disruptors to public attention for the first time.

When the Silent Spring Institute was established, research into the link between chemicals like endocrine disruptors and breast cancer was in its infancy, but some scientists were coming to a greater understanding about how some synthetic chemicals used in common household products could play a role in the proliferation of breast-cancer cells. One of the most astounding discoveries of this kind had occurred just a few years earlier, in 1989, in a laboratory at Tufts University in Boston. Two doctors, Ana M. Soto and Carlos Sonnenschein, had been working for nearly two decades to better understand how estrogen—a natural hormone produced by the human body—could induce cancer-cell growth. As part of their research, they had added various amounts of estrogen to cells and measured how they reacted. One day, cells that had *not* been exposed to estrogen started to multiply, just as if they had been exposed. There was no known reason why these cells should suddenly act like this. The researchers began a careful process to study how this could have happened. They substituted all the components, and considered the possibility of human error. They found nothing. Finally, they called the company that supplied the plastic tubes for their laboratory and were told that the plastic had been reformulated. Claiming the formulation was proprietary, the company refused to disclose the new ingredients of the plastics. Soto and Sonnenschein began their own analysis. After painstaking research, they found the source of estrogen contamination right in front of their eyes: The plastics manufacturer had used a synthetic estrogenic chemical called nonylphenol *in the plastic tubes*. It was a frightening and stunning realization: that a chemical commonly used in plastics could cause cancer cells to grow.

With this discovery, Drs. Soto and Sonnenschein became part of a small but growing group of pioneering scientists making the connections between environmental toxins and health. Others, like Dr. Devra Davis (now with the University of Pittsburgh), working with Dr. Leon Bradlow and other leading experts, developed and tested the hypothesis that some commonly used pesticides and toxic chemicals could act like estrogens and cause abnormal cell growth or initiate mammary tumors. Shortly afterward, Mary Wolff, at New York's Mount Sinai School of Medicine, found an association between organochlorine pesticides (including DDT) and breast-cancer risk. Later work has been inconclusive in its findings, in part because current levels of DDT are the lowest in modern history. But these research teams led the way and provided an impetus for more work to be done in the effort to discover the combined effects of hormone-mimicking materials on women's health. The women of Silent Spring were determined to do their part to advance that research.

The Cape Cod Breast Cancer and Environment Study, which the Silent Spring Institute launched in 1994, was designed to investigate why breast-cancer rates were higher on Cape Cod than statewide, and how exposure to these hormone-altering chemicals occurs. No other research organization had yet attempted to tease out a relationship between long-term exposure to hormone-altering chemicals, based on geographic factors, and cancer risk. Under the leadership of Dr. Julia Brody, a skilled scientist who had previously served in senior environmental policy positions at the Massachusetts Department of Environmental Management and earlier at the Texas Department of Agriculture, the organization convened an impressive group of researchers and scientists from Boston, Brown, Harvard, and Tufts universities to collaborate in the work of measuring estrogen mimics in the environment. From the beginning, the organization aimed to go beyond science as usual. "We didn't want to fund scientists who would go away and then come back with a report ten years later," said Ellen Parker, who became the chair of the Silent Spring Institute's board of directors. "We wanted the community—especially women with breast cancer—to participate in the process." Cheryl Osimo was hired as the Cape Cod coordinator and helped to organize a series of public meetings with local residents, giving them the opportunity to voice their most crucial concerns.

From that process, the SSI team decided to focus part of their research on pesticides—many of which contain hormone-altering chemicals—and drinking water. On the Cape, all domestic sewage is disposed in septic systems, allowing effluent to leach through shallow, sandy soil into the groundwater, which is also the drinking-water supply. Women at the public meetings expressed concern that something in the water could be leading to breast cancer. After all, everyone drank from a common water source.

Over the next three years, the Silent Spring team worked hard and amassed vast amounts of essential data to locate the sources of possible toxic contaminants and women's exposure to hormone-altering chemicals. Because breast cancer tumors begin years before they are diagnosed, the researchers sought to re-create a picture of the environment of Cape Cod as far back as 1948, when DDT was first used on the Cape. They mapped water-supply pipes, studied historical records documenting pesticide application, and traced septic systems. They interviewed 1,121 Cape Cod women who had been diagnosed with breast cancer and 992 others who had not. They recorded details about the women's family history of breast cancer and their addresses dating back to 1948. They also spent time looking at water-quality measurements for the previous twenty-five years and patterns of land use over the same time period.

Using this information, the Silent Spring team found that for the years 1982 to 1992, breast-cancer incidence was *21 percent higher* on Cape Cod than in the rest of Massachusetts. These higher rates could not be adequately explained by known risk factors, suggesting that environmental factors could be playing a role. Women who had lived longer on Cape Cod were at higher risk for breast cancer: Those who had been there twenty-five to twenty-nine years were at the highest risk, and their level of risk was 72 percent higher than among women who had lived there for less than five years. In addition, breast-cancer risk was higher for women who had lived in or near areas treated for tree pests between 1948 and 1995, near cranberry bogs between 1948 and the mid–1970s, and near agricultural land since the mid–1970s. Risk was higher yet for women who had lived where no tree buffer existed to protect them from pesticide drift.

It was a series of stunning discoveries. These women who had decided just three years earlier to talk over coffee about tackling a problem that had never been tackled—none of whom, remember, were trained scientists—were now helping to bring about some of the earliest evidence to suggest that the environment could, in fact, play a role in a woman getting breast cancer. Their research was also the first to document estrogenic activity in groundwater and to detect estrogenic pollutants in private wells on Cape Cod. Since then, researchers from the United States Geological Survey and elsewhere have found growing evidence of estrogen-mimicking chemicals in surface waters across the nation. These harmful chemicals get into the water supply in many ways: through sewage, from pesticide runoff from farms and lawns, and from pharmaceuticals, such as birth-control pills, that end up in the waste stream. The presence of estrogenic endocrine disruptors in some lakes and rivers has since been found to have serious and unfortunate impacts on aquatic life, causing, for example, the feminization of male fish. In water bodies across the United States, male fish, frogs, and turtles have been found with feminized gonads. In September 2006, male smallmouth bass in the Potomac River and its tributaries, a system providing drinking water to millions of people, were found to be producing a female egg-yolk protein.

Another aspect of the Cape Cod Breast Cancer and Environment Study, launched in 1998, was equally groundbreaking. Because many household and personal-care products contain estrogen mimics, the researchers decided to look at the extent to which people were being exposed to these substances *inside of their own homes.* Silent Spring asked some of the women who had been interviewed in the breast-cancer study to allow researchers to test air and dust samples from their homes for eighty-nine different hormone-altering chemicals. Many people volunteered to participate, including Jane Chase, a Cape Cod grandmother who had been diagnosed with two different types of breast cancer at two different times in her life.

After her first diagnosis, Jane had helped to start a support group for others with cancer, and through the years she had lost many friends to the discase. Some, like Jane, had experienced a recurrence years after their initial diagnosis, and she had also grown increasingly distraught by the mounting number of women in their twenties and thirties who were being diagnosed for the first time. When she agreed to take part in the Household Exposure Study, Jane became one of 120 women whose homes were tested between June 1999 and September 2001. In addition to extracting dust particles and taking readings of air quality, the researchers questioned her about the products she bought and the materials that had been used in the manufacture of her home.

The results of the study were conclusive and, once again, astonishing: People were being exposed to hormone-altering chemicals inside of their homes. On average, the dust contained twenty-six different hormone-altering compounds, and the air contained nineteen. In many of the homes, the concentrations of at least one of the compounds studied exceeded guidelines for safety established by the EPA. The most commonly found compounds in the dust on Cape Cod were phthalates (pronounced THA-lates). These are industrial plasticizers (chemicals that soften plastic and carry fragrance) that are nearly ubiquitous in our environment, particularly in the products we use in our homes: They can be found in anything made of vinyl, including many of our children's toys, our wallpaper and flooring, our car seats, adhesives and sealants, and our food wrap and disposable containers. Because they are also used to attach fragrances to products, they can be found in many cosmetics and other personal-care products.

The researchers were concerned to find phthalates in so many homes because these chemicals are understood to be potentially harmful to human health. Phthalates have been shown in laboratory tests to cause breast-cancer cells to grow. Research has also shown that exposure to certain phthalates can be incredibly dangerous to developing fetuses, especially males. In August 2006, researchers from the University of Rochester published a truly groundbreaking study in the government journal *Environmental Health Perspectives.* After testing the level of phthalates in blood samples from pregnant women in Los Angeles, Minneapolis, and Columbia, Missouri, they found that the higher the level of phthalates, the greater the chance that these mothers would give birth to baby boys with defects of the reproductive tract. These defects at young ages mean that, later in life, these males face increased risk of serious reproductive problems, including difficulties becoming fathers themselves and increased risk of testicular cancer as young adults.

Although DDT hadn't been used on Cape Cod since it was banned in 1972, the SSI study found that it was still present in the dust of many homes, as were PCBs (polychlorinated biphenyls), also banned in the 1970s and since identified as a probable human carcinogen by the EPA. These results demonstrated just how persistent these chemicals can be once they enter the environment. The household study made it clear that chemicals known to cause cancer in animals when tested could still be found indoors years after they had been banned.

The research team was most surprised to find that chemicals called alkylphenols, which are used in some detergents, disinfectants, hair-care products, and spot removers, were abundant in the air inside these homes. Manufacturers have claimed that these chemicals do not volatize, or break down and escape into the air. But the manufacturers were apparently mistaken. "The finding of our widespread exposure to alkylphenols was troubling," said Ruthann Rudel, a senior scientist at Silent Spring, "because we know they are estrogenic. Even more alarming, though, is that no one has conducted enough research to know their full impact on our health."

The team at the Silent Spring Institute are continuing to push the envelope on this issue. Soon, they will conduct a study exploring the potential exposure to endocrine-disrupting and other harmful chemicals in cleaning solutions. But, as Ellen Parker explained, this problem is not one that will be solved in the laboratory alone. "We were so naive when we began our activism that we were surprised to learn that the burden was on proving the evil of chemicals rather than their safety," she said. "Our ultimate hope is that the research we are doing will enhance people's understanding of why it's necessary to pass legislation and enact policies that follow the commonsense idea of 'do no harm.'" Working in coalition with other groups, the members of the Silent Spring Institute have helped to lay the scientific groundwork for such policies.

GREENER, BETTER

Of course, breast cancer is just one of the potential consequences of the toxic soup that surrounds us, and many pioneering Americans are working to help identify the link between the way we steward our environment and our own health.

John Spengler, director of the Environmental Science and Engineering program at Harvard's School of Public Health, has devoted his career to studying and understanding the effects of indoor and outdoor air pollution on human health. He pioneered the development of personal monitors to measure how air pollution affects individuals as they go about their daily activities. This breakthrough has helped researchers gather data critical to understanding the link between pollution and human health.

Spengler has shown that exposure to indoor pollution can be even more harmful to human beings and their health than outdoor exposure. His work led to the recommendation by the National Academy of Sciences to ban smoking on airlines in 1986. He has not been satisfied with merely showing that fungi, molds, radon, mildew, asbestos, lead, and tobacco smoke indoors can adversely affect health. Spengler has also taken the next step to improve air quality through sustainable-development strategies at Harvard and elsewhere, involving the design of more healthful living conditions, taking into account energy efficiency, comfort, and indoor air quality. Dr. Spengler has identified the environmental health triggers in the air that cause illness and other adverse health reactions.

There's also a growing interest in this subject among chemists, some of whom are exploring how to counter the ill effects of toxins released in industrial processes. Five of the most eminent green chemists in the U.S. are John Warner at the University of Massachusetts, John Hutchinson at the University of Oregon, Paul Anastas at Yale, Eric Beckman at the University of Pittsburgh, and Terry Collins, a member of Carnegie Mellon University's (CMU) Mellon College of Science faculty. Collins is noted in his field for his seminal contributions to green chemistry, his dedication to education, and his public advocacy for greater use of green chemistry to achieve a sustainable civilization. Credited with creating a new class of oxidation catalysts with the potential for enormous positive impact on the environment, Collins heads the Institute for Green Oxidation Chemistry (IGOC). At CMU, the Institute aims for nothing less than replacing polluting, chlorine-based technologies with benign processes. Working with leading Pittsburgh health care facilities, Collins is currently evaluating the use of several nontoxic disinfectants and cleaning products that may revolutionize modern business. Green chemists like Collins are forging ways to add safer and cheaper detergents to hot water, replacing toxic solvents, and reducing wastes.

Dr. Devra Davis, who leads the Center for Environmental Oncology at the University of Pittsburgh's Cancer Institute, is certainly an inspiring leader in the effort to advance an integrated and preventive approach to environmental health. The center takes a proactive approach to identifying the "goods" that can prevent cancer or keep it from recurring, and the "bads" that should be avoided to reduce risks of the disease. The nation's busiest cancer treatment center, the UPCI is the only National Cancer Institute–designated Comprehensive Cancer Center in western Pennsylvania and is ranked among the top hospitals in the nation by *U.S. News and World Report.* Not content with the conventional approaches, its research activities are looking into the ways that regularly encountered pollutants can interfere with chemotherapy and affect the chances that cancer will occur or recur. It is the locus of activities for hospital greening for the entire medical system of the University of Pittsburgh Medical Center (UPMC), and it sponsors cutting-edge research on the environment-disease link. On any given day, the center may be conducting community education programs or offering training for physicians and nurses on the latest scientific findings linking environment to disease. A special focus of activities involves looking at potential environmental factors that may lie behind the puzzling and persisting increased death rates for many forms of cancer that occur in African Americans.

The UPMC story is one of a health-care system that increasingly understands it must act to prevent illness and promote health alongside its efforts to detect and treat diseases. The system spans the tri-state region and provides care and insurance to patients across thirty counties, spanning a range of facilities—from full-fledged major medical centers, to doctors' offices, to cancer centers, to in-home care and nursing homes. This institution is serving as a living laboratory for the community, setting standards for doing more with fewer resources and greater efficiency, and introducing technologies that promote efficiencies and waste reduction throughout the system. This model of health care, which seeks to prevent disease rather than merely treating its consequences, is one we should all demand in our communities.

Deirdre Imus is a different kind of pioneer in the medical world. In 1998, she and her husband, national radio personality Don Imus, founded the Imus Cattle Ranch for Kids with Cancer. It is a 4,000-acre working cattle ranch in northern New Mexico that provides the experience of the American cowboy for children suffering from cancer and various blood diseases, and to children who have lost a brother or sister to Sudden Infant Death Syndrome (SIDS). More than 700 children have experienced the program since the ranch was founded in 1998. Since starting the ranch, Deirdre Imus has become a true pioneer of the movement to seek solutions to the toxins in our environment.

"As I got to know these kids," she said, "I had to ask myself: Why is this happening? Why are so many kids getting sick?" Like the women who met in Ellen Parker's living room, Deirdre did not have the training to answer that question. And also like them, that did not concern her. She just did what she needed to do to better understand the problem. "I read Rachel Carson's book. I started researching, talking to doctors, and looking at epidemiological studies. I couldn't believe what I was finding. Even the World Health Organization tells us that well over 80 percent of all these chronic illnesses, including cancer, could be prevented if we weren't constantly bombarded and exposed to all these environmental toxins."

In fact, exposure to environmental toxins has been linked to childhood cancers. The U.S. National Cancer Institute has noted that exposure to pesticides may play a role in the development of childhood leukemia, brain tumors, non-Hodgkin's lymphoma, Wilms' tumors, Ewing's sarcoma, and soft-tissue sarcoma. Solvents that are commonly used in paints, gasoline, varnish strippers, degreasers, and some glues have also been linked to brain tumors and leukemia in children.

Children are more susceptible to the harmful effects of chemicals than adults because their developing bodies are less equipped to handle them. Pesticides, for example, are particularly harmful to young children because the central nervous system—including the brain and the spinal cord—is not fully developed until the age of about six, and pesticides have known neurotoxic effects. The National Academy of Sciences issued a somber warning about the existence of pesticides in baby food: "Exposure to neurotoxic compounds at levels believed to be safe for adults could result in permanent loss of brain function if it occurred during the prenatal and early childhood period of brain development." In 2003 a University of Washington study found that children who ate a diet of organic food had a level of pesticides in their bodies six times lower than children fed conventionally produced food.

Baby food is not the only problem: Chemicals that go into the manufacture of other products intended for young children also pose a dilemma for parents. Polyvinyl chloride (PVC) softens because of the existence of phthalates, yet it is still used in the manufacture of many children's toys, such as bath books, rattles, beach balls, plastic raincoats and boots, and even teething rings. It can be absorbed from the products during use into a young child's body.

What's more, it's impossible to fully shield a child from toxins because their exposure actually begins in the womb. A biomonitoring study, coordinated by the EWG, tested the umbilical cord blood from ten babies who had been born in the United States in August and September 2004. These newborns were found to have absorbed in the womb a combined total of 413 chemicals. At birth, each child carried an average body burden of *200 chemicals*. The chemicals included components of pesticides, flame retardants, and other persistent organic compounds or by-products from burning gasoline and garbage.

The EWG also tested the breast milk of twenty first-time mothers from across the United States for the presence of components of chemical flame retardants that are used in computers, TVs, and foam furniture, all of which can cause thyroid toxicity, and some of which have been banned in Europe. The results were sobering. The breast milk of each new mother tested positive for components of flame retardants. The average level of brominated fire retardants in the milk samples was seventy-five times higher than the average for women who had been tested in Europe, and were at levels associated with toxic effects in studies on lab animals.

Children cannot excrete harmful compounds as effectively as adults because their kidneys are less mature. Young people also have lower levels of the enzymes known to break down certain insecticides in the body. The fact that children take in more air than adults—the normal respiratory volume of a resting infant is twice that of a resting adult—makes them more susceptible to the chemicals that volatize in the air and dust. As reported in a 1993 environmental journal, researchers in one study found that children living in homes where the pesticide pentachlorophenol (PCP) was found in the air had nearly twice as much PCP in their bloodstreams as their parents.

As Deirdre Imus came to understand the extent of the problem through her work with children at the Imus Ranch, her research, and the many talks she had with experts like Dr. Devra Davis and Dr. Deborah Axelrod of the New York University Medical Center, she began to look at the world in a whole new way. She began to realize that hospitals—meant to be healing environments—could be very toxic places. "As soon as you enter most hospitals," she said, "right away you're breathing industrial cleaning products and pest controls, while the various building materials used can seep into the air, in the form of gases. And of course, we don't even know what the effects are when all these different chemicals bump into each other in our bodies."

In fact, in 2002, the Food and Drug Administration (FDA) conducted a safety assessment of one chemical, a type of phthalate called DEHP, that is used in the manufacture of much of the equipment used in hospitals. The FDA concluded: "Exposure to DEHP has produced a range of adverse effects in laboratory animals, but of greatest concern are effects on the development of the male reproductive system and production of normal sperm in young animals. We have not received reports of these adverse events in humans, but there have been no studies to rule them out. However, in view of the available animal data, precautions should be taken to limit the exposure of the developing male to DEHP."

Deirdre decided to take on the fight against toxins in order to reduce their impact on children. In 2001 she founded the Deirdre Imus Environmental Center for Pediatric Oncology, which is housed at the Hackensack University Medical Center, a not-for-profit corporation in New Jersey, the nation's fourth-largest hospital in terms of patient admissions. The pediatric center represents one of the first hospital-based programs with the specific mission of identifying, controlling, and ultimately preventing exposures to environmental factors that may cause cancer and other health problems in children.

Through her work with the Center, she developed a line of nontoxic industrial cleaners under the name "Greening the Cleaning" and helped to implement them hospital-wide. Not only did the use of of Greening the Cleaning products mean a more healthful environment for patients, their use has also cut the hospital's expenses for cleaning products by 15 percent. Since then, nearly 200 institutions, from schools to hospitals, have begun to use the products. Imus has also launched a retail line of household nontoxic cleaning products that are now available in many stores. All of the profits from the sale of these products are used to support the work of the Center in Pediatric Oncology.

But Deirdre wasn't content to stop there. Rather, she began to lobby local governments to adopt a more environmentally friendly approach to the cleaning of schools and other public buildings. Her efforts have had a tremendous impact. Her organization has helped usher in "Green Cleaning" Executive Orders from governors of three states (New York, New Jersey, and Connecticut). In January 2005, New York Governor George Pataki recognized Deirdre Imus in his State of the State Address for her time and energy in raising awareness of the hazards of chemical cleaning products. The governor issued an Executive Order the same day, requiring all state agencies and authorities to begin using non-toxic cleaning products that are free of harmful chemicals. And, under a New York state law passed last in August 2006, all schools in the state will begin using "Green Cleaning" alternatives beginning in the 2006–2007 fall school term as soon as existing inventories are depleted. In January 2006, with information from the Center and their award-winning Greening the Cleaning® program, former New Jersey Governor Richard J. Codey signed Executive Order 76, requiring all state agencies and authorities to begin using environmentally-responsible cleaning products that are free of harmful chemicals. In April 2006, Connecticut Governor M. Jodi Rell signed Executive Order 14, mandating the immediate use of "green cleaning" products in state facilities. Governor Rell recognized the legislation as a move to minimize risks to health and the environment.

Even after all that Deirdre Imus has accomplished, there is one question she remains unsure about: Does she consider herself an environmentalist? "I guess I am, but I don't know," she said. "I don't call myself that. Maybe I'd say green activist, or humanitarian, or children's advocate. I'm not a doctor, I didn't go to school for anything I'm working on right now. I think what I'd call myself is just a 'commonsense thinker.'"

A FLAWED SYSTEM

The news that we are so surrounded by an alphabet soup of toxic, unregulated chemicals may seem, at worst, alarming, and at best, overwhelming. In response, Rachel Carson's words from *Silent Spring* are worth remembering: "The public must decide whether it wishes to continue on the present road, and it can do so only when in full possession of the facts," she wrote. Near the end of her book, she concluded: "The choice, after all, is ours to make. If, having endured much, we have at last asserted our 'right to know,' and if knowing, we have concluded that we are being asked to take senseless and frightening risks, then we should no longer accept the counsel of those who tell us that we must fill our world with poisonous chemicals; we should look about and see what other course is open to us."

We know another course is possible. A profound shift in the

chemical-management paradigm has been adopted by the European Union (EU), where chemical producers are now required to provide authorities and the public with toxicity data on all high-volume chemicals. It is simply common sense: Before you release something into the environment, you must tell us about its health and environmental effects. Japan has banned the use of some phthalates in toys, and soon, certain phthalates will be permanently banned from use in all toys in Europe. In July 2006, the EU imposed a ban on all new TVs, computers, and other electrical and electronic equipment containing a toxic flame retardant called deca-BDE. By June of 2007, a major new legislative initiative will govern the way the EU treats chemicals. The program, called REACH (Registration, Evaluation, Authorization, and Restriction of Chemicals), affects all firms that make or import more than one ton of a chemical substance each year, requiring detailed information on chemical safety that will be made publicly accessible.

Contrast that with what happens in the United States. The Toxic Substances Control Act (TSCA), passed in 1976, was intended to provide complete evaluations of existing chemicals in commerce and to regulate new ones, but its goals have gone largely unfulfilled. Common chemicals we encounter every day are supposed to be "regulated" under the TSCA. However, at the time of its passage, nearly 62,000 chemicals being manufactured and sold in the United States were all exempted from any mandatory review or testing.

In 1998, the federal government and the chemical industry established a voluntary program whereby industry leaders agreed to begin testing chemicals that are produced in high volume (defined as more than 1 million pounds each year). The intention here is good, but the reality is that for much of the chemical revolution we have been flying blind, without solid tests on which to base our decisions about chemicals. Certainly, the fact that we are only now, half a century after the start of the chemical revolution, engaging in this sort of testing program shows how far we still have to travel.

We also need to question whether industry-sponsored research will provide the sort of independent information required. Consider, for example, what science tells us of phthalates. In laboratory tests, they have been shown to cause breast-cancer cells to grow and harm the reproductive tract of developing fetuses. In one study, a team from Boston's Tufts University, led by Professor Soto, studied the effects of phthalate exposure in rats. They exposed pregnant rats to bisphenol A (BPA), a chemical used in the manufacture of some plastics, and which is found in many containers, including baby bottles and the linings of canned foods. The levels to which rats were exposed mirrored levels that humans can encounter daily. The results? By the time they reached puberty, rats that had received even the lowest doses of BPA had four times more precancerous growths in breast tissue than those that had not been exposed at all to this compound.

But what does the industry say about these chemicals? These are the falsely reassuring words a concerned consumer would find on the Web site of the Phthalates Information Center administered by the American Chemistry Council, the industry's lobbying organization: "Phthalates have established a very strong safety profile over the 50 years in which they have been in general use. There is no reliable evidence that any phthalate has ever caused a health problem for a human from its intended use. . . . Despite the strong body of evidence that indicates phthalates may be used safely in a wide variety of products and applications, some individuals and organizations have 'cherry picked' the results showing impacts on test animals to create unwarranted concern about these products." In point of fact, testing is done on animals in order to predict and prevent human harm, not to prove that such harm will take place. When adequately tested, every chemical proven to cause cancer in humans has been found to cause cancer in animals. This means that we must pay careful attention to animal testing.

Given these incongruities, what is our best course of action? Do we wait for definitive human evidence of harm, basically treating people like laboratory rats in an uncontrolled experiment? Or do we make choices based on the technical information at hand to reduce potential risks, while encouraging research to develop safer alternatives?

Is it enough to trust the claims made by manufacturers about the chemicals we use today, or should we be requiring them to test these substances and *prove* that they are not harmful?

The bottom line is this: The absence of definitive proof of human harm should never be confused with proof that there is no harm. We have to do a better job of relying on basic science to guide us in predicting and preventing harm, rather than waiting for enough illness to amass that it becomes undeniable—as we did with cigarettes and, more recently, Hormone Replacement Therapy (HRT). No one doubts today that we should have acted sooner to control both.

Hormone replacement therapy was stopped when it became clear that the use of synthetic estrogens increased the risk of breast cancer, heart attack, deep vein thrombosis, and stroke. One report speculates that a drop in breast cancer among white women in the United States in 2003 could have been in large part due to the fact that so many women stopped using synthetic HRT just one year earlier. The jury is still out on this issue. But if synthetic hormones like those used in HRT are now understood to increase the risk of cancer and other diseases, shouldn't we be sure to test the effect of other endocrine disruptors before letting them into our lives?

Because we do not require that the toxicity of chemicals be determined before they are sold, citizens are left to battle a powerful chemical industry on their own. In the late 1990s, a coalition of organizations began to question the use of PVC in toys and petitioned the Consumer Products Safety Commission (CPSC) to ban the chemical in the manufacture of products intended for children. The CPSC denied the petition in 2003 (though some companies have agreed to voluntarily discontinue the use of PVC in at least some of their products). Some states have attempted to take on the matter locally. A bill banning the use of phthalates in toys was recently introduced in the California State Assembly, but it was ultimately defeated under heavy lobbying from the toy industry. Some other states are proposing similar legislation, but they are sure to face a similar fight.

One of the most disturbing instances of industry influencing government regulation occurred in 2005, when the EPA was evaluating a pesticide called atrazine, which is used on most of the corn and sugarcane grown in the United States. Scientific studies have found that atrazine is a reproductive toxin and can cause cancer. Reports from Italy found that the incidence of ovarian cancer in women with high exposures to atrazine was two to four times higher than in women without such exposures. In addition, the chemical has been detected at levels higher than the EPA's safety standard in the drinking-water supply for more than a million Americans in the Midwest. The *Chronicle of Higher Education* reported that when researcher Tyrone Hayes, now a professor at the University of California at Berkeley, worked for Syngenta, the primary manufacturer of atrazine, his lab found that the pesticide caused deformities in frogs. The company actively discouraged him from publishing these findings, however.

Despite this information, the EPA ruled that atrazine could remain on the market. The European Union saw it quite differently and moved to ban atrazine based on the same research available in the United States. Furthermore, the Natural Resources Defense Council (NRDC) has found, through government documents obtained through a Freedom of Information Act lawsuit, that representatives of the EPA secretly met, *more than forty times,* with lobbyists from Syngenta during the evaluation process. "We're flabbergasted," said NRDC senior scientist Jennifer Sass at the time. "We've reviewed the science on atrazine, and it is clear that it is dangerous at levels the EPA says are harmless. And we're shocked that EPA would abdicate its responsibility to protect the public and allow the manufacturer to write the rules."

Another reprehensible example of the federal government's failure to protect its citizens from avoidable harm occurred in 2005, when the EPA proposed a study to test the effects of pesticide use on children's health. Named the Children's Health Environmental Exposure Research Study and nicknamed CHEERS, the study, according to the EPA, "was designed to fill critical data gaps in our understanding of how children may be exposed to pesticides (such as bug spray) and chemicals currently used in households. Information from the study was intended to help EPA better protect children."

How would the research be done?

Sixty families from Duval County, Florida, would agree to record how their children, aged thirteen months and younger, responded to toxic chemicals in their homes. In exchange, the families would each receive $970, children's clothes, a camcorder, and a framed certificate of appreciation. The study was to be funded by the EPA with the help of a $2 million contribution from the American Chemistry Council, formerly the Chemical Manufacturers' Association.

There were many problems with this approach, most significantly, the families likely to respond to this survey would have been poor—families for whom $970 meant at least one month they did not have to choose between paying the rent and buying groceries—a fact that the EPA did not even attempt to hide. A proposal explaining the program stated that participants for the study would be chosen from six health clinics and hospitals in the county. "Although all Duval County citizens are eligible to use the [health care] centers," the EPA report stated, "they primarily serve individuals with lower incomes. In the year 2000, seventy five percent of the users of the clinics for pregnancy issues were at or below the poverty level." The EPA proposal went on to say that "the percentage of births to individuals classified as black in the U.S. Census is higher at these three hospitals than for the County as a whole."

Mercifully, the EPA canceled the CHEERS study after a number of organizations and several senators—including my husband and his colleague, Barbara Boxer—expressed outrage.

THE PRECAUTIONARY PRINCIPLE

As hard as people like the women of the Silent Spring Institute and Deirdre Imus are working to fix this problem, they certainly cannot do it alone. Part of the answer clearly lies with necessary government safeguards. As a society, we need a prevention-based policy, and that means testing chemicals for their possible harmful effects *before* they are released into the environment and allowed to end up in the products under our sinks, in our medicine cabinets, and inside women's purses.

The precautionary principle—which is being adopted in many places outside of the United States, including the European Union—is based on this very simple and logical idea: The burden should be on the manufacturer to prove that the chemicals they sell do not have harmful effects, rather than on the consumer to prove that they do. It is certainly the wisest, cheapest, and best approach to the toxic dilemma. Manufacturers should not sell products to us until we have proof that they will not harm us. Period. Other nations accepted the wisdom of this. In December 2006, the European Union formally adopted REACH regulations, which makes industry more responsible for managing the risks from chemicals and for providing safety information on them. As the world's leading industrial nation, the United States must embrace this practice as well.

Convincing elected officials of the harmful effects of toxic substances can be difficult in part because the manufacturers are working hard to convince them otherwise. Manufacturers may claim that the level of exposure to particular chemicals is so low as to be insignificant. However, even small exposures can add up over time. A fundamental problem with the way that the EPA evaluates the possible toxic impact of a chemical is that it considers that chemical in isolation; in other words, what are the effects to a single person exposed to that *one chemical* at *one point in time?* This is the wrong question in the wrong context. One cannot ignore the cumulative effect of the body burden. Our bodies are being bombarded with a range of chemicals every day of our lives. Biomonitoring tests conducted by many groups make it clear— our bloodstreams are threatened by a cocktail of different chemicals.

We must not allow our bodies—particularly the bodies of women and children—to be used as part of an uncontrolled experiment without our knowledge and without our consent. And we do not need to quietly accept the presence of industrial and synthetic chemicals as a necessary condition of living in today's world. Any discussion about our relationship to the Earth needs to take these issues into account. We must examine how we use the Earth's resources and how we manage and understand the choices we make about the natural and artificial chemicals in our everyday lives. For nearly a decade, the Heinz Family Foundations have been bringing together scientists, advocates, and researchers who are working hard to explore the link between the environment and women's health. The kinds of questions these researchers ask—and that all of us should ask—and the decisions we make every day can guide us to healthier lives.

Our current system has put us in a position of forever managing crises and fears and panic instead of preventing them. It keeps us on the defensive and in the demeaning position of feeling victimized. By taking the kind of proactive approach that people like Devra Davis, Deirdre Imus, and the women of Silent Spring have taken, we can discover ways, both as individuals and as a society, to change all this, and as a result, to promote better health for ourselves and our children. The solutions can occur on many levels—both personal and political, in the corporate world, in the halls of educational institutions, in the nonprofit world, and in small entrepreneurial start-ups with vision.

As individuals, there are many choices we can make each day that can help us to at least keep our homes more free of toxins, and we have included a list (see appendix) of some recommendations on doing that at the end of the book. But, if nothing else, we hope that all of us will join the discussion about toxins in our homes. Think about the skyrocketing asthma rates, the high cancer rates. Make a list of the products you use each day with ingredients you may not completely understand, and which may not even appear on the label. Individually, maybe they are not a problem. But if you use them regularly—or use some of them every day—maybe your body is taking a beating. Talk to your friends and family members about these issues. Maybe some of you will be inspired to do what Ellen Parker did—invite people over for coffee and figure out if you are all asking the same questions. Then ask how you might find the answers. Maybe some of you will choose to call your legislators and ask them what they think about the issue of PVC use in toys, or whether they could support legislation incorporating the precautionary principle. Maybe you will decide to buy organic berries or broccoli, or to clean with vinegar. Maybe you can get your school board to adopt safe cleaning products in the schools. You may find yourself making first one change, and then another. Incrementally, the small changes will add up.

I often think about something Cheryl Osimo said to me, in her unmistakable Cape Cod accent: "The key is, as women, we must all work together as a team in order to do whatever it is we need to do to find the preventable causes of the diseases we see." It really is a matter of strength in numbers. The *New Yorker* magazine recently ran a ditty that illustrates this concept in a way that struck a chord for me: "Tomato ketchup in a bottle: first none'll come, and then the lot'll." With a special affinity for ketchup, I especially like the analogy. But what it makes clear is that once we reach the so-called tipping point, small actions can produce dramatic changes.

I agree with Cheryl Osimo about the tremendous role that women can play in this process of bringing about change to heal our world. I have come to think that women often possess a special strength: the skill for managing chaos. After raising three boys, "growing up" with one adult male, my late husband, and now with my second husband John, I've concluded that mothers and wives should be given the professional title of Chaos Manager. And no pay is sufficient. The only coin is love.

Nearly three decades ago, I traveled to the Amazon to observe the slash and burning of the rain forest with then Senators John Heinz, Al Gore, and Tim Wirth and his wife Wren, all of us in the capable hands of a brilliant biologist, Tom Lovejoy. I was awestruck by the remarkably high trees, some as tall as 200 feet, which created the forest canopy. Each stood in soil of less than a foot deep, propped up by a tripod of roots—much like flying buttresses in a cathedral. The soil in which these massive old trees rested was home to mushrooms, fungi, and more than 30 million insects. The loss of any single member of this forest family could mean the death of the system on which these mighty trees depended.

As humans, we tower over much of the world around us today. In truth, however, science tells us that we are no less dependent on our environment than the trees of the Amazon are on theirs. In fact, the Amazon region has been called the lungs of the earth, because its vegetation provides so much of the world's oxygen. Recognizing that exquisite connection we have to the natural world today provides us with a renewed urgency to ensure that the world we leave to our children and grandchildren will be less toxic, and more hopeful, than the one we find ourselves living in today. For all of us, whether in our homes or communities, that begins with the principle: first, do no harm.

CHAPTER THREE

Abuse of Power

Many of the problems facing our planet today can be addressed if we accept the connections between our actions and the consequences— as people like the women of the Silent Spring Institute have, and as Rachel Carson did before them. DDT can be extremely harmful, so we shouldn't be exposed to it. Some cleaning products are potentially toxic, so we shouldn't be using them in hospitals. Some ingredients used to manufacture plastics might harm our children, so they shouldn't be used in toys. These are not radical ideas or political notions, they're simply common sense, follow-the-logic thinking.

Our leaders in Washington, and in some boardrooms across the nation, have failed to make these connections. There is no mystery, for example, about why our air today remains polluted. Air pollution can be traced back, in part, to the more than 500 coal-fired power plants in this country, many of them decades old, that generate the electricity used in our homes, offices, and factories. It can also be traced to hazardous waste sites, petroleum refineries, chemical plants, waste-treatment facilities, and the like. And though the government may be failing to do much about it, there are some individuals who are challenging the status quo and bringing about change for the better in their communities.

DIRTY POWER

We know that coal-fired power plants release a mix of toxic chemicals, including mercury, into the atmosphere, and that, spewed through the smokestacks, it eventually settles in lakes, rivers, and oceans. Once in the water, mercury mixes with bacteria and becomes methylmercury, a highly toxic compound. It is easily ingested by fish and becomes more concentrated as it travels up the food chain. Nearly every fish sold in our grocery stores today contains some mercury. Some types of fish—including tuna, swordfish, and king mackerel—have particularly high levels. We also know that mercury is a dangerous neurotoxin to humans, especially fetuses and children. Two years ago, scientists with the Environmental Protection Agency announced that approximately one in six infants—or 630,000 of the 4 million babies—born in the United States each year has a blood mercury level above what the agency considers safe, and high enough to cause learning disabilities, impair motor skills, and affect intelligence.

The connection is very clear: Out-of-date, low-tech, coal-powered plants can gravely injure children and adults alike, even miles and states beyond where they are located. But we know something else. Controlling mercury emissions from power plants—especially our oldest and dirtiest power plants—can result in reduced mercury levels. The state of Florida, for example, through the application of existing technologies, was able to achieve sharp reductions in mercury pollution. In the Everglades, mercury levels went down by approximately 80 percent in less than fifteen years. In Wisconsin, a 10 percent a year decrease in mercury deposition resulted in a 5 percent per year decline in mercury levels in yellow perch, amounting to a 30 percent drop over six years, according to a Natural Resources Defense Council report.

Prompted by a 1998 report on toxic pollution put out by the Environmental Protection Agency, President Bill Clinton declared mercury a "threat to human health." The EPA data suggested that mercury was the most dangerous toxin in our environment. In 2000, under provisions of the Clean Air Act, Clinton ordered coal plants to reduce their mercury emissions. To achieve this, power plants were required to install control technology for mercury emissions and other toxic air pollutants by the end of 2007, and then further limit any unacceptable health risks that remained. In 2001, EPA acknowledged that mercury pollution from utilities could be reduced by nearly 90 percent by 2008.

Common sense told us that this was the right course of action—a simple matter of connecting the dots, and then acting to thwart a preventable problem.

When President George W. Bush and the Republican Congress took power in 2001, guess what happened? The Clinton rule on reducing mercury emissions was wiped off the books, and in its place the president proposed a policy allowing power plants to emit *more than five times as much* mercury through 2018, and three times as much after 2019, than under existing law. An EPA analysis noted that this revision to the act allowed more than 100 power plants to actually *increase* mercury emissions.

These policy changes were not without consequences. In all, more than 100,000 of our nation's lakes and 846,000 miles of our rivers were under fish advisories in 2003—and 76 percent of all the advisories were attributable at least in part to mercury contamination. The administration would not back down, despite the fact that in 2006, the EPA issued advisories in forty-six states warning the public—pregnant women and children in particular—not to eat some varieties of fish.

But there's yet a more disturbing connection at work here: Why would the Republican majority overturn a law that made so much sense, one that could protect our air and water, and ultimately help keep people safe? The reason: Because of the lobbying power of large corporate interests resistant to change and generous with campaign contributions. Since 1999, the thirty biggest utility companies in the nation, operating some of the dirtiest and most polluting power plants, have contributed $6.6 million to President Bush and the Republican National Committee, making them one of the Republicans' largest financial supporters.

Now, when a father or mother applies for a fishing license in some states, hoping to take their children fishing, they also receive a booklet that lists all of the rivers, lakes, and streams where it is no longer safe to fish. Washington's casual indifference has jeopardized the great American rite of passage of a parent taking a son or daughter fishing. The experience and wonder of dropping a baited line and hooking that first fish has turned into a different kind of event. Now, if able to find a clean fishing hole, a child lucky enough to catch a fish may no longer be allowed to eat it. In many communities, families cannot participate in one of our oldest national pastimes. Even fish bought at a grocery store could place someone's health at risk—all because huge campaign contributions have leveraged a president and Congress to be more beholden to powerful and polluting utility companies than to the American people and their well-being.

The connection between politics and powerful special interests stretches well beyond the issue of mercury contamination in fish. These interests also played an important role in helping to actually dismantle the Clean Air Act, which since its passage in 1972 has been one of the cornerstones of U.S. environmental standards. The Act targeted the six common industrial pollutants that affect air quality the most: nitrogen oxide, sulfur dioxide, ozone, particulate matter, carbon monoxide, and lead. Statutory deadlines were set to reduce automobile emissions levels, America's leading source of pollution at the time. These mandated a 90 percent reduction in hydrocarbon and carbon monoxide levels by 1975 and a 90 percent reduction in nitrogen oxides by 1976.

The Clean Air Act achieved some stunning results. The concentration of air contaminants, especially in urban areas, has decreased dramatically over the past thirty-five years. Total emissions of the six targeted pollutants dropped by 53 percent in the first two decades after passage of the act, and according to the EPA, the reductions in air pollution prevented 206,000 premature deaths; 674,000 cases of chronic bronchitis; 209,000 hospital admissions; and 227 million respiratory ailments. Most impressively, these reductions were achieved during a period of tremendous economic growth: The U.S. economy grew by more than 187 percent, the number of vehicle miles traveled increased by 171 percent, and U.S. energy consumption grew by 47 percent. Furthermore, with a net monetary benefit of $21.7 trillion, despite all the predictions of economic doom to the contrary, the Clean Air Act is often considered one of the most cost-effective and efficient regulatory programs ever passed.

But a law is only as powerful as the consistency of its application. Today, according to the American Lung Association's *State of the Air: 2005* report, more than 152 million Americans—half the nation—still live in counties where they are being exposed to unhealthy levels of air pollution. The two most pervasive air pollutants today are particle pollution and smog-causing ozone, stemming primarily from emissions from dirty power plants, factories and from diesel exhaust.

The Clean Air Act has been under heavy attack in recent years. This is due in large part to the continued pressure and opposition of those powerful interests that have had the administration's ear. This cozy relationship led to a proposed initiative in February 2003 that hid behind a name of Orwellian deceitfulness.

The Senate refused to weaken the Clean Air Act and defeated the president's initiative. But that didn't stop the Bush Administration from bowing to corporate polluters. Instead, the White House decided to pursue a series of administrative rule changes aimed at undermining the Clean Air Act, starting with what's known as New Source Review.

Due to a loophole included in a 1977 amendment to the Clean Air Act, many of today's older plants lack modern pollution controls. Because these dinosaurs faced certain extinction, the industry argued at the time, it would be a waste of scarce resources to require they be retrofitted in the last days of their lives. Congress did not require immediate controls for these older plants, but they wisely put in place a key provision to keep this loophole from being abused—a provision that still exists today. Under New Source Review or NSR, plant owners are required to adopt or upgrade pollution controls to modern standards whenever they make plant changes that significantly increase emissions.

In the last ten years, however, evidence started to mount documenting how broadly this provision had been ignored. In the 1990s, under the leadership of President Clinton, the Environmental Protection Agency and the U.S. Department of Justice began to investigate electric power producers for violations of New Source Review. The investigation showed that for years many plant owners had been making major capital investments, extending the lives of their plants while increasing pollution by thousands and even tens of thousands of tons each year, without adopting or upgrading pollution controls—all in clear violation of the Clean Air Act. By mid–2001, the Department of Justice and the EPA had filed lawsuits against or issued violations to fifty-one power plants owned by thirteen companies in twelve states.

Since George W. Bush has taken office, however, similar enforcement measures have stalled. The result has been an illegal and harmful assault on the health and rights of American families across the nation, not to mention an overt rebuff of congressional intent.

According to the Justice Department and EPA, the failure of an owner to install new emissions controls when these plants were upgraded has resulted in the emission of tens of millions of tons of sulfur dioxide, nitrogen oxides, and particulate matter. From 1992 to 1998, electric generation from these sources increased by more than 15 percent—producing as much smog-forming pollution as emitted by 37 million cars a year.

Many of these plants are in the Midwest, but, because air pollutants can travel far, they impact a broad area of the Midwest, Southeast, and Northeast United States, increasing airborne concentrations of smog and fine particles. And that pollution has been directly connected to making Americans sick. According to a report released by the Clean Air Task Force, a coalition of scientists, economists and other professionals, the pollution stemming from the 51 violating power plants has shortened the lives of as many as 9,000 people and causes as many as 170,000 asthma attacks each year.

Despite this sobering reality, the George W. Bush administration significantly weakened New Source Review protections, and undermined NSR enforcement plans. In November of 2002, without sufficient scientific, health or environmental justification, the President announced rules that significantly rolled back the NSR provision. The changes adopted a series of loopholes allowing approximately 20,000 facilities nationwide to avoid installing modern-day pollution controls when upgrading their facilities and increasing their annual pollution. Additional changes implemented in August of 2003 weakened the regulations even more drastically, effectively exempting coal-fired power plants and other industrial polluters from the need to install NSR pollution controls.

Again, it's necessary to ask a straightforward question: why would our government allow industries to so freely pollute, especially when we are fully aware of the potential health impacts? It was later discovered that some of the EPA rules were adopted verbatim from lobbyists for the utility industry, who secretly met with White House officials to help develop the national policies impacting clean air.

These types of linkages between the policies enacted, the interests behind them, and the impact on each of us require vigilance and individual action. Every parent in America, no matter where we come from, shares an interest in breathing air that doesn't make us ill and serving food that isn't loaded with mercury. When we make these connections we will understand what is at stake every time we make a choice—particularly the choice we make at the ballot box.

A MATTER OF JUSTICE

John: After working for twenty-five years as a lieutenant governor and senator on a wide range of environmental legislation, from laws to combat acid rain to rejuvenating our lakes and rivers, one dimension of this struggle leaps out at me: While all Americans are at risk of suffering the ill effects of air pollution—and all pollution—not all are suffering equally. In the United States, poor and minority Americans have a much greater chance of becoming ill from environmental toxins because they have a greater chance of living near a polluting industry, and living with highly polluted air, than do white, wealthier Americans. A 2005 investigation conducted by the Associated Press found that people of color were *79 percent more likely* than whites to reside in communities where pollution posed the highest health risks (in 1996, that number was 49 percent). The average annual income in the most polluted areas was just $18,806, and one of every six people lived in poverty.

A tour of most American cities makes this far too apparent. A region along the Mississippi River between Baton Rouge and New Orleans, dubbed "Cancer Alley," contains literally hundreds of hazardous waste sites. The area is now one of the poorest in the country and also one of the most polluted. About 200 miles west, the largely African American community of Mossville, Louisiana, in Calcasieu Parish, is home to more than fifty-three industrial factories, more than forty of which are located within a 10-mile radius. The South Bronx, a largely African American and Latino community, bears far more than its fair share of New York City's polluting industries, from power plants to waste-transfer sites. Roxbury, Massachusetts, a central neighborhood of Boston, is also a predominately minority community, and while it has a huge shortage of the assets of wealthier communities, there is no shortage of toxic waste sites. The list, unfortunately, goes on.

The practice of local governments encouraging the placement of noxious industries in poor neighborhoods goes back to the early part of the twentieth century. In the early 1900s, as many cities began to enact zoning policies, it was not unusual for local municipalities to zone minority communities as "industrial"—while, at the same time, zoning similar white communities as "residential." This made it easy for polluting industries to move into these neighborhoods, forcing them to shoulder an unfair portion of environmental nuisances. The trend continues today. Poor and ethnic communities are often assumed to be politically powerless and therefore are targeted when it comes time to locate a new power plant, toxic dump site, or other polluting facility.

For generations, our country appeared to be quietly resigned to this fact, but there has been a change in recent decades, thanks, in large part, to the residents of a small, rural community in Afton, North Carolina, who in 1978 decided they would no longer sit back and allow their homes to be destroyed by powerful interests. That year, the governor of their state announced some very disturbing news: Nearly 60,000 tons of oil, laden with dangerous levels of recently banned PCBs, had been illegally dumped along hundreds of miles of roads across the state. An investigation found that the oil had been dumped there by the operators of a Raleigh-based trucking company who had purchased the oil for resale. After the EPA barred the resale of such material, the company chose to dispose of it by filling tractor trailers with the toxic oil and secretly spilling it from trucks in the dead of night.

The level of PCBs discovered along the roadside was so noxious, and posed such a grave health risk, that the EPA was prompted to name the contaminated areas a Superfund site, the designation given to the nation's most polluted sites. Governor James B. Hunt issued stark warnings about avoiding the affected roadways, cautioning state residents to stop grazing cattle on land near them and to destroy crops grown there. The news precipitated a health panic across the state.

The people responsible for illegally dumping the toxic oil were eventually fined and jailed, but it was the community of Afton, in Warren County, that would suffer far graver consequences. In 1979, as the cleanup effort began, the state chose a 3-acre wheat field in this small rural town for a landfill where the contaminated soil, scraped from the roadside, would be buried. State engineers claimed Afton was the safest and most economical location to dump the material, despite the facts that the water table in Warren County was very high—merely 5 to 10 feet below the surface—and that the town's drinking water came from local wells. Even under the best conditions, landfills often leak, and the risk of groundwater contamination in Afton was high. Before long, the first of what would be more than 6,000 truckloads of the PCB-contaminated oil began to arrive in Afton.

Almost immediately, local residents started to demand answers. If the roadside areas where the oil had been spilled were considered so dangerous, what would it mean to have 60,000 tons of it buried in their backyard? They wanted an explanation of why their community had been chosen as the location for the landfill. Could it have something to do, they wondered, with the fact that more than 84 percent of county residents were African American? Or that Warren County was one of the state's poorest, with an annual per capita income of just $6,984 at the time?

By the time the first truckload arrived, crowds of local residents had gathered at the landfill's entrance to demonstrate their unwillingness to ignore those questions. With each day and each new truckload, the protests swelled. People marched arm in arm to the dump, singing the words to *We Shall Overcome,* the song made famous in the civil rights marches of a decade earlier. They gathered in front of a Baptist church in town, attempting to block the trucks, and even laid down on the asphalt in front of the landfill's entrance, refusing to move. The demonstrations captured the attention of the national media. Soon, representatives of national civil rights groups, churches, and labor organizations and black elected officials arrived in Afton to join in the fight. State troopers in riot gear were called in. By the end of two weeks, more than 500 protesters had been arrested.

Afton, North Carolina, may have seemed at the time an unlikely place for the birth of a political movement, but that's exactly what happened. Although the protesters were ultimately unable to stop the landfill from opening and the PCB-contaminated oil from seeping into their communitys water supply, their actions had more far-reaching effects. For the first time, the issue of environmental justice, or the fact that poor and ethnic communities carried a disproportionate share of environmental risks, entered the national dialogue and the budding environmental movement. As newspapers across the country reported on the efforts of the Afton protesters, people were forced to confront this harsh reality.

Soon after these events, prompted by Congressman Walter E. Fauntroy, a member of the Congressional Black Caucus, the U.S. General Accounting Office, the investigative arm of Congress, began to look into the siting of hazardous waste landfills in relation to the racial and socioeconomic characteristics of people living in the surrounding communities. It was the first time this issue had been examined, and the results, released in 1983, proved what the citizens of Afton had assumed: There was a clear correlation between the location of hazardous waste landfills and the number of African Americans who lived nearby.

Several similar investigations followed, the most significant conducted in 1987 by the United Church of Christ (UCC) Commission for Racial Justice. The UCC study found that race was the single most significant factor in determining the location of a hazardous waste facility. The areas with the highest number of polluting facilities consistently had the highest mean percentage of minority residents, many of them poor, while the areas without any facilities were largely white. In 1994, a UCC follow-up report found that the problem had only worsened in the ensuing seven years. According to the authors of the 1994 report, people of color were 47 percent more likely than whites to live near a commercial hazardous waste facility.

Another study at the time, which was published in the *National Law Journal,* uncovered significant discrepancies in how federal environmental protection laws were enforced in poor communities. For example, the EPA took 20 percent longer to place contaminated sites located in minority communities on the National Priorities List, which designates hazardous sites that are eligible for long-term remedial action financed through the Superfund program; and companies found to have illegally polluted in poor communities paid fines that were 54 percent lower than those levied for similar actions in white communities.

In 1994, President Bill Clinton took action. He signed Executive Order 12898, requiring the federal government to abide by environmental justice principles—namely, to ensure that programs or activities affecting human health or the environment do not discriminate on the basis of race, color, or national origin. The order required the

EPA and other agencies to incorporate these principles into their overall missions.

This was a bold and necessary move, and since then, the idea of environmental justice has become an integral part of the environmental agenda. But despite these efforts, the problem has only grown worse with time. Today, more than two-thirds of all African Americans in this country live within 30 miles of a coal-fired power plant, and 60 percent of African Americans live in communities with uncontrolled toxic-waste sites, according to the National Black Environmental Justice Network (NBEJN). This proximity destroys quality of life and leads to feelings of powerlessness, and, most significantly, coal-fired power plants pollute the air, putting local residents at greater risk for health problems such as respiratory disease, lung cancer, and, as we're seeing in exploding numbers across all races and demographics, asthma.

We know that asthma is related to pollution. According to Environmental Defense, when it comes to asthma, "genetics loads the gun, but environment pulls the trigger." In Atlanta during the 1996 Summer Olympics, the city, hoping to avoid unmanageable gridlock, went to great lengths to encourage people not to drive. Their plan worked: During the seventeen days that the Olympic games took place, auto use decreased by 22.5 percent. But the results were far more significant than averted gridlock. The concentration of ozone dropped by nearly 30 percent, and the benefit to people who suffered the impact of dirty air was immediate. During that period, the number of asthmatics who visited a doctor decreased by 40 percent, the number admitted to hospitals dropped 19 percent, and the number who went to emergency rooms dropped 11 percent.

Asthma, one of the leading health problems among all Americans, is reaching epidemic proportions. In 2004, the American Lung Association estimated that 20.5 million Americans suffered from asthma; close to 1.8 million emergency-room visits were attributed to asthma;

and it accounted for an estimated 14.5 million lost workdays in adults. Asthma is now the most common chronic disorder in children, affecting more than 6 million children in the United States. It is one of the leading causes of school absenteeism in this nation and the third leading cause of hospitalization among children under the age of fifteen.

But again, there is a discrepancy in who is suffering the most. According to the Centers for Disease Control and Prevention, families with annual incomes below $10,000 suffer more than twice the rate of asthma than families who earn more than $35,000. African Americans seek emergency care for asthma attacks at more than four times the rate of whites, and African American children are five times more likely to die from asthma than white children. Although African Americans represent 12.8 percent of the U.S. population, they account for 23.7 percent of asthma deaths.

There is no justice in these statistics. But given the fact that in 2002, 71 percent of African Americans lived in counties where violations of federal air-pollution standards were taking place, compared to 58 percent of the white population, they are hardly surprising.

BUCKET BRIGADES

As daunting as the challenge may be, communities from coast to coast are fighting to protect their neighborhoods and the health of their children from powerful special interests and an administration willing to side with them, inspired by the example of the struggle for environmental rights that began in Afton, North Carolina.

In Boston, for example, the Roxbury Environmental Empowerment Program (REEP) is helping to develop the next generation of leaders by actively engaging young people in working to improve the future of this largely African American community. So far, the young people working with REEP have convinced the city to completely redesign and renovate two parks in Roxbury, persuaded a major developer to spend half a million dollars to clean up a hazardous waste site, educated hundreds of their peers on the environmental links to asthma, organized an ongoing campaign for clean air, and played a key role in developing strategies to improve public transportation in communities of color.

The Bucket Brigade is a program that is having tremendous results in Louisiana. This program was started in 1995 by attorney Edward Masry, who worked with the now well-known Erin Brockovich, after they were both made ill by fumes from a petroleum refinery that Masry was suing on behalf of citizens of Contra Costa County, California. When he called the local, state, and federal environmental authorities to inquire about the air pollution and explain what was happening to the citizens, he was told that their monitors detected no problem. This so angered Masry, whose clients were being exposed to these toxic releases daily, that he hired an environmental engineer to design a low-cost device, called the "bucket," which the community could use to monitor their exposure themselves.

The "bucket" is a device that captures air, which is then sent to a laboratory to measure for about 100 toxic gases. Because the buckets are both inexpensive and simple to use, they gave residents of Contra Costa County living near refineries, chemical plants, and other toxic air–emitting sources a chance to take on the indifferent regulators and corporations who were telling them that the air they were breathing was fine, even as they were choking and dying.

Working closely with Masry, Denny Larson, an organizer with a local group called Communities for a Better Environment, proceeded to promote the use of these buckets in seven other communities in the refinery belt of Contra Costa County. The biggest hurdle was getting the authorities, who belittled the idea of citizen bucket brigades, to accept the results. Larson met with EPA officials in 1996 and asked the agency to approve and fund bucket air sampling. To their credit, the regional EPA office invested in a quality-assurance evaluation of the bucket results and ended up accepting them. With the EPA acceptance, Larson was able to work with grassroots groups around the country to launch local bucket brigades.

As Larson discovered, typically there are no monitoring devices in industrial zones. Instead, they are often located 10 or 20 miles away, sometimes even upwind of the sources. When the public complains about bad smells and choking fumes, the regulatory authorities and industries scoff and ask for proof. Thanks to the buckets, according to Larson, with just a few air samples a community can demolish the industries' claims that pollution doesn't cross their fence-line.

Although the program started in California, the greatest success of the bucket brigadiers was in Louisiana in the late 1990s, when the largely African American community of Mossville in Calcasieu Parish, cited earlier as the home of more than fifty-three industrial factories, were infuriated by lackadaisical government enforcement and frequent accidental toxic releases. In September 1998, Mossville residents of "fence-line communities" formed a bucket brigade and began taking samples. Two of the five original samples found violations of Louisiana standards for vinyl chloride, dichloroethane, and benzene, all very harmful toxins. Subsequent samples were even worse. In fact, one later sample found carcinogenic benzene in excess of 220 times the state's standard.

This got the attention of the media and the enforcement authorities. By 1999, the bucket brigades had spread throughout "Cancer Alley" in Louisiana, leading to the formation of a new nonprofit group, the Louisiana Bucket Brigade. The local EPA office moved in with their own high-priced monitoring devices, which confirmed pollution levels even higher than those detected by the buckets. Fines were levied against the polluters, and state-of-the-art fence-line monitoring devices were required of some facilities. The regional EPA office has since given grants to community groups to continue bucket monitoring. Pollution has been significantly reduced, all of which stemmed from a few citizen activists with their buckets. Bucket brigadiers are now active in California, Ohio, Louisiana, Pennsylvania, and Texas with a proven track record of effectiveness.

CLEANING UP A COMMUNITY

The South Bronx—and Majora Carter, who grew up there—provides an inspiring example of what one community can achieve. Majora's father, Major Carter, the son of a slave and a Pullman porter, moved there in the 1940s. He met Tinnie, Majora's mother, and after they married they purchased a house in the Hunts Point section of the Bronx, just north of Manhattan. At the time, the neighborhood was largely white and working class, and it was supported by a thriving manufacturing industry. Many people, including African Americans and other minorities, moved to the area to find work at one of the factories and warehouses within walking distance of the brownstones that lined the leafy streets.

But as Majora's parents settled into their new home and their new marriage, the neighborhood began to change rapidly. The influx of minorities led, unfortunately, to a period of white flight. By the time Majora was born in 1966, one of ten children in her family, Hunts Point barely resembled the neighborhood her parents had claimed as their home. Its residents were almost exclusively members of minority groups, and because of a New York City housing policy that concentrated a large number of impoverished families in the area, they were increasingly poor. Before long, the neighborhood was redlined by many banks and financial institutions, leading to large-scale disinvestment. Arson became rampant during the late 1960s and early 1970s, and many of the fires were believed to have been started by the buildings' owners, who, it was charged, preferred to torch their property and collect insurance rather than repair the homes that increasingly housed many of the city's poorest families.

The neighborhood was further devalued by the work of Robert Moses, one of the most influential and polarizing figures to ever serve in New York City government. As an official in charge of numerous public works projects, he spearheaded an intense highway expansion campaign, and five major highways were proposed for the Bronx, principally to make it easier for the residents of the wealthy neighborhoods in Westchester County to get to Manhattan. The South Bronx, which is located between these two wealthy areas, paid the price. Residents were often given just one month's notice before their buildings were razed and highway construction began. More than 600,000 people were displaced. Prostitutes and drug pushers took over the neighborhood, and selling heroin became the new industry.

"I grew up as a child seeing stretches of burned-out, abandoned buildings everywhere I walked," Majora remembered. "As a kid, you never fully understand what makes that sort of thing happen, but it teaches you that you're probably not worth much." When she was just seven years old, her older brother Lenny was killed by gunfire. "He had survived fighting in Vietnam," she said, her voice still cracking at the thought, "but he couldn't survive the South Bronx in the 1970s. That was really a pretty big year for me. The buildings at either end of my block burned down and Lenny was killed."

Perhaps that was the day she decided that when she was old enough, she would move out, leaving behind the poverty, the burned-out buildings, the dealers, and the trash, and never return to Hunts Point. She worked hard to get out. A smart young girl and a good student, she was accepted at Bronx Science, one of the city's leading public schools and often hailed as one of the best high schools in the nation. Afterward, she studied film and art at Wesleyan University in Connecticut. "The older folks were just pleased as punch and super proud that I was

in college, period, that I didn't become a statistic, that I wasn't pregnant at fourteen the way many of my friends were," she said. She was
just glad to have gotten out. At college, she rarely admitted she was
from the South Bronx, which by this time had earned a national reputation as one of the poorest and most forbidding parts of the country.

Majora graduated from college in 1988 and later pursued a master
of fine arts degree at New York University. She was thrilled at the
prospect of studying at NYU and becoming an artist and a writer, but
she understood that in order to make that happen, she would have to
break the promise she had made to herself. As young and broke as
she was, she returned to the South Bronx, moving back to her parents' house to make ends meet. "I can't say I was too happy about it at
the time," she said. "But coming home was one of the best things that
would ever happen to me." She accepted a job with a not-for-profit
arts organization in Hunts Point, hoping to deepen the emphasis on
arts in the community.

Before long, Majora began to look at her neighborhood in a new
light. Hunts Point—which is in the poorest congressional district in the
entire nation—hosted a large share of the city's polluting industries. In
this relatively small area, there were *thirty-five* waste-transfer facilities. At
these sprawling, unsightly complexes, most of the trash collected in the
city—about 50 percent of its commercial waste and 30 percent of its
noncommercial waste—was shifted from collection vehicles to long-
haul trucks. There was also a factory that processed half of the city's
sewage sludge into fertilizer pellets, as well as the Bronx Lebanon incin-
erator, where "red bag" waste from hospitals in several surrounding
counties—including bedsheets, bandages, and syringes—was burned.

These facilities were not only eyesores but also hazards. They emitted noxious chemicals, creating a smell that permeated the Hunts
Point peninsula. Thousands of heavy diesel trucks traveled through
the community each day to access these facilities. In addition, two of
the world's largest wholesale food distribution centers were located in

Hunts Point, and these brought even more trucks into the neighborhood. It did not escape Majora's attention that an area where only 27 percent of the households had cars was crossed by nearly 50,000 cars and trucks each day. All of these factors greatly reduced the quality of life and property values of Americans who were trying to improve their marginal economic status.

Diesel fuel, which is largely used to power commercial trucks, is particularly harmful to people's health. No one who has ever driven with their windows down while following a commercial truck along the highway needs to be told that diesel fuel is toxic. The exhaust, which is considered by the National Toxicology Program to be a carcinogen, contains more than forty air contaminants, and a diesel engine emits more than a hundred times more particulate matter than a conventional gasoline engine. Long-term exposure can cause chronic respiratory symptoms, impact lung health, and lead to kidney damage. Even short-term exposure is dangerous, leading to headaches, increased blood pressure, and eye, throat, and lung irritation.

The health impact of the land use in the South Bronx seemed clear. The rates of asthma-related deaths in the borough were almost *three times* the national average, and hospitalization rates were seven times higher than the national average. Asthma was an epidemic particularly among the children of the South Bronx, but this was not necessarily surprising, as nearly one-fifth of all elementary students attended schools within 500 feet, or less than two city blocks, of a major highway, where air pollution concentrations exceeded healthy levels.

Majora became disgusted by the state of her neighborhood. But this time, rather than determining to leave, she vowed to stay. "There was a general feeling among the population here that this is the South Bronx and of course everything bad happened here," she said. "But then I began to realize that many of its problems were brought on the community from the outside."

She was happy at her job, working on projects that created public art and encouraging students to explore the arts. But that changed in 1997 when the city announced plans to build yet another waste-transfer station along the Hunts Point waterfront. Majora remembers that when she heard the news, she felt like she had been punched in the stomach. "I said to myself, 'Wait, we already handle 40 percent of the city's commercial waste, and this plan would bring in another 40 percent of the city's municipal waste.' I began to realize that we could talk about revitalizing the community through the arts as much as we wanted, but if they built a 5,200-ton-per-day waste facility on the waterfront, what was already bad was just going to get much worse. . . . I just couldn't believe something like this—something that seemed criminal to me—was going on in New York City."

Though she knew it was wrong, she also understood that part of the problem stemmed from the defeatist attitude of people in the community itself. "Nobody saw us as anything except a dumping ground, and often we internalized that," she said. She decided to try to change that attitude and to help residents understand that they could play a role in halting the city's plan for the waste-transfer station in its tracks. With other local residents, she started by knocking on people's doors and inviting residents to attend every meeting scheduled about the waste-management plan. She staged local protests, at one point convincing her colleagues, coworkers, and neighbors to march down the street wearing blue plastic recycling bags and strings of aluminum cans. To help raise awareness outside of the community, she organized boat trips down the Bronx River and "toxic tours" of the existing waste-transfer sites. She invited elected officials to come and witness the number of truck fleets that passed through Hunts Point, the source of the South Bronx's record-breaking asthma rates.

"Mobilizing the community certainly was not easy," she said. "We'd all been so demoralized and dejected by the idea that ours was just a forgotten place, that it was hard at first to inspire interest and hope." But she explained to parents that the asthma rates among the children could have something to do with the polluting industries and the number of trucks in the community. She talked to them about what their waterfront could be: a place with trees and rocks and open space. She talked about how bike routes and parks could better link the community and provide much-needed green space.

After three years, her tenacity paid off. In 2000, at a public meeting held at Majora's former junior high school, more than 700 people came to tell representatives of the city that they would not stand for additional garbage in the South Bronx. After the meeting, the city officials announced they would look elsewhere for a place to site the waste-transfer station. "I have to say," she told me with a smile, "it was one of the proudest moments of my whole life."

Rather than hang up her activist boots, Majora built on the momentum created by the garbage fight. She helped to organize a forum for people to voice their ideas. She wanted to get them thinking not just about what they *didn't* want to see in their community, but what they *did* want to see there. "It might sound strange," she said, "but a lot of people were just beginning to realize the extent of the waterfront we had right here." Studying maps and talking through ideas at a series of neighborhood meetings, local residents began to overwhelmingly express their interest in building parks and having access to the waterfront.

"This was not a major process, it was more a series of small meetings," she explained. "But little by little, people were coming to say to themselves, 'You know what, the way this community is right now is not the way it has to stay.' They began to understand why the asthma rate was so high. And with that understanding, they began to believe that their opinions actually did matter and that they did have a right to have dreams for their neighborhood." Still working at the arts organization, and entering her thirties, Majora had been approached by a local group called Partnership for Parks, which offered her a $10,000 seed grant to help plan for a waterfront park. "It was really nice and I appreciated the offer," Majora said, "but the reality was that with all the facilities located here, we couldn't even get to the river."

She had an idea, though. In 1998, she had come upon what appeared to be a garbage dump, with mounds of debris. The dump ended at the banks of the Bronx River. She looked into it and discovered this was not a city dump, but a city street. Why, she asked herself, couldn't that be a waterfront park? Within weeks, she had written what would be the first of several proposals to turn the garbage-strewn street into a waterfront park. But she didn't want to stop there. "I knew that the dreaming and visioning and thinking were important," she said, "but I also knew that somebody had to take the initiative to actually make the things happen. And I decided at least one of those people would be me."

She left her job at the arts organization and, in 2001, founded Sustainable South Bronx, an organization dedicated to encouraging sustainable development in order to advance the environmental and economic rebirth of the area. Since then, Sustainable South Bronx, under Majora's leadership, has had tremendous success, earning a national reputation as a leader in the environmental justice movement. Their office, housed in a converted factory, is abuzz with activity. "From the beginning," Majora said, "I was never on a moral crusade as much as I was focused on economic development. I wanted this group to plan our community's future, not just react to environmental blight caused by pernicious city planning. I wanted to play offense, not just defense. And most of all, I wanted to give the residents of our community permission to dream."

One of the first projects: New York City's first green roof—that is, a special rooftop garden that can help a building maintain proper heating and cooling—designed as a demonstration project atop her offices. The project was meant to be a springboard for a green-roof installation business, providing training for people interested in working in the field and technical assistance to residents who wanted to build green roofs at their own homes and offices. Because green roofs can retain up to 75 percent of the rainwater that falls on them, they can help reduce the need to build water-treatment facilities, the majority of which, of course, are located in poor communities.

Sustainable South Bronx also runs an ecological-restoration job-training program called Bronx Environmental Stewardship Training, or BEST. Local residents, many of whom had relied on public assistance or had never gone beyond getting their GED, are trained to secure jobs in areas such as landscaping and brownfield remediation. "Little by little," Majora said, "we are seeding the area with a skilled 'green collar' workforce that has both a financial and personal stake in their environment."

Majora believes sustainable development means considering not just environmental matters, but quality-of-life issues as well. The Bronx has a very high incidence of obesity and diabetes, particularly among children. "People don't want to leave their houses and go for a walk if they're surrounded by nothing but pollution," Majora explained. To address this, she is working with the city and other local organizations to spearhead the South Bronx Greenway, which would create bicycle and pedestrian paths around the Hunts Point waterfront. So far, she has helped secure nearly $30 million for the greenway project, and the initial stage of development is slated to begin in 2007.

Though she was motivated in part by a strong desire to heal her neighborhood, Majora considers herself more of an entrepreneur than a typical environmentalist. "Our organization is beginning to prove that we can implement our strategy in a pretty darn economically and fiscally responsible way," she said. "Things like parks and green roofs and decent zoning policies and green-collar jobs and public transportation don't cost a huge amount, but can make a tremendous difference that has long-term economic advantages both locally and nationally."

Majora has rightfully been recognized as a true hero of the environmental justice movement. In 2005, she was named one of the

MacArthur Foundation's twenty-five MacArthur Fellows. This honor, which is commonly known as a "genius grant," comes with a five-year $500,000 grant. "I still have a hard time believing that I was chosen for this. But I know that this is as much a testament to the residents of the South Bronx as it is to me as an individual."

There seems to be almost no limit to what Majora can accomplish in the South Bronx. Currently, she is working with other local groups to expand access to the Bronx River by convincing the state of New York to replace the lightly used Sheridan Expressway, an elevated highway that cuts Hunts Point in two, with affordable housing, positive economic development, and parks. The New York State Department of Transportation recently agreed to study the costs and impact of removing the roadway. She is also working to change the way that the city of New York views the South Bronx, hoping that many more people, both in and out of government circles, will begin to see it as more than a toxic dumping ground.

And the trash-strewn street that Majora stumbled upon? She leveraged the initial $10,000 seed grant 300 times, ultimately raising $3 million to create the first waterfront park to open in the area in more than half a century.

.   .   .

Dealing with toxic hot spots and air pollution is as much a moral challenge as it is an environmental one. We must return to the principle that polluters should pay to clean up the mess they make; that our poor communities cannot—and should not—carry the burden.

The stunning successes—in terms of advancing the welfare, health, and economic well-being of a community—of groups such as Majora Carter's Sustainable South Bronx and the Bucket Brigades make the indifference, or malevolence, of the federal government to environmental justice an affront to logic as much as to decency.

In 2004, the Office of Inspector General (IG) of the EPA issued a report criticizing the Bush administration's failure to integrate environmental justice into its operations, accusing the administration of having "changed the focus of the environmental justice program by deemphasizing minority and low-income populations." The IG report urged the EPA to reaffirm its commitment to environmental justice principles. Despite the warning, the EPA's draft Environmental Justice Strategic Plan released the following year weakened protections for low-income and minority communities and disregarded race as a consideration for determining environmental justice. It also diverted resources away from conducting environmental justice reviews.

In September 2006, the Office of Inspector General issued another critical, and aptly titled, report: "EPA Needs to Conduct Environmental Justice Reviews of Its Programs, Policies, and Activities." The report said that 60 percent of surveyed EPA program officials responded that they had not performed environmental justice reviews as required under Executive Order 12898, and 87 percent said EPA senior management had not requested them to perform such reviews. Eighty percent reported that they did not even *know how to do an environmental justice assessment* and that protocols, frameworks, or additional direction would be useful. According to the report authors, "Until these program and regional offices perform environmental justice reviews, the Agency cannot determine whether its programs cause disproportionately high and adverse human health or environmental effects on minority and low-income populations."

This report is further evidence that federal regulators charged with responsibility for protecting minority and low-income neighborhoods have turned a blind eye, instead helping to turn them into America's industrial dumping grounds. Federal leadership is desperately needed to help communities bearing the brunt of pollution problems, but the Bush Administration has spent its time trying to turn back the clock.

As Bill McDonough urges, and as Majora Carter proves, there is value in examining the intent that accompanies our actions. If, decades ago, we set out to discriminate against our less powerful citizens, dumping on them the burden of toxic air and waste, then we have done a great job of fulfilling our intent. But in thinking about the frightful damage caused by pollution to all Americans, and particularly to the most vulnerable Americans, let's remember one basic fact: The most fundamental responsibility of any government is to protect its citizens from physical harm. Sometimes that harm comes from hostile foreign powers, or from terrorists, or from criminals. But as this chapter shows, it also comes from toxic materials, from air and water pollution, and from those who carelessly expose others to the real and horrible consequences of their own greed or negligence. The environmental justice movement was founded on the simple expectation of American citizens that their government will fight, not tolerate, such harm. Taking up that fight does not involve an expansion of government, or an intrusion of government into private matters, but a vindication of public trust in democratic government itself.

CHAPTER FOUR

The Water of Life

John: The oceans that surround our land, and the rivers and streams that run through it, have always defined the spirit and culture of this country. Native Americans excepted, most early Americans came here by sea, and much of our development as a nation is owed to commerce on the oceans, rivers, and canals.

I was blessed to grow up in a family that reveled in our connection to the sea—a connection that many families in Massachusetts shared, given our fortunate geography. On my mother's side of the family my ancestors were sea merchants, and I grew up learning how to sail and appreciate the wonders of the ocean. My father was a recreational fisherman and passionate sailor who, in retirement, sailed across the

Atlantic several times for the sheer pleasure and adventure of it. He taught me navigation and the rules of the sea, not to mention countless other lessons of the forces of nature that are more powerful than any of us. I particularly remember struggling on a bobbing boat in the high seas, several hundred miles offshore in the Atlantic, learning how to use a sextant to navigate by the sun, moon, and stars.

The places my family often visited—Boston, Nantucket, Martha's Vineyard, the Elizabeth Islands, and famous fishing ports, such as Gloucester and New Bedford—were home to great stories and storytellers of the sea. Herman Melville wrote *Moby Dick* based on the whaling industry that was centered in Nantucket during the nineteenth century and his own experiences on a whaling vessel out of New Bedford. Rudyard Kipling's *Captains Courageous* tells the story of a young heir to a fortune who falls overboard from a liner at sea and is rescued by Portuguese fishermen from Gloucester. He gains new values and a new perspective from the rough-and-tumble life of this unique community. Many Americans were recently introduced to the port of Gloucester and the perils of fishing in the chilling account of *The Perfect Storm* by Sebastian Junger. Another author, Richard Henry Dana, Jr., left his studies at Harvard to become a common seaman on board a brig out of Boston, the *Pilgrim,* and turned his journey into an American classic, *Two Years before the Mast.* Perhaps he captured the wonder we all share when he wrote: "There is a witching in the sea, its song and stories, and in the mere sight of a ship, and the sailor's dress, especially to a young mind. . . . I have known a young man with such a passion for the sea, that the very creaking of a block stirred up his imagination so that he could hardly keep his feet on dry ground, and many are the boys, in every seaport, who are drawn away, as by an almost irresistible attraction."

American history and culture remind us that this attraction is not reserved to the ocean. Mark Twain gave us a way to forever appreciate the Mississippi in his classic tale of boyhood innocence, *Huckleberry*

Finn. And from the Ohio to the Mississippi and on to the Missouri, Snake, and Columbia rivers, Meriwether Lewis and William Clark forever linked rivers to the spirit of American discovery and courage.

But our connection to the water, the sea especially, is more than cultural or historical; it is primal. Water covers three-quarters of the Earth's surface and is the source of life for all people and all species of every continent. Without safe, clean water, we cannot survive.

As President John F. Kennedy said in a speech he gave in Newport, Rhode Island, in 1962: "All of us have in our veins the exact same percentage of salt in our blood that exists in the ocean, and therefore, we have salt in our blood, in our sweat, in our tears. We are tied to the ocean. And when we go back to the sea—whether it is to sail or to watch it—we are going back from whence we came." Water accounts for up to 90 percent of the weight of cells in the human body and three-fourths of the body's total weight.

Essential to our survival, so powerfully linked to our history and culture, such a precious resource ought to receive the highest level of protection—nothing but uncompromising stewardship. But, tragically, the callous disregard with which lakes, streams, rivers, estuaries, bays, harbors, and oceans are treated tells a very different story.

Today, more than one-third of our river and stream miles, and almost half of all lake acres, do not meet the water-quality standards established under the 1972 Clean Water Act. Nearly one-fourth of our total supply of beach areas is considered marginal or completely unsuitable for swimming, fishing, or supporting marine species. In 2003, there were more than 18,000 closings and advisories declared at ocean and lake beaches, mostly due to unsafe levels of bacteria in the water stemming from the runoff of untreated human sewage and animal waste. The fish in our lakes and rivers are now so poisoned with mercury from industrial pollution that in nineteen states they are considered altogether unsafe to eat, and in forty-eight states there are similar advisories specific to certain locations. Even our drinking water is often unsafe: About 6 million Americans are sickened annually from drinking contaminated water from their taps.

The threats to our waters are nothing new; this is news we began hearing decades ago. But we have not heeded it. In the late 1960s, just as I was returning from service in Vietnam, the health of the nation's inland waters had reached a critical low. I'll never forget picking up the newspaper one day in June 1969 and seeing the stark photographs of Cleveland's Cuyahoga River on fire. The flames reached five stories high, and a large plume of black, dirty smoke wrapped the sky in darkness. In shock and disbelief, I—like many other Americans—learned that the river was so polluted that it had literally caught on fire. It was later reported that the fire had started from a spark that had landed on oil and debris floating on the waters of the Cuyahoga from a railcar crossing above it. Two years later, the problem persisted. In 1971, I traveled to Cleveland, Ohio, and as I approached the Cuyahoga, which snakes through the city before emptying into Lake Erie, I could see the river smoldering. The oil and debris littering the river water remained, and the river still periodically lit up. It was as unnatural as it was unbelievable.

The images of the Cuyahoga River fire quickly became a symbol of the growing crisis of urban pollution. I couldn't help but wonder: How had it come to this? Just twenty or so years earlier, when I was a child, my mother, Rosemary Kerry, would take me and my brother and sisters to Buzzards Bay on Cape Cod, where we would spend some summer afternoons digging our toes into the sand and seaweed, searching for clams and mussels—which thrived in the cool, clear water, and were as abundant as they were delicious. We'd carry them home in buckets, and as my mother served a steaming bowl of food pulled from the ocean that day, Diana, Peggy, Cameron, and I felt a great sense of connection to the Earth.

Those seeds of awareness planted by my mother grew through the years into a passionate concern for our surroundings and our relationship to them. When I watched wisps of somke rising from the Cuyahoga that day, I was saddened by the realization that few areas remained as pure as the Buzzards Bay of my youth. Instead, many rivers, lakes, and coastal areas had become veritable dumping grounds. Before the use of sewage treatment plants, many cities routinely dumped their human waste—totally untreated—into the nearby waters, turning harbors along the nation's coasts into open sewers. Few laws existed to prevent factories or other polluting industries from discharging their waste into the rivers, and those that did exist were largely ignored.

This neglect spread from coast to coast, seriously damaging the fishing economy, human health, and Americans' quality of life. New York's Hudson River, for example, was extremely polluted, both from the industries that operated along the river from New York to Albany and from the 1.5 billion gallons of raw sewage that New York City slopped into it *each day*. The same was true for Boston Harbor, in my backyard, which was at the time considered one of the dirtiest harbors in the nation owing to high levels of untreated sewage and industrial waste from surrounding communities.

Fish kills stemming from pollution, which had become almost commonplace, were another significant sign of neglect. About the same time as the Cuyahoga fire, the largest-ever fish kill to date occurred in Lake Thonotosassa, Florida. There, more than 26 million fish were found dead in an event caused, authorities believed, by toxic runoff from four local food-processing plants. Simultaneously, DDT was being detected in national waters at nine times the government's allowed limit. Drinking-water samples were found to be laden with chemicals. The list of polluted waters and the associated problems continued to grow.

CALL IN THE MARINES

Discontent with the situation also began to grow, and not just among those who lived near the troubled waters. Across the nation, people from all political, social, and economic backgrounds joined together to voice their growing disgust about the deterioration of the environment and our poor stewardship. Fueled in part by the images of the burning Cuyahoga River, people began to demand a response.

This was especially true of residents of Crotonville, New York, about 40 miles north of New York City on the Hudson River. One evening in 1966, nearly 300 people gathered at the American Legion Hall to discuss what to do about the declining state of the Hudson. That meeting marked the beginning of one of the most successful stewardship organizations in our country: Riverkeeper.

It's highly unlikely that the men and women who packed into the American Legion Hall that night in 1966 would have referred to themselves by any of the terms used at the time to define people who were active in environmental causes. As Robert Kennedy, Jr., Riverkeeper's chief legal counsel, explained, "The people of Crotonville were not your prototypical tweed-jacketed environmentalists like those who were trying to protect areas in Wyoming, Montana, and the Rockies." Many of them were former marines with blue-collar jobs: factory men, carpenters, and electricians. They were bound together by fierce patriotism and a sense of connection to the Hudson River. For many, it was because they fished there. For others, it was because they were descendants of families that had been pulling striped bass, bluefish, and shad from the cool waters of the river since the days the area was controlled by the Dutch.

Others simply felt a deep sense of wonder for the river. They knew that while they might never see Yellowstone National Park or Yosemite or climb the Rocky Mountains, they would always have the

Hudson. "It was their Riviera, their Monte Carlo," was how Kennedy explained it. They were not willing to quietly stand by and watch the Hudson be turned over to polluters; and that evening, the discussion was focused on what they were going to do about it. The crowd at the American Legion Hall was rowdy. They pressed against the rifle racks in a room filled beyond capacity. Part of what fueled them was a deep-seated frustration with government agencies like the Conservation Department and the Coast Guard, which had proven they'd rather yield to the powerful businessmen of then polluting industries, like the Penn Central Railroad and General Electric, than do their job of protecting the waters.

One by one, individuals took the microphone to express their concerns, and the discussion eventually took a dangerous turn. Though these men (and they were all men at the time) were not radicals or lawbreakers—many of them had seen combat in World War II and Korea—the idea of violence entered the debate. Someone suggested floating a raft of dynamite beneath the Con Edison piers, where it would be sucked into the intake. Another person proposed using a mattress to plug the Penn Central Pipe at the Croton-Harmon Railroad, which spewed oil into the river, leaving the beaches blackened and the taste of diesel in the shad, a bony, herring-like fish. Or perhaps, someone offered, they could ignite the pipe with a match.

But then Bob Boyle rose to speak. A former marine, a devoted fly fisherman, a guru of dry fly tying, he was also the outdoor editor for *Sports Illustrated*. He explained to the crowd that in the course of researching an article about angling in the Hudson two years earlier, he'd stumbled across an ancient navigational statute, the 1888 Rivers and Harbors Act. Not only did the statute forbid any pollution of American waters, it also provided a bounty reward to people reporting violations. Boyle explained that the law had never been enforced. As Bobby recounted the story, Boyle said to the crowd: "We shouldn't be talking about breaking the law, we should be talking about enforcing it." The room erupted with excitement, and the residents of Croton came to a quick and solid decision: They would officially organize themselves and set out to enforce this little-known statute. Step one: They would personally track down the Hudson's worst polluters. Step two: They'd bring them to justice and make them pay for their actions. They named themselves the Hudson River Fisherman's Association, and Ritchie Garrett was elected their first president. Standing before the packed room, this grave digger told the crowd: "I'll be the last to let you down."

Within several years, the Hudson River Fisherman's Association had achieved something that had once seemed impossible. In a testament to gumption and perseverance, they permanently shut down the Penn Central Pipe in 1969, preventing further pollution from a source that had already sullied miles of the river. For their work in identifying and prosecuting this case, the association was awarded $2,000, the first bounty ever bestowed under the 1888 Rivers and Harbors Act. There were two weeks of wild celebration in the town.

They kept at it, and before long they had successfully prosecuted some of the most powerful companies in the nation: Standard Brands, Ciba-Geigy, American Cynamid, and others. They collected a bounty in every case. In 1973, the association successfully prosecuted the Anaconda Cable and Wire Company for dumping toxins into the river at Hastings, New York. The bounty in this case, $200,000, was then the highest penalty in U.S. history levied against a corporate polluter. With that money, the association built a boat, named *Riverkeeper,* which members used to patrol the Hudson in their continuing effort to search for polluters. In 1983, they hired their first full-time "Riverkeeper," activist and former commercial fisherman John Cronin. The following year, Bobby Kennedy, Jr., joined Riverkeeper as its chief prosecuting attorney, and in 2000 Alex Matthiessen became the organization's executive director.

Bobby, John, Alex, and others have made Riverkeeper one of the most successful organizations in the nation. The Hudson River, once described as an "open sewer," is now the richest water body in the North Atlantic. It produces more pounds of fish per acre than any other waterway north of the equator, and it is the last major waterway on both sides of the Atlantic that still has all of its historical species. "It's a Noah's Ark, the last refuge for many of the animals that are going extinct elsewhere," Bobby said. "These fish support recreational and commercial fisheries along the Atlantic coast worth hundreds of millions of dollars."

But as Bobby pointed out, his battle to protect and improve the quality of the Hudson River is about more than just the shad or the sturgeon or the striped bass. "I believe my life will be richer, and my children and my community will be richer," he said, "if we live in a world where my children can see the traditional gear of the commercial fishermen on the Hudson, whose livelihoods, rights, culture, and values I have spent twenty-two years fighting for."

Riverkeeper's ambitions have extended beyond the Hudson River. Today, there are 117 similar programs across the United States. Men and women committed to these programs patrol every major river on the West Coast, from Alaska to Canada to San Francisco to Baja, Mexico, and almost every major river on the East Coast from Canada to Florida. There are also now twelve programs in India, seventeen in Australia, and more in Latin America, Canada, Europe, and Africa. In total, there are now 155 "Waterkeeper" programs—which include Riverkeepers, Baykeepers, Soundkeepers, and Coastkeepers—on six continents, all connected by an international organization known as Waterkeeper Alliance.

TURNING AWAY FROM SUCCESS

That original meeting at the American Legion Hall in Crotonville, New York, was part of a much larger movement that had started to develop across the country at the time. Television programs and various symposia raised the burning question: "Can Man Survive?" At the April 1969 celebration of the Centennial of the American Museum of Natural History, Undersecretary of the Interior Russell E. Train boldly announced: "If environmental deterioration is permitted to continue and increase at present rates, [man] wouldn't stand a snowball's chance in hell [of surviving]."

Also at this time, a young man named Denis Hayes had recently left graduate school at Harvard to help Senator Gaylord Nelson of Wisconsin organize a national event to raise awareness about the declining health of our planet. They wanted the event to bring people together to demand that greater attention be paid to solving these serious problems. In an October 1969 editorial, the *New York Times* said of the growing unrest: "Call it conservation, the environment, ecological balance, or what you will, it is a cause more permanent, more far-reaching, than any issue of the era—Vietnam and Black Power included."

These efforts culminated in the first Earth Day celebration on April 22, 1970, in which figures from both political parties and a remarkable one in every five Americans—more than 20 million people —participated. They took to the streets, gathered in parks, and convened in auditoriums of high schools and colleges to demand better protection for our natural resources. I joined in the Massachusetts organizational effort and spoke to students who were excited to safeguard their environmental future. Legislatures from forty-two states passed Earth Day resolutions to commemorate the historic day, and Congress adjourned so that more than 500 of its members could attend rallies, "teach-ins," and marches dedicated to the protection of our air, water, forests, and land.

It was a wonderful moment and it had notable political consequences. Within months, unable to ignore the public outcry, President Richard M. Nixon announced the creation of the Environmental Protection Agency, whose sole purpose was to protect human health and the environment. The president admitted that he had first been reluctant to propose setting up a new independent agency. Eventually, however, he had been convinced by all "the arguments against placing environmental protection activities under the jurisdiction of one or another of the existing departments and agencies."

As the Nixon administration was preparing for the EPA to open its doors, a group called Environmental Action, made up of Americans from both major political parties, was gearing up for the nation's first-ever "Dirty Dozen" campaign. Based on congressional voting records, they selected the twelve congressmen with the most dismal records on the environment and targeted them for criticism. Their campaign received enough publicity to have an effect in the next election cycle. That fall, seven of those named were defeated, and the public rejoiced.

The victories achieved on Earth Day were far from merely symbolic. They ushered in an extraordinary string of legislative reform measures: the Clean Air Act, the Clean Water Act, the Endangered Species Act, the Marine Mammal Protection Act, the Safe Drinking Water Act, and the Coastal Zone Management Act. Significantly, in light of the divisions separating the major political parties today, these laws were adopted with overwhelming support from Democrats and Republicans alike. These victories also proved that while local control is always preferable, there are certain moments when responsible stewardship of the Earth is unachievable without federal regulation and leadership.

These laws remain the bedrock protection for our environment: If anything, their relevance and value have increased in the quarter century since they were passed. In contrast to the gridlocked Washington of today, in 1972 a large partisan coalition in Congress agreed that there should be "zero discharge of pollutants into navigable waters by 1985, and fishable and swimmable waters by 1983." Industries could no longer recklessly discharge toxic waste, and all municipalities were required to build and operate wastewater treatment plants to treat raw sewage.

The Clean Water Act helped to prevent billions upon billions of pounds of pollution from flowing into our rivers, lakes, and streams. The number of waters safe for swimming and fishing has doubled since 1972, helped by a federal government commitment to funding water-remediation and pollution-control efforts—efforts that local municipalities could never have afforded on their own at the time, nor can they today. A measure of the progress made is the Cuyahoga River, now clean enough to be safe for swimming and fishing. Boston Harbor has also been largely cleaned up, thanks to a $3.5 billion remediation effort launched in 1985 by the Massachusetts Water Resources Authority.

Despite the achievements of the Clean Water Act, today, for the first time since its passage, water quality has begun to decline. Today's water pollution is different but no less damaging than the water pollution that occurred in the past. It stems primarily from what are called "non-point sources." Pollution is no longer usually caused by a direct release from one point of origin, such as a pipe from an industrial operation. Instead, pollutants are carried to our bodies of water indirectly and from many different sources—including our own backyards. Every time we litter or spray our lawns with chemicals, every time our cars leak gasoline or oil, this waste is swept up in rain and melting snow and carried to our waterways via storm drains. Heavy metals seep into the water during mining operations, and inadequate sewage collection systems in cities and towns across America habitually overflow during heavy rainstorms, dumping an estimated 1.3 trillion gallons of raw sewage into waterways each year. Just half an inch of rain in Washington, D.C., for example, can lead to the overflow of raw sewage into the local Anacostia River.

Most water pollution today, however, can be directly linked to agricultural practices. Pesticides and manure are frequently washed by rain and snowmelt into our rivers, lakes, and streams, contributing 60 percent of the pollutants in our water today. In recent decades, agricultural production has largely shifted away from sustainable practices toward industrial farming techniques. While the industrialization of agricultural activities may have resulted in lower prices at the grocery store, those prices certainly do not reflect the true cost of the switch from sustainable family farming to factory farming, especially when we take into account the cost of the damage that has been done to our waterways.

Imagine for a moment what would happen if American cities implemented waste-management plans in which human waste was not treated but, rather, stored in uncovered pits in populated neighborhoods and then sprayed on nearby crops and pasturelands. In rainstorms, the waste would run from the fields, and the pits would overflow onto the streets, down drainpipes, and into our waterways. The pits themselves might leak, causing waste to seep into the groundwater and down into drinking wells. This may seem unthinkable, yet that's exactly how waste is handled at industrial farms.

Nationally, according to EPA figures, there are approximately 18,800 factory farms in operation known as Confined Animal Feeding Operations, or CAFOs, and 431,200 smaller factory farms, called AFOs. CAFOs generate an immense amount of waste—nearly 500 million tons annually, the Sierra Club estimates. In eastern North Carolina alone, an area that has become the nation's second-largest producer of pork, there are 10 million hogs being farmed, most of them in confined conditions. As a whole, these 10 million hogs produce as much fecal matter as all of the people in North Carolina, California, New York, Texas, Pennsylvania, New Hampshire, and North Dakota combined. And that's just one part of one state. In Iowa, livestock produces an estimated 50 million tons of excrement each year.

How do the operators of these industrial farming operations deal with the disposal of all this material? Typically, the waste produced at factory farms is stored in containment ponds called "lagoons": open pits brimming with thick, black excrement that, at such a high concentration, becomes a toxic soup of nitrogen, phosphorous, ammonia, and bacteria. Included in this mix are some of the unabsorbed antibiotics and growth hormones that were given to the animals. The waste from these lagoons is often applied to cropland. In theory, the pits are lined to prevent the waste from seeping into the ground, but according to a paper by the Global Resource Action Center for the Environment, lagoon specifications allow leakage at a rate of up to 0.036 inch per day. This would allow a 3-acre lagoon to legally leak more than a million gallons of waste each year. Regulations require the lagoons to be large enough to contain rainwater, but spills during rainstorms are common, and lagoons are always vulnerable to leaks, breaks, and spills.

Last year, CAFOs contributed to the pollution of 129,000 river miles, 3.2 million lake acres, and more than 2,800 estuarine square miles across the United States. The U.S. Fish and Wildlife Service says that manure runoff has led to the contamination of fisheries along 60,000 miles of streams. Pollution from factory farms does not just threaten the fish and animals that dwell in the water, however; it can have serious and sometimes fatal impacts on human health. When pathogenic microbes in animal waste spread to drinking-water supplies and are ingested by humans, they can cause such symptoms as acute gastroenteritis, fever, kidney failure, and even death. Also, the practice of pumping huge quantities of antibiotics into confined animals to ward off disease and promote growth has contributed to the rise of bacteria resistant to antibiotics in humans, making it more difficult for us to treat diseases.

Rick Dove knows far too well the potential health impacts of agricultural pollution. He has lived along the shores of the Neuse River near New Bern, North Carolina, for more than twenty-five years. After graduating from the University of Baltimore Law School in 1962, he joined the Marine Corps and served two tours in Vietnam. In 1987, he retired as a colonel and settled back into civilian life in North Carolina. "I fell in love with the place," he said simply. "All I ever really wanted to do was to be a commercial fisherman. So after I retired, I decided to pursue that dream and couldn't think of any place better than the Neuse River." He remembered that years earlier the river had seemed like "a paradise" to him. With the help of his son Todd, Rick Dove bought three boats, from which they worked over 600 crab pots and more than 2,000 feet of gill nets. They opened a little seafood outlet store, and for two years enjoyed the life of commercial fishermen.

But then, father and son began to notice a change in the water. Many of the fish floating by their boats had open, bleeding sores. At first it was only a few, but as time passed, the numbers of bleeding fish grew larger and larger. It was a disturbing sight, but not nearly as disturbing as what happened next. Soon, both Rick and Todd began to develop similar sores on their arms, hands, and legs. Rick began to experience memory loss. As he talked to other fishermen, he heard similar, equally horrifying stories. Some men reported losing consciousness at sea. Others found themselves in their boats unable to remember how to get back to the dock, or after a long day of fishing, couldn't find their way home.

The situation escalated. The next year, more fish were developing the bleeding lesions, and Rick's health also worsened. Frustrated and disappointed, he knew he was too sick to keep going. He stopped fishing and gave up his business.

Then, in 1991, the Neuse River suffered the largest fish kill ever recorded in the state's history. Over 1 billion fish died in a six-week period during September and October. There were so many dead fish that some had to be bulldozed into the ground. Others were left to rot on the shore and river bottom. The stench produced by this kill was overwhelming, something Rick Dove says he'll never forget.

What was happening? Though Rick did not at first make a connection between his declining health and the growing number of sick and dying fish, it was all related. The problem, which wasn't identified until 1995, was found to be *Pfiesteria piscicida,* a toxic microorganism, often referred to as the "cell from hell," that is an extremely powerful neurotoxin. It paralyzes fish, sloughs their skin, and eats their blood cells. It is also volatized into the air and is capable of sickening humans who breathe it. How had it gotten to the Neuse? Primarily from nutrient pollution from the industrial hog farms.

"It was really an awful thing," Rick said. "We didn't expect this because, thanks a lot to the work of the local Riverkeeper, we had succeeded in removing 98 percent of point source pollutants, like industrial pipes. But in the 1980s, when the hog industry got going in North Carolina, everything changed very quickly, in a matter of just a few years. It was as if they were building cities of hogs. In a typical city, of course, you have to put in water and sewer lines and treatment plants, but even with 10 million hogs, that's not how these operations work. The industry calls themselves farmers and hold on to so-called farming practices, but it doesn't work that way. A lot of that fecal matter, full of antibiotics and pathogens, was going directly into the Neuse. It changed a lot of people's lives."

Rick Dove eventually was able to return to the water in 1993, this time as the Riverkeeper of the Neuse, where he continues the tradition of identifying and suing local polluters. Listening to Rick talk about his work is inspirational. Sixty-seven years old—a marine—he could have been doing almost anything else; he'd earned it. But his personal sense of responsibility and love for the river kept him on the job. "Semper Fi"—"Always Faithful"—the motto of the Marines, was his for life. His story conclusively demonstrates the connection between the choices we make and the health of our communities. Few of us likely give much consideration to how our everyday choices— such as the seemingly straightforward decisions we make at the grocery store to provide food for our families—may have an impact on people we will never meet, in places we may never visit.

It also shows us how connected we are as Americans. In recent times, particularly since the 2000 presidential election, we have generally bought into the idea of blue states and red states. But it takes people like Rick to remind us that, regardless of how we vote or which party we align ourselves with, we all share many very basic ideals. All of us certainly want clean water. No fisherman should be sickened by toxins in the water. No mother should worry that her child will become sick from swimming at the local beach. Nobody among us—young or old, farmer or artist, Democrat or Republican—should demand anything less than safe, available water. This is not a matter of politics; it is a matter of common sense, morality, and responsibility.

Rick's work, for example, is closely related to something that is happening on the other side of the country, in Washington State. Helen Reddout, a cherry farmer in the Yakima Valley, has faced a similar hazard.

THE IMPROBABLE VICTORY OF CITIZEN FARMERS

Yakima County, in south central Washington State, is a beautiful part of the country, bounded on all sides by striking mountain ranges: the Cascade Mountains on the west, the Wenatchee on the north, the Rattlesnake Hills to the east, and Horse Heaven Hills to the south. Mount Rainier, a volcano in the Cascades that rises near Seattle, nearly 150 miles to the northwest, can be seen in the distance, its silhouette made gauzy and ghostlike in the summer heat. The land here is dry but fertile, and thanks to the Yakima River, which runs through the region before meeting up with the Columbia, the Yakima Valley supports a vibrant and diverse farming economy. Throughout the year, the fields are ripe with a wide variety of crops near ready for harvest: There are orchards full of Washington State's famous apples and cherries, vineyards, fields of asparagus and hops, and endless rows of corn. But by far the largest agricultural activity here is dairy production, and Yakima County is now the state's largest milk producer.

You can smell the dairy farms long before you see them. Like other agricultural activities in the United States, the dairy industry here has, in recent decades, shifted largely from sustainable family farming to large-scale industrial farming. From Granger to Grandview, an area that covers a 16-mile corridor, there are now seventy-two industrial dairies, each location housing many thousands of cows. They are visible everywhere. Throughout the area, cows stand crowded into pens that dot the landscape and, in some places, line the very edge of the road. Hundreds of them stand together—squeezed so tightly they can barely move. They eat from piles of hay stacked just outside their pens, and they stand in pools of their own waste—their legs, underbellies, and udders soaked black from excrement. Mountains of dry manure surround the pens near large, open-air ponds of wet manure. Like most animals raised under industrial farming practices, these dairy cows will spend most of their lives in these conditions, inside of these pens, never stepping foot on a blade of live grass. The only "exercise" they get is when it is time for them to be milked or slaughtered.

Helen Reddout understands the problems associated with the industrial dairies in her area far too well. She is a sixteenth-generation farmer, and her family owns apple and cherry orchards on 170 beautiful, shady acres around Outlook, near the large, white colonial-style house where she lives. Canned fruits and vegetables line shelves in her kitchen, and in the backyard wildflowers reach up to the windows. The walls are lined with framed portraits of her five children and eleven grandchildren. Just recently, one of her grandsons, who served in Iraq, became the father of Helen's first great-grandchild. Her home and orchards are surrounded by large dairy farms. Though the nights here are cool and comfortable, the windows of her house remain shut at all times to keep out the smell of the dairies, and each day, as she drives to one of her orchards, she knows where to roll up the windows and hold her breath.

Helen was born in Missouri but has lived in the Yakima Valley since

1954. When she was younger, her parents would take her with them in the summer as they traveled from their farm in Missouri to Washington State to earn extra income by picking fruit for a few weeks at some of the local orchards. During a trip in 1954, when Helen was eighteen, she came with them to pick, as usual, but never went back. One morning, as she brushed her teeth outside of the cabin for migrant farmers where her family was staying, she looked up, her mouth covered in toothpaste foam, and spotted a young man hauling buckets across the gully.

"He looked at me and I looked at him," she remembers, "and it was as if I stuck my finger in an electric socket." She learned that his name was Don Reddout and that he also worked in the orchards. Getting dressed to go work in the orchards that day, she pulled on her favorite chartreuse shorts, hoping they would help her stand out and be noticed. "Every time I saw him driving down the row on his tractor, I'd move my ladder so that it would be in his way," she said. She spent so much time climbing up and down the ladder that she only made a few dollars that day, but her strategy worked: He asked her on a date. Three months later, they were married. "On our twenty-fifth wedding anniversary, I finally admitted to my husband that the reason I made so little money that day was because I spent all my time trying to get his attention," she said with a laugh. "That's when he told me that he spent the whole day looking up and down the rows, trying to spot those chartreuse shorts."

When they were first married, Don and Helen vowed that they would work hard to someday own an orchard of their own. For seven years, they saved as much money as they could, and in 1964 they bought a small cherry orchard not far from their home. They were also the parents of four young children by that time, and things were certainly not easy. Income from the orchard was not enough to support their family, but like many other farmers, Don found additional work. For ten years, he worked as a foreman on a neighboring farm, and then later managed a food warehouse, running the orchard in his spare time. Helen took care of the children, and when they got a little older she decided to pursue her dream of becoming a teacher. She went to college when she was thirty-three, after her youngest son started school, and then took classes toward a master's degree in education. For the next twenty-five years, she taught at the local elementary and high school, and she retired in 1997. She and Don had a happy life and a wonderful marriage, and today, the Reddout Orchards, which are close to becoming certified as organic, are among the largest producers in Yakima County. Sadly, Don passed away two years ago, just five weeks before the couple's fiftieth wedding anniversary. Helen, now seventy, manages the Reddout Orchards with the help of her children.

When she first moved to the area, there was a robust dairy industry, but it looked nothing like it does today. At the time, most of the farms were owned by families, who raised only as many animals as they could properly care for. The cows grazed on pastureland and ate a natural diet. Though this is now considered "organic farming"—a practice for which we'll pay high prices at the grocery store—it was once just simply how we farmed. In the early 1970s, as regulations governing dairy operations in California became more stringent, company heads began to consider other locations. Washington State became a popular choice, and Yakima Valley in particular. The land was cheap and fertile, and the regulations were considered to be loosely enforced, at best. Several large dairy businesses moved from California into Yakima Valley, bought up small farming businesses, and brought in thousands of cows. Most of them set up their farms along the Granger Drain, which empties into the Yakima River. By the 1990s, there were more than 40,000 head of cattle along the Granger Drain.

Helen and Don Reddout, and many other local farmers, watched the dairy industry change with growing concern—concern not just for the way industrial agriculture was moving away from sustainable farming practices, but also for the impact on their quality of life. One dairy cow produces about 120 pounds of wet manure each day, according to the EPA, and with 40,000 head of cattle in Yakima County, that translates to more than 4 million pounds of waste each day. That amount of waste creates an overpowering smell of sewage and ammonia. When it is sprayed on cropland, as is typical, the wind can carry pathogens for several miles, where they end up in waterways, on roads and lawns, and in people's homes, as well as their bodies. "We were becoming prisoners in our own homes," Helen said. "You'd see rags stuffed into people's windows to try to keep out the smell. We had to stop using air conditioners, because that just sucked the smell in. The Health Department reported increasing rates of asthma and diarrhea in county residents. The flies became incessant, and we stopped entertaining outdoors. Can you even imagine living like that?"

One night in the early 1990s, Helen decided that she had had enough. "Don and I were asleep upstairs, and we had left the windows open," she said. "All of a sudden, I just woke up. It was as if someone had taken sewage out of a septic tank and dumped it right in my face." She closed the windows, but the smell remained. She got air freshener, even perfume, and sprayed it everywhere, but she could not get rid of the smell. The next morning, she got into her car to try to determine where the smell had originated. A few miles away, at one of the larger dairy farms in her area, she saw that liquefied waste was being sprayed from an irrigation gun onto an open field. The smell of ammonia was so strong that it made her gasp. She watched as the waste formed puddles along the field and ran down the furrows into the Granger Drain.

"Watching what these dairy operations were doing to our home, to our community, and to our land—it was just like that 1975 movie *Network*, with Peter Finch and Faye Dunaway," Helen said. "All I wanted to do was to open my window and scream as loud as I could, 'I'm mad as hell and I'm not going to take it anymore!' That's basically what I did."

Helen began by contacting every agency she thought might be able to help get the dairies to clean up their smell: the EPA, the Department of Ecology, the Department of Agriculture. She read the Health Department regulations and got a copy of the zoning laws. She talked to her neighbors and other farmers' wives. Understanding that strength often comes in numbers, she twice tried to start an organized coalition of concerned citizens, but both times, frustrated by the lack of response they were getting from the local agencies and elected officials, the groups lost interest and the organizations folded.

For seven years, she struggled to get something done. Just when she was about to drop the issue herself—resigned to the idea that things would never change—she and Don met a neighbor while they were browsing at a local yard sale who complained that one of the dairies was planning to build a calving operation adjacent to her property. The site was just a few yards from where her drinking well was located. Helen had begun to grow tired of the work, having accomplished almost nothing, but she knew she had to keep going.

Not long after that, she received a call from an organizer with the Columbia Basin Institute, an environmental organization based in Portland, Oregon. The institute had heard that Helen was an environmental activist working on the CAFO issue in Washington State and offered assistance. "I really didn't think of myself as an environmentalist," she said, "and I still wouldn't strap that term to myself. I'm a farmer. And all farmers understand the importance of taking care of the land and the air. If you don't nurture it, it won't nurture you, and you won't have anything left to pass on to your kids." But she welcomed the help, and that day, the seeds of a new organization were sown.

The neighbors she spoke to at the yard sale, and others who offered to help—all of them farmers—began to meet. Though their original concern was the smell and the flies, they began to realize that the factory farms were contributing to much wider, and more consequential, problems. "It was like dropping a pebble into a still pond," Helen said. "The ripple just kept getting bigger and bigger and bigger." Helen had her well tested and discovered it was polluted with nitrates. Nitrates can make people very sick, and in high doses in children can lead to "blue baby syndrome," a circulatory ailment that is often deadly. High nitrate levels in drinking water near feedlots have also been linked to spontaneous abortions. A few years earlier, in 1993, health officials in LaGrange, Indiana, had found that nitrate pollution in private wells had caused several women living near a hog operation to experience miscarriages in their eighth week of pregnancy. Helen immediately imposed a ban on drinking the tap water in her home. She also began to take notice of how many of the waste lagoons were overflowing onto the roads and, more disturbingly, into the local irrigation ditches that fed the Yakima River.

That's when Helen discovered the Clean Water Act. Like other polluting industries, CAFOs are subject to its regulations. They are prohibited from discharging pollutants into the waters of the United States and must obtain a permit through the National Pollution Discharge Elimination System (NPDES). "In the beginning, I'd see mention of the Clean Water Act, but I didn't really pay it much attention," Helen said. "But then I read it, and everything became clear to me, because it was right there in black and white: Dairies cannot discharge their waste into the water." What the dairies were doing, she understood, was not just bad for the environment; it was illegal. And the answer was not to advocate for new laws or new regulations. The practical solution was simply to demand that the existing regulations be enforced.

Once again, Helen and the others hit the phones. They asked agents from the Washington Department of Ecology (WADOE), which administers the Clean Water Act in the state, to come and see the problem and offered to give them a tour of the polluting farms. Helen spent time with the organizer from the Columbia Basin Institute.

They took photographs of manure spilling into the drainage canals, of dead cow carcasses piled in a ditch, of CAFO lagoons sited in areas that were designated as wetlands on the county map. But still, nothing happened. Agents claimed the problem wasn't under their jurisdiction or that they were too short staffed to send anyone out. In the rare instances when inspectors did come, she'd never hear from them again.

The group, meanwhile, decided it was time to become official. Adopting the name Community Association for Restoration of the Environment, or CARE, they registered with the Washington secretary of state and applied for nonprofit status. Nine people were named to the board of directors, and Helen agreed to serve as vice president. "We knew we were really at the beginning of something big, and we expected it to be a long fight," Helen remembers, but their first hurdle was harder to overcome than any of them had expected. The names and phone numbers of the board of directors were now public information, and within a week, the group of nine had shrunk to three. "Many of the people had contracts with the dairy industry in the area, and they were all contacted and told that if they didn't back off, they'd lose their work," she recalled.

It was an immediate and serious setback, but Helen and the remaining members of CARE refused to be intimidated. They also knew that they had another option. The Clean Water Act includes what is called a "citizen suit provision." It provides that any individual can bring suit against an industry he or she believes is polluting the waters of the United States. The group did not necessarily want to take this route. CARE had no budget, the members worked mainly out of Helen's dining room, and they were farmers, not attorneys. But after months of frustration, and aggressive and intimidating responses from the CAFO owners, they decided they had no other choice. The organizer of the Columbia Basin Project put the group in touch with Charlie Tebbutt, an attorney from the Western Environmental Law

Center. The nonprofit law firm agreed to take on, and fund, the case, should CARE decide to pursue legal action. "Without the Western Environmental Law Center's help and expertise, we would not have been able to do what we did," Helen emphasized.

The team began by doing careful research. They went to WADOE and studied the records relating to the CAFOs. They checked into who had a permit and who did not; which operators had received complaints from neighbors; and who had been cited for violations of the Clean Water Act in the past. They found that, at most, only 14 percent of the industrial dairies in the Yakima Valley were operating in compliance with Clean Water laws. A few operators were notorious —one was Henry Bosma. With more than 5,000 head of dairy cattle on two adjacent properties, Bosma's operation was clearly subject to regulation under the Clean Water Act. He had established one dairy in 1973, and another in 1990, but for nearly all of that time, he was operating without an NPDES permit. He also had a long list of citations for illegally dumping waste into the waterways, mainly into a ditch that flowed into the Granger Drain and to the Yakima River.

The instances of illegal discharge were flagrant: Bosma had received his first citation just a few months after he began operations in 1973. Others followed in 1984 and 1988. By 1986, he was under WADOE order to get a permit, but he still failed to do so. In fact, after complaining that the agency had been "promoted to some type of deity," he returned a permit application saying he didn't "understand any of it." In 1993, he was cited for two instances of discharge into the drainage ditch; three years later, he was fined $9,000 for additional violations. He appealed the fine and was granted relief. But he didn't obtain a permit until 1996, and even then, only for one of his two dairies. At the time that CARE was researching the matter, he still had no permit for the other.

Even after getting the one permit in 1996, the Bosma dairy did not stop its illegal dumping. WADOE found illegal discharges from the

Bosma dairy on at least four occasions between January and September of 1997. Manure from the operation had spilled into the ditch, and it had been overapplied on the fields. In April 1997, one neighbor reported that a pipe leading from Bosma's dairy had been spilling manure directly into the canal for several weeks. He had taken photos to document it.

"When we saw this information, and how long the polluting had been happening and how little the state had done to address it, it was just absolutely shocking from a public standpoint that an agency could be that derelict in their duties," said Charlie Tebbutt.

Through their research, the members of CARE came to understand the extent to which the waters were being polluted. In September 1997, in conjunction with an investigation into a reported discharge violation, WADOE agents had tested the water in one of the irrigation ditches that abutted Bosma's dairies. They found that the water contained fecal coliform bacteria—a dangerous pathogen found in the intestines of animals—in an amount exceeding 48,000 colonies per 100 milliliters. State law allowed a level of just *200 colonies per 100 milliliters.*

In addition to reading the records, CARE members set up a "Dairy Watch" in which they each chose a time to patrol the dairies and photograph obvious violations, while keeping a journal describing what they saw. This was no easy task. A few dairy operators tried to intimidate them—Helen was nearly run off the road on several occasions, and CARE members and supporters received threats that if their investigation did not stop, their businesses would suffer. Still, the group was able to document many violations at several of the dairy operations over the course of a few months, and they knew they had enough evidence to support legal action. Finally, on October 31, 1997, CARE sent letters to ten operators expressing their intent to sue.

According to the citizen suit provision, citizens must wait sixty days between sending the intent-to-sue letter and filing suit, in hopes that the issue can be resolved without having to go to court. According to Charlie Tebbutt, agents from WADOE reported at the time that during the sixty-day waiting period, there was more activity to clean up among the dairies than there had been in the previous ten years combined—and not just by the ten dairies that had received notice. That, ultimately, was what the members of CARE wanted: to resolve the issue without having to go to court. To this end, they invited the ten dairy operators to sit down with concerned members of the community to discuss the problems and consider solutions. "It was probably a long shot," Helen said, "but I really thought, we're all farmers, we can fix this together."

The meeting took place at the Outlook Grange, a fitting location, and reminiscent of the meeting three decades earlier at the Crotonville American Legion Hall. Built in 1908, it was the first Grange in the Yakima Valley and had long been a gathering place for farmers to come together to discuss politics, market prices, and agriculture. On the evening of November 20, 1997, pickup trucks lined Van Belle Road in front of the Grange. When Helen arrived for the 7 P.M. meeting, people were spilling out the door. Hundreds of people were inside, many of them wearing yellow buttons reading "Dairy Dollars Support the Community." The dairy farmers, she discovered, had taken out a full page advertisement in the local newspaper announcing that Portland activists were attempting to shut down local farms. The meeting was mostly polite, but it was strained. Some in the crowd shouted out that they didn't need Portland attorneys to tell them how to run their farms, making it difficult for the organizer from the Columbia Basin Project to complete his presentation. In the end, no resolution was found.

"I walked out of that meeting in disbelief," Helen said, "but I knew we had our answer. We were going to sue." On January 15, 1998, CARE filed suit in U.S. district court against four dairy operations: those owned by Henry Bosma, Jake DeRuyter, Herman TeVelde, and Sid Koopman. CARE members believed that of the many dairies they had investigated, these four had the worst records. The group alleged that these operations were acting in clear violation of the Clean Water Act, leading to the pollution of the Granger Drain, the Sunnyside Irrigation Canal, and the Yakima River.

CARE v. Henry Bosma Dairy was the first trial scheduled; it was set to take place before Federal District Judge Edward Shea. Helen and the others were nervous, and Charlie Tebbutt remembers how tense this time was for everybody involved. "A week before the trial began, Helen said to me, 'If we lose, I'm going to have to move out of this valley.' That's how much this meant to her and how invested she was and what it meant for the people there. She was stepping so far out on a limb, and if she wasn't right about things, or couldn't prove what she knew was happening, the threats and intimidations she had been receiving for years would have become even worse. I think she really would have had to leave the area."

But before long, the tension eased a bit, as CARE won a few very important victories in a pretrial ruling before Judge Shea. First, he ruled that the definition of a CAFO included not only the pens or locations where the animals were confined, but also the lagoons and the equipment used to distribute the animal waste to fields outside of the confinement area. This was the first time that CAFO had been defined so widely. Judge Shea also ruled that the Clean Water Act applied to all storage ponds and all devices for application of animal wastes and wastewater, including trucks, wheel lines, center pivot irrigation systems, and spray guns. Finally, he concluded that overapplication of manure constituted a violation of the NPDES permit, as it could lead to discharge into waters.

"This was a very important ruling," said Charlie Tebbutt, "because it was one of the very first to recognize that the whole facility is used as a disposal area and therefore is subject to Clean Water laws. The pens are a problem because the excrement builds up there, the lagoons that handle the excrement are a major source of contamination, and the fields where the operators spread manure can be a significant source of contamination because overapplying it means it's going to run into the waterways and leach into groundwater. This ruling made those points very clear."

The trial began on June 1, 1999. Helen testified before the judge, as did Shari Conant, the president of CARE, whose family owned 40 acres of pear and apple trees. Helen held up the photos that members had taken showing animal waste flowing into the rivers and piling up along the banks of the irrigation ditches. She explained that when water is low, their orchards were irrigated with water pumped from the Granger Drain. But often, their pump became clogged with manure, despite filtering. She talked about how Don had fished for trout in the Yakima River as a young man, and even in the Granger Drain, now almost fully devoid of life. When their children were young, she said, she and Don had enjoyed taking them to the back of the orchard, 10 acres of which abutted the Yakima River, to have picnics, gather wildflowers, and bird-watch. But in recent years, they were no longer able to enjoy these activities. The river smelled like manure, and animal waste had collected along the banks. She also described how her well had been polluted, making it necessary for them to purchase bottled water, at their own significant expense, for years.

"I have to admit," she remembers, "I was pretty nervous up there. But I also had read the Clean Water Act, and I knew without a doubt that what we were doing was right. So I stopped looking at the audience and just told it like it was."

The first part of the trial lasted three weeks, and when it was over, Helen and the other members of CARE waited nervously to hear the judge's decision. To their delight, and the shock of many in the dairy industry, CARE won the suit. They had proven that Henry Bosma was guilty of sixteen violations of the Clean Water Act, and that his CAFO operation had contributed to the pollution of the irrigation ditch and the Yakima River. Bosma—who had until that day paid only a nominal penalty for all his documented violations—was eventually penalized $171,000 in civil penalties and had to pay $428,000 in CARE's legal fees.

Helen Reddout and the other members of her organization were thrilled with the victory—and with what came next. CARE negotiated settlements with the three other dairies they had filed suit against. In the weeks following the court's decision, members of CARE watched with satisfaction as new lagoons were dug that could store the waste without overflowing. Berms were established on dairy operations throughout the county. For Helen, "it was wonderful to see these operators finally realize that the Clean Water Act did, in fact, mean something, and that citizens could make sure they weren't allowed to pollute."

The penalties imposed against Bosma went to the U.S. Treasury, but both sides agreed that the money would be directed to CARE to continue its work. CARE decided to fund two water studies in the Lower Yakima Valley: one to determine the extent to which pollutants from the CAFOs had spread in the groundwater; and the other to help provide free well-water testing to low-income families in the area, along with information about how to protect their families from the potential health impacts of polluted wells. CARE is currently working on issues related to air pollution stemming from the CAFO waste. Helen and the other members have solicited the help of air-quality professionals and are providing the results to government agencies. They are also educating people on how to protect themselves from air pollution–related health problems.

Though this was a stunning victory for the organization and led to significant cleanup in Yakima Valley, the larger significance of *CARE v. Henry Bosma Dairy* was that the ruling reached far beyond Washington State, setting precedents that changed how the Clean Water Act is regulated and enforced nationally. The landmark ruling that the regulations apply to the entire CAFO—including the land where the liquefied waste is sprayed and the machines used to dispose of the waste—was the first of its kind; as was the ruling that the irrigation ditch is considered "waters of the United States" and therefore is subject to the protections of the CWA.

Charlie Tebbutt believes that CARE's work elevated the issue of CAFO pollution to the national level, leading, in part, to a subsequent decision by the EPA to adopt new regulations governing CAFO pollution. In 2003, the EPA established rules requiring industrial dairy operators to adopt a Nutrient Management Plan outlining how they will store waste, how they will prevent their animals from coming into contact with surface waters, how they will handle dead animals, and how they will ensure that manure is applied to croplands at the appropriate agronomic rate. "These cases helped force EPA to address the problem. Unfortunately, the rules still left loopholes large enough for manure trucks to drive through," lamented Tebbutt.

Since then, Helen has spent a lot of time traveling around the country, speaking to communities to help them seek ways to get the regulations enforced where they live. Helen and the other members of CARE proved that the Clean Water Act is as relevant today as it's ever been. The answer is not always to write new laws or regulations to deal with our problems. Rather, we sometimes need simply to enforce the laws we have on the books and protect them from being dismantled by corporate special interests.

In 2001, Helen was selected as an Environmental Hero by the Washington Environmental Council. But even after what she has accomplished, she still struggles with the idea of being called an environmentalist. "I wouldn't say that's what I am," she said. "I would never strap myself to a tree, or go to extremes to save something. All I know is that we are lucky to live on this Earth, and we have a responsibility to take care of it. If we don't, it is not going to support us. And after thirteen years of this work, I won't say that I don't feel some burnout. People sometimes ask me why I keep going and I say if I don't keep going some individuals will believe they have a free hand at polluting, and I don't want to see the state of our land, or our air, or our water, if that happens. Someone has got to try and stop that."

OCEANS AT RISK

The work that people like Helen Reddout and Rick Dove are doing is part of a much bigger picture than even they may realize. Part of their achievement is to bring to light the connections we all share. Clean water and the right to drink from our wells, or go fishing and swimming without having to worry about getting sick—whether on the Neuse, the Yakima, the Cuyahoga, or Buzzards Bay—is not a local concern but should be a shared right for all Americans.

Just as the fishermen of North Carolina are in principle connected to many farmers in Washington State, so are our rivers and streams connected. Eventually, they must empty into our oceans. As Rachel Carson so eloquently described in *Silent Spring,* "For all at last return to the sea—to *Oceanus,* the ocean river."

There's no better example of this than the Mississippi.

The river originates as a stream draining from a small glacial lake, called Lake Itasca, in northern Minnesota. This simple brook blossoms into the Mississippi, the nation's mightiest river. At St. Louis, it meets the Missouri River to form the largest river system in North America, and the fourth largest in the world. Traversing or bordering ten states, the river drains most of the area from the Rocky Mountains to the Appalachians—or 41 percent of the 48 contiguous states—before traveling more than 3,000 miles to empty into the Gulf of Mexico in southeastern Louisiana.

The Mississippi Basin supports a diverse agricultural economy, producing 92 percent of our agricultural exports, 78 percent of the world's exports in feed grains and soybeans, and most of the livestock and hogs produced nationally, according to National Park Service figures. But unfortunately, that means the Mississippi also carries a lot of the waste that stems from unsustainable agricultural practices. Today, the river that Mark Twain once described as in "all ways remarkable" now carries roughly fifteen times more nitrate load from agricultural runoff than any other U.S. river, three times more than the levels recorded in the 1950s.

And because the Mississippi eventually feeds into the Gulf of Mexico, the pollution has spread there, bringing its own devastation. Each spring, the buildup of nutrients causes massive algae blooms to proliferate. The algae, and the bacteria that live off of it, are so abundant that they deplete the water of oxygen—a state known as hypoxia. Without sufficient oxygen, many bottom-dwelling fish and aquatic plants cannot survive, and by summer, everything is dead. This gulf "dead zone" covers an average of 5,000 square miles each summer—the approximate size of the state of New Jersey—and dissipates by October. But it impacts many people who may never even see it. The dead zone jeopardizes the gulf's $26-billion-a-year fishing industry, which supplies much of our country's seafood, including about three-quarters of the shrimp harvested domestically. Fishermen are forced to travel further and further for their catches. And although the Gulf of Mexico is the worst case of hypoxia in or adjacent to our country, many other bodies of water also develop dead zones, including the Chesapeake Bay in Maryland and Virginia, the western Long Island Sound in New York and Connecticut, and the Neuse River in North Carolina.

Apart from the creation of dead zones—which number approximately 100 worldwide each year—there are a number of other hazards that threaten the oceans. According to a United Nations Environment Programme report released in the summer of 2006, ocean degradation is "rapidly passing the point of no return." The watery deep, home to more than 90 percent of living organisms, faces danger from pollution, litter, shipping, and climate change.

Moreover, water temperature is up, alkalinity is down, and over half of the world's coral reefs are threatened by human activities. So severe is the threat that the United Nations was compelled to call for countries to initiate more protection, regardless of territorial boundaries; it also called for more research, as only 10 percent of the ocean has been explored.

Then there are the biological and economic consequences of overfishing. Driven by the growing global demand for seafood, we have been steadily taking more fish than we should from our oceans, threatening the sustainability of the stocks. The largest fish are not as large as they used to be. Anyone who has spent a lifetime fishing for the seafood industry knows this is true: Today's skippers no longer see the massive tuna and swordfish that used to fill their boats, and they have to go farther away to find any at all. You can go into a restaurant almost anywhere in America and order a variety of fish that bears the designation "fresh." How fresh depends on where you are and what your own definition is, but for most people the supply seems endless. In reality, it isn't: Fish stocks are dwindling in bodies of water across the globe, and certainly here in the United States. Last year, the National Oceanic and Atmospheric Administration categorized nearly a third of the federally managed fisheries as "overfished"—meaning their populations are depleted and will not rebound without deliberate action to limit fishing activity. In my home state of Massachusetts, the cod population has not yet recovered from decades of overfishing and the subsequent collapse of the fishery in the early 1990s. Cod were once abundant in the waters here, helping to support a thriving fishing industry. Losing this permanently would mean losing a critical part of our region's heritage, and would be one more step in the dangerous worldwide trend toward depletion of fish stocks.

In fact, in November 2006, a team of international scientists released a report that found that about one-third of all fishing stocks worldwide have collapsed. Should current global fishing trends continue, the report said, *fish stocks worldwide risk collapse, perhaps as soon as fifty years from now.*

As sometime chairman or ranking member of the Senate Oceans and Fisheries Subcommittee, I have learned over almost a quarter of a century that one simple law of economics continually threatens fish stocks and stands in the way of local assumption of responsibility: There is too much money chasing too few fish. Fishermen with generations of fishing in their families, large mortgages on their boats and homes, and inexact science to guide them obviously are reluctant to give up their livelihoods. Marketplace demand, coupled with the increasing worldwide growth of high-tech fishing fleets—whose catching capacity is far outpacing any sustainable harvest levels—are major contributors to the problem. And although the United States has been working over the past decade to reduce its domestic fishing capacity, a number of other nations have supported increased fishing on the high seas. In addition, a number of new techniques threaten the long-term sustainability of global fish stocks, especially longlining, in which very long monofilament fishing lines—some of them more than 60 miles long, with up to 10,000 baited hooks—are suspended at different depths in the ocean. Each year, commercial fishing operations set as many as 2 billion of these longlines worldwide. Sharks, sea turtles, and seabirds such as the albatross are particularly vulnerable to longlining, and thousands of them, adding up to as much as 88 billion pounds of life by some estimates, are accidentally killed every year. Massive high seas longliners—which dwarf our U.S. vessels—are increasing in number, and plans for nationally subsidized construction continue unabated. The growth of these fleets, as yet unchecked by international and national management bodies, has led to a tragic, unnecessary destruction of fish.

Trawlers that capture deepwater species by dragging a weighted net along or near the bottom of the sea are as destructive. Worldwide, bottom trawlers—which some have likened to fishing the seafloor with bulldozers—scrape an area 150 times larger than the total area of forests clearcut on land each year. The trawlers simply take everything in their path. And the oceans are not free of the perils of drift nets, even though they were banned in 1992 by the UN. The desire for profit still drives many to cheat. The practice of drift-net fishing continues in the western Pacific; absent sufficient monitoring and enforcement of the UN ban, bandit use adds to the miles upon miles of monofilament netting abandoned long ago. These nets capture everything in their wake, essentially strip-mining the ocean. In storms or accidents, these nets are sometimes lost. Once loose, these "ghost nets," as they are then called, continue to ensnare and kill fish, attracting predators, which also then get caught, die, and decay. When weighted down with their new, accidental catch, the nets sink into the ocean until scavengers or decay lightens the load, and then rise to the surface to begin the cycle of killing again.

The tough but necessary alternative to overfishing is overall fleet reduction, beginning with the most voracious commercial predators who put immediate return on investment ahead of sustainable fishing practices, supported through a federally funded or an industry-funded buy-out plan. Essentially, it would allow for compensation for those agreeing to exit the fishing industry under the buy-out, and then make use of tools such as quotas, sector allocations, and fishery cooperatives to ensure that conservation and safety goals are achieved. The large commercial fleets simply take too much from the sea, outstripping the ocean's capacity to replenish itself. Reducing them offers a real future for small-scale local fishing squeezed out by the leviathans.

Although most of the news about fish stocks worldwide is dire, we should be encouraged by success stories—which have occurred even in New England. This is a problem we can solve if we have the right tools. The solution, in theory, is simple: We must make our fisheries sustainable and keep them that way. That means, at the very least, taking no more fish of any species than will allow us to maintain that species at current harvesting levels. Rather than depleting fish populations, we should be trying to replenish them. Fish stocks can recover when overfishing stops. For instance, on Georges Bank, haddock have rebounded quickly as a result of fishing restrictions imposed in the late 1990s. But one of the most encouraging success stories I know of relates to the astounding recovery of Atlantic striped bass populations from the brink of total collapse. Striped bass, which migrate through coastal waters from North Carolina to Maine, are highly prized by both commercial and recreational fishermen. But in the late 1970s, a sharp drop in commercial striped bass harvests signaled a serious decline in these stocks that could not be stemmed under existing laws. At the time, each state was free to manage harvests independently and without regard to any coastwide fishery management plan, creating a classic "tragedy of the commons."

In 1984, continuing problems in the fishery provided the impetus for the Atlantic Striped Bass Conservation Act, which called for federal-state cooperation in implementing and enforcing an interstate fisheries management plan for striped bass. The act played an important role in the recovery of striped bass stocks. The secretary of commerce and the secretary of the interior were jointly authorized to declare a moratorium on striped bass fishing. An aggressive conservation program was carried out by the states, and uniform management across several state jurisdictions was achieved. In Massachusetts, we endured an almost ten-year ban on striped bass fishing. As a result, the striped bass recovered, and today commercial and recreational fishermen are enjoying an unbelievable resurgence of "keepers," some measuring over 36 inches in length. By 1995, the Hudson River and Chesapeake Bay striped bass stocks were restored, and a few years later the stocks of the Roanoke River, the Albemarle Sound, and the Delaware Bay were also declared recovered.

Building on the success of this approach, Congress passed the Atlantic Coastal Fishery Cooperative Management Act in 1993. This act extends the same enforcement mechanism to other species. Today, all Atlantic coast states included in a fishery-management plan must comply with certain conservation provisions or face a moratorium on harvesting the species in question. This innovative approach is a good template for coordinated management of coastal migratory fisheries nationwide. It could also serve as a model for ecosystem-based management under regionally developed plans. In fact, it could pave the way for management of migratory species on the high seas through regional fishery management organizations.

.   .   .

The ills suffered by our marine environment do not end with overfishing. Some of the problems being experienced by our fisheries—and fishermen—are the direct result of actions taken by people who do not fish for a living. For example, though striped bass are now plentiful, we are finding lesions and diseases in those affected by pollution and coastal runoff, a development that is demoralizing to the managers and the recreational and commercial industry leaders who were so instrumental in the stock's recovery. A more integrated approach is essential. When our fish stocks recover at sea, their health must not be compromised by harm we are causing on land.

The pressure on our coastal areas has outstripped the capacity of many states—which are suffering severe budget problems—to stem the tide of development. The Coastal Zone Management Act (CZMA) includes provisions to strengthen federal oversight, reduce polluted runoff, and encourage state innovation, but much more will need to be done to stop the land from poisoning the sea.

No job is finished just because a law has been passed. The laws must be enforced, and as the evidence in this chapter makes clear, regulatory officials all across America have not been doing their job. There are too many stories of major business interests exerting all their power to avoid responsibility for pollution. Too many people live with the consequences of this irresponsibility, and some are dying from it. Too often, public officials have their own conflicts of interest, and frequently people are appointed to positions of oversight precisely because they have those conflicts. We must create a new era of vigilance in our development and farming practices to prevent non-point source pollution from killing rivers, bays, and lakes and destroying the life that inhabits them. We have to reinvigorate and expand international co-operation to protect the oceans. We must demand that existing laws are enforced. We must restore the full power of the Clean Water Act and re-create the federal partnership that helps local communities with expensive infrastructure projects essential to the health of citizens and the Earth alike.

It's too easy to think of the great oceans as vast expanses of water filled with inexhaustible life that mankind could hardly adversely affect. The mighty Pacific, Atlantic, and Indian oceans seem too big to be influenced by us. But the truth is, they are being changed by us every day, at an increasing pace, with potentially irreversible consequences not merely to aquatic life forms but to entire weather systems that depend on them, from the Gulf Stream to the Humboldt Current. We cannot continue to ignore the fact that our oceans are in jeopardy, and we need to realize, as was concluded in the seminal Pew Oceans Commission's 2003 report to the nation, that "the root cause of this crisis is a failure of both perspective and governance." The Pew report went on to say, "We have failed to conceive of the oceans as our largest public domain, to be managed holistically for the greater public good in perpetuity."

There is another reason why we have to cherish the oceans and absorb profoundly the lessons of what is happening there, and it is a selfish one. Because it is here, in these deep, dark waters, that the single largest threat to all species—and all humankind—is slowly playing out: global climate change.

CHAPTER FIVE

Global Climate Change: The Decisive Decade

John: For far too long, the national debate about climate change has been hijacked by irresponsible skeptics, many of them in Washington. There is a wealth of scientific evidence and a consensus in the scientific community that climate change is happening. Nonetheless, the George W. Bush administration has refused to acknowledge the scale of the problem or to take any meaningful action. Even the proposals in his 2007 State of the Union address—which was the first time President Bush said he would work to halt the growth of U.S. global warning pollution from oil—do not measure up to the urgency of the threat. Some in Congress have even continued to argue that the current wave of unprecedented warming is due only to "natural changes."

For example, until control of Congress changed hands in January 2007, Senator James Inhofe (R-Okla.) was entrusted with stewardship of the nation's environment. As chairman of the Senate Environment and Public Works Committee, which has major oversight of climate change policy, he publicly and forcefully declared: "God's still up there. George Soros, the Hollywood elitists, the far left environmentalists on the committee that I chair—all of them want us to believe the science is settled and it's not." On another occasion, he called the threat of climate change "the greatest hoax ever perpetrated on the American people" and even compared the idea to Nazi propaganda in the lead-up to World War II. In just a few breaths, Senator Inhofe managed to deny what nearly every credible scientist in America says about the reality of climate change and the role of man-made forces in accelerating it, while also impugning as anti-American the motives of his colleagues in promoting a measure that President Bush himself embraced (and then ignored) as recently as his 2000 campaign. In Congress, the climate skeptics have even trotted out the author of *Jurassic Park* as an expert witness to argue that climate change is fiction—despite stunning evidence to the contrary. That is a pretty good measure of how the debate on environmental issues has degenerated, and how radical a position many conservatives are currently taking.

And these efforts have been well supported by big oil and their Republican allies in Congress. For more than a decade, ExxonMobil has gone to great lengths to both muddle the facts and stifle efforts to address climate change. Oil companies have given money to advocacy organizations that deny the science behind global warming theory and have even taken out full-page ads in major newspapers questioning the role of man-made emissions in climate change. When Americans can pick up a paper and see an ad like that, and hear their leaders in Washington claiming that climate change is a "hoax," no wonder we are one of the few nations that have not wholeheartedly embraced both the science and the urgent need to act.

Here, then, is the reality of global climate change. At both poles and nearly all points in between, the temperature of the Earth's surface is heating up, and at a frightening and potentially catastrophic rate. Just how hot is it becoming? According to the most recent report by the United Nations Intergovernmental Panel on Climate Change (IPCC) in February 2007, global surface temperatures have increased about 1.4 degrees Fahrenheit over the last century. The Earth is very probably hotter today than at any time in at least the past thousand years. The years 2005, 1998, 2003, 2002, 2006, and 2004 were, respectively, the six warmest on record, and all but one of the twenty hottest years on record have occurred since 1980.

Science tells us that this heating is the result of human activity. In fact, *Science* magazine analyzed 928 peer-reviewed scientific papers on global warming published between 1993 and 2003. *Not a single one* challenged the scientific consensus that the Earth's temperature is rising due to human activity. During the past century, humans have burned such a large amount of fossil fuels and cut down so many forests that we have literally changed the composition of the atmosphere and, with it, the Earth's energy balance—the climate-regulating balance between incoming energy from the sun and outgoing heat from the Earth. It is this activity that has compounded the greenhouse effect, a naturally occurring process that serves to warm our planet. Water vapor and other greenhouse gases—carbon dioxide, methane, nitrous oxide, and halocarbons—in the Earth's atmosphere are transparent to incoming solar energy but partly opaque to the heat energy radiating upward from the Earth's surface. Much like the glass panels of a greenhouse, these gases help to trap heat and thereby keep the surface temperature at an average of about 57 degrees Fahrenheit. Without the greenhouse effect, the temperature at the surface of the Earth would be too cold to sustain life.

Since the Industrial Revolution, the greenhouse effect has been significantly amplified by changes in the atmospheric composition brought about by human activities. The most important of these changes has been an increase of over 35 percent in the atmospheric concentration of carbon dioxide (CO_2), caused in part by deforestation, but in even greater measure by the burning of fossil fuels to generate electricity, heat our homes, power our industrial sector, and fuel our cars. The atmospheric concentration of carbon dioxide is now at its highest level in at least 650,000 years, and it continues to rise as the use of fossil fuels grows and deforestation continues.

Human-caused increases in the concentrations of other greenhouse gases—notably methane, nitrous oxide, ground-level ozone, and halocarbons—are together exerting a further warming effect about equal to that of the CO_2 increase. A variety of particles in the atmosphere have also increased as a result of human activities, some of them tending to warm the Earth and others tending to cool it. Until now, the net effect of all the particles appears to have been a cooling influence that roughly equals the warming influence of the greenhouse gases other than carbon dioxide. As a result, the combined effect of all of the human influences on the atmosphere to date has been approximately the amount of warming that would have resulted if carbon dioxide had been the only concentration that changed.

The concept of human-induced climate change is not a recent discovery. As early as 1896, Svante Arrhenins, a Swedish scientist, began studying rapid increases in human-caused carbon emissions, determinng that "the slight percentage of carbonic acid in the atmosphere may, by the advances of industry, be changed to a noticeable degree in the course of a few centuries." In 1979, the U.S. National Academy of Sciences reported with "high confidence" that an increase in global average temperatures of 1.5 to 4.5 degrees Celsius (2.7 to 8.1 degrees Fahrenheit) was likely if carbon dioxide levels doubled. It was greeted by a chorus of skepticism. Then, in the particularly warm summer of 1988, NASA climatologist James Hansen of the Goddard Institute for Space Studies, in New York, testified before a congressional committee that the human influence on global climate was already detectable in measured temperatures.

Not all climate scientists were convinced in 1988 that Hansen was right. Some thought that the observed warming trend could be part of natural climatic variability. But the continuation of the trend through the 1990s and into the 2000s, the emergence of supporting lines of evidence from both contemporary observations of climate-linked phenomena and from the study of past climates, and steady improvements in computer models of climate have all contributed to a growing consensus among the experts that human influences are the main cause of the ever more pronounced global heating being observed.

Today, in fact, nearly every researcher professionally engaged in the study of climate change, from across the political and ideological spectrum, agrees that the increased concentration of greenhouse gases in the atmosphere caused by human activity is responsible for the current warming trend. At a climate change symposium hosted by the New York Botanical Gardens in September 2006, one scientist described the feeling among climate scientists in these plain terms: "The more one reads and understands the proven science about global warming, the more terrified one becomes."

Another leading scientist, Dr. John Holdren, has been studying the causes and consequences of global environmental changes for more than thirty-five years. He is currently the director of the Woods Hole Research Center and a professor at Harvard University in both the Kennedy School of Government and the Department of Earth and Planetary Sciences. In 1995, as Chair of the Executive Committee, he accepted a Nobel Peace Prize on behalf of the Pugwash Conferences. Sitting in his office at Harvard recently, he explained that skepticism about this issue has largely abated in recent years. "To be credible," he said, "the skeptics about human causation of current global climate change would need *both* to explain what alternative mechanism could account for the pattern of changes that is being observed, *and* explain how it could be that the known, human-caused buildup in greenhouse gases is *not* having the effects predicted for it by the sum of current climate-science knowledge (since, by the skeptics' assumption, something else is having these effects). No skeptic has met either test."

In fact, even the Environmental Protection Agency under the Bush administration has endorsed this conclusion. In May 2002, the EPA published a report stating, "There is general agreement that the observed warming is real and has been particularly strong within the past 20 years . . . due mostly to human activity." That sentiment was again reiterated in a statement issued in June 2006 by eleven national academies of science, including that of the United States. Their joint statement said that "the scientific understanding of climate change is now sufficiently clear to justify taking prompt action." Similar conclusions have been expressed by the United Nations Intergovernmental Panel on Climate Change, the American Meteorological Society, the American Geophysical Union, and the American Association for the Advancement of Science, among others.

It seems that new scientific evidence about the urgent threat of climate change is being released on nearly a daily basis. But it is not just scientists who are learning more about the problem. Al Gore's book and documentary, *An Inconvenient Truth,* masterfully explained the global warming threat to a wider audience, exposing millions of people to the harsh realities of this challenge. For people the world over, the scientists' theories should come as no surprise: One doesn't have to read the reports or even study the science to understand the dangerous effects of climate change, because the effects are already upon us. In many places, it's simply enough to walk outdoors and look around.

According to the National Climatic Data Center, average temperatures in the U.S. in 2006 were 2.2 degrees Fahrenheit above the twentieth-century mean. In 2006, the hottest year ever recorded in the contiguous United States, a summer heat wave blanketed large swaths of the country. In California, more than 130 people died as a result of the heat. Chicago officials were forced to evacuate hundreds of families from buildings in the city's South Side that had lost power as temperatures climbed into the 90s for a fifth straight day. As the Northeast braced for temperatures to soar above 100 degrees, the lights atop the Empire State Building and the East River Bridges in New York City were switched off to save power. The city, fearing an overload of the energy grid, was trying to prevent a potential blackout as millions of New Yorkers sought refuge from the heat by cranking up their air conditioning.

Winters are also getting warmer. Ice on lakes is freezing later and melting earlier in the season. During a few recent winters, New England's Lake Champlain—renowned for its ice fishing—did not freeze at all. And, of course, this warming knows no borders. The summer of 2003 in Europe was the hottest on record, and probably the hottest there in at least 500 years. A brutal heat wave in the first half of August, in which temperatures reached a record 100.2 degrees Fahrenheit in England and 104 degrees in France, claimed an estimated 35,000 lives.

FAR-REACHING CONSEQUENCES

As unsettling as it is to have to endure increased summer temperatures and prolonged heat waves, the consequences of climate change are potentially far graver. As Dr. Holdren explains, "Climate is the 'envelope' within which all other environmental conditions and processes operate," including precipitation, humidity, winds, ocean currents, sea level, and all of the biological and even economic processes affected by these. Distortions of this envelope can have potentially deadly and destructive ramifications and a significant impact on life on Earth, determining what we can grow where, where humans can live, the geography of disease, the distribution of species and pests, and so many other factors.

Drier conditions and reduced precipitation, if severe, can mean widespread drought and problems with growing crops. Our 1999–2002 national drought was one of the three most extensive of the past forty years and had sweeping and complex impacts on agriculture, forestry, water supply, tourism, and recreation. From coast to coast, streams and wells dried up, and river levels fell dramatically. People were told not to water their lawns, and public fountains in many urban centers were dry and dusty. The most dire result, however, was the resulting wildfires.

Just ask Toby Richards, a fire-management officer for Gila National Forest in New Mexico. In an October 2006 interview with Grist, an environmental news Web site, he told a reporter about a fire that had ignited in mid-winter above 9,000 feet. "We went up to a lookout and watched this fire burning in an area that was normally under six feet of snow," he said. "Every once in a while you will get a lightning strike up that high that burns a tree or two in the winter, but this fire grew to a hundred acres." Stories like this confirm what the science has been telling us about the fire season in the West—the season is lasting longer, it's less predictable, and the fires are larger.

According to scientists at California's Scripps Institution, drier conditions, caused in part by earlier snow runoff, are correlated to an increase in violent wildfires throughout the western region. Thomas Swetnam, a scientist who took part in the Scripps study, said in a statement, "I see this as one of the first big indicators of climate change impacts in the continental United States." He added: "Lots of people think climate change and the ecological responses are 50 to 100 years away. But it's not 50 to 100 years away—it's happening now in forest ecosystems through fire."

We are also experiencing more extreme weather events due to shifts in the climate system. In certain regions of the United States, extreme precipitation events, defined as rainstorms that produce more than 2 inches of rain in 48 hours, have been more frequent than in the past. For example, in New York City between 1950 and 1970, there was on average only one of these events each year. But they now occur an average of five times a year. Many coastal regions of the northeastern United States are experiencing twice as many extreme precipitation events today as in the 1950s. These heavy rainstorms create flooding, affect agriculture, and pose a critical challenge to the management of municipal storm runoff. And as we learned from the recent tragedy in New Orleans, hurricanes are becoming more intense, as warmer sea water contributes to more powerful storms. The number of Category 4 and 5 hurricanes globally has nearly doubled since the 1970s.

The Senators from North Dakota, Byron Dorgan and Kent Conrad, can speak directly to the local impacts of changing climate. Farmers and ranchers in their home state have seen a dramatic cycle of natural disasters, including floods and frost in 2005 and severe drought in 2006. Millions of acres of cropland were either prevented from being planted or lost to the floods and heat. Drought also devastated livestock production in south central North Dakota. Is this a sign of what's to come?

The list, unfortunately, goes on. Signs of climate change are evident the world over. In India, researchers have found that extreme monsoon events became more common between 1951 and 2000, resulting in a greater number of landslides and flash floods as well as damage to crops. The Sahel, the southern fringe of the Sahara, is getting drier and drier; monsoon patterns in China have been observed to be significantly altered; and glaciers in the Tibetan and Himalayan plateaus are disappearing at a rate that will affect the flows of China's and India's great rivers, with serious human impact. As noted in the UN's 2006 Human Development Report: "Almost all glaciers in China have already shown substantial melting. . . . This is a major threat to China's over-used and polluted water supplies. The 300 million farmers in China's arid western region are likely to see a decline in the volume of water flowing from the glaciers."

Even plant and animal species are feeling the effects, as the warming trend has forced species everywhere to adapt or risk extinction. Lilacs are blooming earlier each spring, and the vineyards of Bordeaux now flower three weeks earlier than just a few years ago. Birds are migrating north earlier and nesting earlier, and their eggs are hatching earlier. In fact, a recent study published in the proceedings of the National Academy of Sciences found that 130 plant and animal species in North America, Europe, and Asia have responded to earlier spring temperatures by shifting into new habitats or altering the timing of their normal spring activities, like flowering or migration.

People everywhere are noticing the changes and speaking up about what they are seeing. In Louisiana, a 2005 *Shreveport Times* story quoted duck hunters who said that hunting had been getting worse for several years. The ducks, it seems, were just not arriving in the numbers they had previously arrived. The story was written following a National Wildlife Federation report warning that a warmer planet would mean that traditional duck-breeding grounds in North America's prairies could dry up and that traditional wintering wetlands in the South could flood. In South Carolina, another newspaper, *The State*, reported that without farm-raised mallards, there would be virtually no duck hunting in the state, because the wintering wild population of mallards has dropped over the past half-century from 200,000 to 3,000. In Arkansas, the winter duck population has shrunk from a million to half a million during this same period. Last year, drought dropped the population to 160,000. Hunters everywhere should be concerned about climate change. Many hunters fight hard for their rights to gun ownership through their membership in sporting or gun-owner associations, but they have yet to become equally engaged in efforts to thwart climate change, thereby preserving the prey they hope to hunt.

The same goes for fishermen, because life under the sea is also different today than just thirty years ago. Oceans act as a sink, or sponge, absorbing carbon dioxide from the atmosphere. When the chemistry of our atmosphere is changed by the burning of fossil fuels, so is the chemistry of our oceans. As journalist Elizabeth Kolbert reported in a remarkable series for the *New Yorker* magazine, researchers released data in 2004 that analyzed more than 70,000 seawater samples from different oceanic locations. They found that nearly half of all carbon dioxide released into the atmosphere since the beginning of the nineteenth century has been absorbed by the oceans, and that these waters now hold 120 billion tons of CO_2.

Why does this matter? Since the dawn of the Industrial Revolution, the world's oceans have become 30 percent more acidic, and because of continuing carbon dioxide uptake, they will continue to become even more so regardless of any immediate steps we may take to reduce greenhouse gas emissions.

Dr. Mark Eakin, coordinator of the Coral Reef Watch Program of the National Oceanic and Atmospheric Administration (NOAA), explained that the problem stems not simply from the *amount* of change taking place in our oceans, but from the *rate* of change. Such significant alterations in the ocean's chemistry have not occurred at such a fast pace in over 20 million years. As one might expect, such rapid changes seriously disrupt the aquatic ecosystem, forcing underwater species to adapt dramatically in a very short period of time. Not all can.

A continuing increase in the acidity of the oceans could mean the disappearance of many species and ecosystems that used to thrive in our waters. Sea creatures that construct their skeletons from carbonate minerals in the ocean—such as corals, shellfish, sea urchins, and starfish—are likely to suffer the most from a more acidic ocean, because the higher level of acid will make it difficult for them to form and maintain their skeletons and shells. Scientists project that by the year 2050, corals could be very rare on tropical and subtropical reefs, including Australia's Great Barrier Reef. Should corals decline, this would have serious ramifications for the thousands of species of fish and other aquatic organisms that depend on the reefs for survival, not to mention for the fishing and tourism industries.

The effects of climate change on our oceans are not just threatening the creatures who live in the water, but also those of us who live near the water. Over the past century, the sea level has risen some 4 to 8 inches. Most of this rise is due to thermal expansion: As global ocean temperatures rise, the water expands, simply because warmer water takes up more space.

The accumulation of evidence of climate change can be overwhelming, but there is simply no avoiding it. We have no choice but to face the reality that as the temperature gets warmer, the climate system has to respond to a new atmospheric chemistry. Today, for example, from where I sit at my desk at home, I can hear the birds chirping outside. That's because the windows are open, and the temperature is around 70 degrees. It sounds like a perfectly comforting day, except for the fact that it's November 29, and this is Boston.

As unseasonably warm days become more frequent, the reality of climate change certainly becomes harder to either deny or ignore. And there are some places on Earth where the evidence of climate change is obvious enough to convince even the most stubborn skeptics. One of those places just happens to be among the most majestic and breathtakingly beautiful places in this country, Montana's Glacier National Park.

In 1850, when the land that would become our nation's tenth national park was surveyed, there were 150 glaciers. These massive mountains of ice, snow, and rock were formed thousands of years ago, and they have helped scientists and biologists unlock many secrets of the past. But, as a team of government ecologists are now discovering by studying the twenty-seven glaciers that remain today, they may be the clearest sign of exactly what's to come.

John Kerry and Teresa Heinz Kerry

THE CANARY IN THE COAL MINE

Dr. Daniel Fagre, an ecologist with the United States Geological Survey (USGS), has been studying the impact of climate change in Glacier National Park since 1991. After a brutal heat wave plagued the midwestern United States, Congress enacted the 1990 U.S. Global Change Research Act, which established a program aimed at understanding and responding to climate change. The National Park Service was asked to implement long-term research programs to measure the impacts of warming within the parks. Because most national parks are not directly impacted by dense population or industry, climate change can be detected and studied more easily.

Dan is most comfortable in hiking boots and shorts, and most of the photos one is likely to come across of him show him standing at the edge of a cliff, one of the snowcapped mountains of Glacier National Park looming in the background, a huge backpack strapped to his back. Dan is an avid outdoorsman, and getting a tour of the park from him, bouncing along Going-to-the-Sun Road, with its mystifying views and hairpin turns, is a tremendous gift. He talks easily about his concern about climate change, his Minnesota upbringing still detectable in his accent.

He compares the study of national parks and what they say about the future of climate change to the caged canaries once used to detect danger in a coal mine. Just as a canary would signal imminent distress underground, parks often provide the first tangible evidence of the effects of climate change. The glaciers at Glacier National Park provide a particularly useful tool in climate research. First, it is possible to observe their response to the climate by noticing how quickly they are either growing or shrinking (a measure unlike, say, the acidity of oceans, which humans cannot readily observe). Also, unlike other things in nature, glaciers do not have the ability to adapt to climatic changes.

"It's very complicated to measure all kinds of things in the ecosystem at large because it's very spread out," Dan explained at his office, which is housed in a small cabin tucked under pine trees at the park's headquarters. "But glaciers are compact. They also react only to climate. Trees can get bugs and can adapt to changes in carbon dioxide concentration or water-use efficiency that affect their response to climatic change. Glaciers have none of those adaptive mechanisms. They can't migrate or hibernate or anything, so they just sit there and act as barometers of climate change."

For a glacier to be maintained, he explained, there has to be, over time, more input (snow accumulation and freezing in cold months) than output (melting in warm months). Over the past century, the average local temperature within the park has increased at least 1.4 degrees Fahrenheit and perhaps as much as 2.9 degrees Fahrenheit. These warmer temperatures have led to an increased rate of summer melting. At the same time, the average maximum snowpack has declined, and melting has started earlier and earlier in the springtime. This combination has led to a deficit in the snowpack at the end of each year for several years running. When Dan first began his work in 1991, his team adopted a plan to measure the park's glaciers every ten years. But to their surprise, the glaciers were melting so rapidly that they had to change the study period to every five years. "We misjudged how sensitive the globe is to climate change, and a lot of things were happening faster than projected," he said. "Things that we thought would happen fifty years from now have, in some cases, already happened." In the end, the glaciers were changing so fast that the researchers again had to change their strategy: They now take measurements every year.

The glaciers in the park sit atop mountain ranges, and measuring them can be tricky because of the gradual movement. Strapped with a precision Global Positioning System (GPS), Dan and his colleagues hike up to a glacier and walk the perimeter to measure its size. They then get a mass balance of the glacier—which includes the amount of snow on top of the glacier and the ice mass below it. To measure the snow and ice loss each year, they use a steam drill that bores a hole down to the ice mass below and insert a long stake. At the end of the summer, they record the position of the ice surface on the stake and calculate the drop in ice height. They also use ice radars to bounce a wave through the ice to the rock underneath it. This allows them to determine the total depth of the ice.

In addition to these modern tools, Dan's team relies on photographs of the glaciers taken through history. Because Glacier National Park has long been a fascination for tourists, there is a wealth of photographic evidence chronicling the life of the glaciers, beginning back in the very early 1900s. Using repeat photography, Dan can easily show visible evidence of what all of his research is finding: a steady recession of the glaciers.

By 1993, the park's largest glaciers had all melted to less than one-third of the area they covered in 1850, and many of the smaller glaciers had either disappeared completely or were too small to be considered glaciers anymore. In 1910, for example, Grinnell Glacier measured 1,000 feet high. By 1938, it had shrunk to between 600 and 800 feet and had started to separate into two ice masses. The melting created a small lake at the base of Grinnell, which increased the rate of melting. By 1960, the lake covered 20 acres. It now covers 124 acres, and only 10 percent of Grinnell Glacier remains. The story is similar for every glacier in the park. From 2003 to 2005, Sperry Glacier retreated noticeably. Blackfoot Glacier covered 1,875 acres around 1900. It now covers 429 acres. Red Eagle melted by half in five years, dropping below the limit that defines a glacier.

The ecological significance of the loss of glaciers and other ecosystem changes in the mountains cannot be overstated. As Dan explained, the entire ecosystem of the park is being forced to adapt to climate change. For instance, before the onset of global climate change, slowly melting glaciers fed streams gradually through the warmer seasons. A countless number of species depend on those streams. But with increased temperatures causing shorter elapsed times between the maximum snowfall, the initiation of runoff, and the peak flow, the spring release of water occurs more quickly. Temporary, short-lived streams that typically ran through August are drying up earlier, and permanent streams have very low flows in late summer. This change is having significant impacts on the aquatic systems that depend on these streams.

Also, the temperature of the runoff is warmer now, which is disrupting the habitat of macro-invertebrates that thrive in cold water. These invertebrates are at the base of the food chain and are necessary for the survival of many other organisms. Changes to those invertebrate populations would therefore likely cause a domino effect on other species. "We may lose our west-slope cutthroat trout, or at least have them diminished, because of the very same things that are going on with the stream macro-invertebrates," said Dan.

As the glaciers disappear, other forms of life are moving in. Ice fields have become green meadows where wildflowers and trees grow. In some lower regions of the park, vegetation that thrives in dry and arid climates is creeping in. "We've projected that grasslands will expand and that plants such as sagebrush will be making incursions into our park in the next forty years," Dan explained. This change in vegetation means the loss of habitat for the wildlife that the park has become known for. Mountain goats, which thrive in cold climates, still pose for tourists at Logan Pass. But as more trees begin to grow in areas where ice and cold weather once kept them out, the mountain goat's habitat will be threatened. "The mountain goats are the icons of the park," Dan explained. "But they don't eat trees, they don't climb trees, and they will be in trouble. Same for the bighorn sheep and marmots and picas that live here."

As things get warmer and drier, the forests are growing faster. "The trees get started earlier," Dan said. "They now have a longer growing season, especially at high elevations, so they grow like crazy." Increased forest density, coupled with drier conditions in late summer and long droughts, may eventually lead to more frequent and serious forest fires. The summer of 2003 saw one of the worst fire seasons in the history of the park to date. Almost no rainfall in July, August, and early September, at the end of a five-year drought, led to a series of fires that burned 136,000 acres, or 13 percent of the park. "We had had a significant fire in 2000, and at the time we thought it was such a big deal that wouldn't be repeated for a long time," Dan said. "But then 2003 was a much bigger fire season and it just made us laugh about it. . . . Now we expect to have more and larger fires into the future."

Of course, Glacier National Park is not alone as an indicator of the existence of global climate change or its effects. "Obviously, a glacier melting in one spot only means that that glacier is responding to the local climate it experiences. It's like trying to take a poll with one person," Dan explained. "It's the population of glaciers here and in other national parks that really tells us what is going on, and they're virtually all melting."

COMMITTED, WHETHER WE LIKE IT OR NOT

As the evidence in Montana shows, climate change is not just a hypothetical notion; we are already seeing signs of it. Moreover, there is broad scientific agreement that no matter what we do, part of the carbon dioxide humans have already dumped into the atmosphere will remain there for a very long time—up to 1,000 years, according to scientists' estimates—and it will continue to influence and change the climate system. We know that even if we were able, as of this very moment, to completely stop emitting greenhouse gases into the atmosphere, the Earth's temperature would still increase for some time, perhaps to 2.5 degrees Fahrenheit above preindustrial levels. In scientific terminology, we have entered a period of "committed warming." In other words, we simply cannot slam on the brakes and expect that we will be able to quickly reverse what humans have been setting in motion for the past 200 years.

What's more, scientists do not yet fully understand the mechanisms by which the climate of the Earth has shifted abruptly in the past under natural influences, and thus they cannot yet predict how and when such abrupt shifts will occur under the growing human influences operating today. Once the threshold, or "tipping point," for abrupt change is reached, the climate will enter a drastically different state, from which recovery could take millennia, no matter what remedial actions might be attempted after the fact. The only sensible strategy is to try to avoid passing the tipping point in the first place. The problem is that we lack precise knowledge of where that threshold lies.

At the current rate of emissions growth, carbon dioxide levels would double from preindustrial levels by around the middle of this century. This would translate into an eventual global average temperature increase of between 3.5 and 7 degrees Fahrenheit compared to 1900, with potentially catastrophic and life-threatening impacts. And, unless society takes serious evasive action, the CO_2 concentration will continue to rise after midcentury, quite possibly reaching a tripling of the preindustrial level by 2100 and a quadrupling in the twenty-second century.

Already at a doubling—and quite probably sooner—crop yields in most tropical and subtropical regions would be reduced. Water would become scarcer in many regions, and the risk of flooding would increase in others. Droughts would be more severe, and tropical storms, if not more frequent, certainly more intense. A study published in the journal *Nature* in 2004 reported that if left unchecked until 2050, climate change could doom up to 35 percent of all terrestrial plant and animal species to extinction.

Heat waves in North America and Europe would become more extreme, more frequent, and longer lasting in the twenty-first century if this scenario played out. Scientists at the National Center for Atmospheric Research (NCAR) have determined that the increase in heat-wave severity in the United States would most likely be greatest in the West and the South. According to a November 2006 report by scientists with Environmental Advocates of New York, summers in New York may resemble summers in the states of Georgia and South Carolina by the end of the century.

We simply cannot let that happen. We must set goals and begin to reduce greenhouse gas emissions before it's too late. But what should those goals be, exactly? What levels of emissions are both reasonable enough to meet and stringent enough to stop these scenarios from happening? The question on many minds right now is what level of carbon dioxide the atmosphere can tolerate before we reach the tipping point and nature proceeds on its own truly devastating course.

Until a few years ago, many analysts were suggesting that society should aim to limit the human warming influences on the atmosphere to the equivalent of 550 parts per million of carbon dioxide. (In this measure, the warming influences of greenhouse gases other than carbon dioxide and the warming and cooling influences of particles are converted into the changes in carbon dioxide concentration that would have the same effect.) This level of warming influence would translate to an eventual global average temperature increase of about 5 degrees Fahrenheit. As Dr. Holdren wrote in an article that appeared in the journal *Innovations,* this level "represented a compromise between the highest level at which climate change impacts might be manageable (taking into account the potential for adaptation) and the lowest level that might be achievable (taking into account the known mitigation options and their estimated costs)."

But the advance of climate science in recent years has made the 550 ppm level look far too dangerous. Given the major climate disruptions, human tragedies, increased warming, and sea-level rises we have observed already—set in motion by a 37 percent increase in carbon dioxide levels—analysts are now arguing that even an increase of 3.6 degrees Fahrenheit is flirting with disaster and that we should make every effort to stay below that level.

The warning signs are stark. Climate change at both poles has been dramatic and more significant than in the equatorial regions of the planet. According to the World Wildlife Fund, air temperatures in the Arctic have risen by a stunning 9 degrees Fahrenheit over the past 100 years. Thawing permafrost has caused the ground to subside more than 15 feet in parts of Alaska, and the oceans are eating away at shorelines, threatening waterfront communities. Animals that Arctic natives depend on for food—including polar bears, whales, walrus, and seals—are altering their feeding and migration patterns, threatening the human population's food supply and way of life. In fact, things are so dire that the Department of Interior on December 27, 2006, was forced to propose listing the polar bear as a threatened species under the Endangered Species Act because of the loss of its sea ice habitat from global warming. This proposal marks the first legally binding admission by the Bush administration of the reality of the global warming phenomenon.

Of particular concern is what a warmer Arctic will mean for the sea levels. The huge ice sheet that covers most of Greenland is losing a greater amount of water through melting than it is gaining through snowfall. The difference gets added to the global sea level. The situation in the even larger Antarctic ice sheet is less clear, but there are signs of accelerated melting and increased motion in the potentially unstable portion called the West Antarctic Ice Sheet. The 2001 IPCC report offered a best estimate of about half a meter of sea-level rise over the twenty-first century, mostly from the expansion of warming sea water, with only a small contribution from the Greenland and Antarctic ice sheets. More recent data about the melting rate of the

Greenland and Antarctic ice sheets raise the possibility of much faster increases in sea level.

The disappearance of the West Antarctic Ice Sheet would mean a rise in sea levels of about 16 feet, submerging numerous coastal cities across the globe, including New York; Washington, D.C.; London; and Bombay. The effects of the complete loss of the Greenland ice sheet would be even more devastating, leading to a 23-foot rise in sea levels. Such a rise would submerge much of the state of Florida. Most scientists believed until recently that complete loss of the Greenland and West Antarctic ice sheets would take millennia; but more recent evidence and analysis have suggested to some experts that a sea-level rise of several meters per century cannot be ruled out.

The floating sea ice that covers the North Pole and most of the rest of the Arctic Ocean is a different problem: When sea ice melts, the sea level doesn't change; but, because open water absorbs far more sunlight than ice does, the disappearance of the sea ice would sharply accelerate warming in the far north. And data released by NASA in September 2006 shows that the sea ice in the Arctic is disappearing far more rapidly than scientists were predicting just five years ago. Satellite monitoring technologies have found that perennial sea ice, which persists year-round, shrank by 14 percent—or 280,000 square miles—between 2004 and 2005. Another study conducted by the Goddard Space Flight Center in Maryland shows that the melting rate has become thirty times faster in the past two winters compared to 1979. This is also a graver reality that what scientists had expected. The release of the NASA reports prompted Jim Hansen, the leading climatologist and director of the Goddard Institute for Space Studies in New York, to issue a stark and critical warning to governments across the globe. In September 2006, he said that the world has a ten-year window of opportunity to take decisive action on global warming and avert catastrophe.

We no longer have the luxury of engaging in a debate that does not lead to action. We must put an end—an *immediate* end—to any discussion other than the one that will lead us forward. We simply have no choice but to face the facts, regardless of how unsettling they are. This is not just an "environmental" issue; it is a moral issue and a matter of life and death. There's no excuse for inertia. Even if, contrary to all science, the proponents of action on global climate change were proven wrong, what harm would the actions to combat global warming cause? We would have produced healthier people with cleaner air, sustainable farming and fishing practices, more healthful food, and more effective sources of cleaner energy, all of which adds up to greater security. But if those who deny climate change get their way and then are proved wrong, we will suffer catastrophe beyond description. Which side of the ledger would you prefer to be on?

Elizabeth Kolbert, describing the attitude of some U.S. government leaders toward the issue, recently offered an enlightening analogy. "It's like people are saying, we know there is a cliff ahead of us, but do not know exactly where it is. Therefore, we'll just keep speeding ahead," she told a crowd gathered at a symposium in New York City, adding, "That captures the Alice in Wonderland–like logic of current U.S. policy."

TURNING OUR BACKS ON THE FUTURE

John: Although the United States has only about 5 percent of the world's population, it is the world's top contributor of greenhouse gases, responsible for about 25 percent of global emissions of these pollutants. American leadership is, without doubt, critical to solving this problem. But rather than assuming the leadership role, and despite the compelling need to act, we are the ones who are falling behind. The United States is currently one of the only industrialized nations in the world that has failed to make a genuine effort to meet the challenge of climate change. A recent study by Climate

Action Network Europe found that, of the fifty-six top carbon dioxide–emitting countries in the world, the United States ranked fifty-third in taking steps to address global warming; only China, Malaysia, and Saudi Arabia did worse.

On February 16, 2005, the Kyoto Protocol went into effect across most of the globe. The 169 countries and other governmental entities that have ratified this international agreement consented to meet targets and timelines to reduce their greenhouse gas emissions. The goal was to reach a total decrease in global emissions of 5.2 percent below 1990 levels by the year 2010.

I was in Kyoto when those negotiations took place, as well as at the meetings that led up to them. In January 1987, two years after I was sworn in to the U.S. Senate, I began service on the Commerce Committee, which shared jurisdiction over climate change. This was a subject most people at the time gave little thought to, though as we know, climate scientists were already studying the phenomenon of greenhouse gases and taking a serious look at the data. Under the leadership of Al Gore, still a senator at that time, we held the first congressional hearings to study the implications of global warming and to encourage the development of environmental technologies to combat it. It was through these historic Senate hearings that we ushered in awareness of global warming in the 1980s.

In June 1992, I served as a member of the official Senate delegation to the Earth Summit in Rio de Janeiro, where representatives from 172 nations convened to discuss what we were going to do about this potentially catastrophic problem. To my surprise and delight, I enjoyed my first real conversations with Teresa, who had been appointed a delegate to the summit by President George H. W. Bush.

Rio produced a ray of international hope, as well as a promise. The hope stemmed from a sense of relief that we had recognized the problem of climate change in time, and the promise was that as members of the global community, we would commit ourselves to address the problem. That hope was translated into the Framework Convention on Climate Change, a treaty adopted at the conclusion of the summit outlining how participating countries would stabilize greenhouse gas concentrations in the atmosphere. The goal was to reach a level that would prevent dangerous interference with the climate system. This Framework Convention treaty was ratified by 189 countries, including the United States. In fact, the U.S. Senate approved the ratification by a unanimous vote. We thought we were on our way to an unprecedented bipartisan implementation of visionary, responsible public policy.

But instead, a period of procrastination and deception began. Trumped-up, industry-funded "studies" began to challenge the scientific assertions that provided the basis for climate change scenarios. Global political leadership was distracted or absent. At subsequent international negotiations held in Buenos Aires and The Hague, conversations that began as healthy exchanges between industrialized and developing nations turned tense. The less developed nations saw industrial countries' efforts to include them in the targets and timetables for greenhouse gas reductions as a "western market conspiracy" to restrain their growth; on the industrial countries' side, those who didn't want any restraints in the first place saw an opportunity to exploit fears of economic dislocation. In December 1997, final negotiations were completed at the meeting convened in Kyoto. To achieve the Kyoto Protocol's goal of reducing global emissions by 5.2 percent below 1990 levels, each nation had its own target goal. The European Union reduction would be 8 percent, Japan's reduction would be 6 percent, and so on. The treaty committed the United States to a target reduction of 7 percent below 1990 levels, to be achieved between 2008 and 2012. In the end, developing countries, including China and India, were exempt from meeting reduction targets until 2012.

In 1997, while the final Kyoto Protocol was being negotiated, the agreement got sidetracked in the U.S. Senate. The issue of developing countries being excluded from reduction protocols was a source of concern. Even then it was clear that India and China, and perhaps other developing countries, such as Brazil and Korea, were about to become significant enough as industrial powers that to exempt them entirely from the Kyoto Protocol would be a mistake—enough of a mistake to convince every member of the Senate that the United States should not ratify the Kyoto Protocol. Rather, the Senate unanimously passed the Byrd-Hagel Resolution, which cautioned the United States from agreeing to binding emissions reductions while less developed nations could grow with whatever practices they chose, and with no responsibility to meet any particular standard. Some people interpret the Byrd-Hagel Resolution as an objection to any mandatory controls on emissions, but that's not the case. In fact, the resolution called for the treaty's renegotiation, not for the issue to be ignored. In one respect in particular, the resolution had particularly damaging consequences: It seeded the idea of American reluctance to lead on this most vital issue.

The United States signed the agreement in 1998, but it was never submitted to the Senate for ratification. His successor, President George W. Bush, and his oil-friendly administration, pulled the United States out of the Kyoto accords altogether, describing it as "an unrealistic and ever-tightening straitjacket." In fact, it was one of the first acts of his presidency. The Bush presidency has spent the majority of two terms empowering those who oppose climate change action and even questioning the validity of the science behind global warming, claiming that millions of jobs will be lost if the United States joins in this world pact. In fact, the president has even gone as far as denying government scientists the opportunity to speak publicly about the severity of the threat. In 2006, James Hansen told a reporter: "In my more than three decades in the government I've never witnessed such restrictions on the ability of scientists to communicate with the public."

ECONOMIC OPPORTUNITY

But it doesn't end there. Aside from failing to acknowledge the most important challenge of our times, the Bush administration is also failing to see that, as with any kind of change, there is opportunity. As a result of this myopia, the United States is ceding its leadership on the development of new technologies that undoubtedly will be a significant economic driver in the future. Other countries are happily filling the void. By abandoning the playing field, we are disadvantaging ourselves economically. In stark contrast to some of our government leaders, many prominent business leaders—Patrick Cescan, CEO of Unilever, and Paul O'Neill, former treasury secretary and CEO of Alcoa, among them—have long accepted the facts about climate change and have pursued visionary policies to respond accordingly.

Rather than arguing against the imagined economic turmoil that will befall our nation, we should be embracing what these business leaders accepted long ago: There is huge economic potential in the response. The new technologies required to reduce emissions, and the means of remedying the harm we have done, should be viewed as our economic future. Every schoolchild learns that the history of this nation has been written through a spirit of innovation—from the Wright Brothers to Henry Ford to Bill Gates. We should certainly not stop now. This is the new frontier in technological ingenuity. It will provide high-value jobs, leading to better quality of life, better technical assistance to the world, and a competitive edge in a new marketplace. Some businesses across the globe and here in the United States are already proving that there are serious profits to be made in developing the technologies to reduce greenhouse gas emissions. And as much sense as it makes from an economic perspective at the business level, it makes economic sense at the government level.

Heads turned last fall when Sir Nicholas Stern, a distinguished development economist and head of the Government Economics Service for the United Kingdom, issued a report on the economics of climate change. It was the first comprehensive, serious cost-benefit analysis of such change. His findings were dramatic and unequivocal. His fundamental conclusion said this: "This Review has assessed a wide range of evidence on the impacts of climate change and on the economic costs, and has used a number of different techniques to assess costs and risks. From all of these perspectives, the evidence gathered by the Review leads to a simple conclusion: the benefits of strong and early action far outweigh the economic costs of not acting."

The Stern report continued:

Using the results from formal economic models, the Review estimates that if we don't act, the overall costs and risks of climate change will be equivalent to losing at least 5 percent of global GDP each year, now and forever. If a wider range of risks and impacts is taken into account, the estimates of damage could rise to 20 percent of GDP or more. In contrast, the costs of action—reducing greenhouse gas emissions to avoid the worst impacts of climate change—can be limited to around 1 percent of global GDP each year. The investment that takes place in the next 10–20 years will have a profound effect on the climate in the second half of this century and in the next. Our actions now and over the coming decades could create risks of major disruption to economic and social activity, on a scale similar to those associated with the great wars and the economic depression of the first half of the 20th century. And it will be difficult or impossible to reverse these changes. So prompt and strong action is clearly warranted.

Stern, like Hansen, identifies the next ten years as our last best chance to tackle global warming and to avoid the scenario in which our children and grandchildren are bequeathed a global catastrophe. It is time to stop debating fiction writers, oil executives, and flat-Earth politicians and address, in a very real way, this mortal threat to America. There are clear principles that should drive and shape our action. We must remember a few simple points. The challenge will become more difficult the longer we wait. The problem and the solution are global, but it is better that we begin locally rather than not at all. Sound domestic policies will contribute to the strength of our economy, our security, and the environment. And at least for now, Washington is far behind the American people when it comes to understanding and meeting this challenge.

Increasingly, homegrown efforts by concerned citizens are outpacing political "leaders" in forcing change. From kids at schools who are engaging in local activities to spread awareness about self-help steps, to dedicated professionals in government agencies like Dan Fagre and Jim Hansen, to creative business leaders like Jeff Immelt of General Electric, to powerful activists like Laurie David, who produced Al Gore's documentary and has founded the StopGlobalWarming.org Web site, to longtime, dedicated environmental leaders like John Adams of the Natural Resources Defense Council, Fred Krupp at Environmental Defense, and Eileen Claussen at the Pew Center, there is a growing awareness that the clock is ticking and that showing responsibility is imperative.

As Teddy Roosevelt once said, "Great thoughts speak only to the thoughtful mind, but great actions speak to all mankind." As imposing as the facts of climate change may be, there are countless practical actions that each of us can take to make a difference. The single most significant thing all Americans can do is elect leaders who understand that there is only one course of action that will *truly* solve this problem: an innovative and strategic national energy policy.

CHAPTER SIX

Drill, Then Drill Some More: Energy Opportunity Lost

John: The majority of U.S. greenhouse gas emissions come from energy use. Energy-related carbon dioxide emissions, resulting from burning fossil fuels—petroleum, natural gas, and coal—represent 82 percent of the total human-derived greenhouse gas emissions originating from the United States. From the automobiles we drive, to the coal-fired power plants used to generate electricity for our homes and businesses, the way we live is changing the composition of our atmosphere. We have no choice but to figure out how to eliminate or contain the greenhouse gas emissions, which threaten our health, our economy, our environment, and our security.

Although climate change is indeed a global challenge, the United States has a particular responsibility to lead the effort to solve it. Our nation contributes more greenhouse gases, in absolute terms and per person, than any other country. Currently we produce about 25 percent of the carbon dioxide emitted globally. We are the leading nation on Earth, economically, politically, and technologically. Therefore, there is no solution to climate change that does not begin with us. We must take dramatic and immediate action and set an example for the rest of the world. And the only way to succeed is to adopt a comprehensive energy policy addressing both how we obtain energy and how we use it.

For decades, we have talked about the need for a better, smarter, more innovative energy policy. Facing record gas prices, a volatile Middle East, and hostile rhetoric from a fundamentalist regime in Iran, a president of the United States once asked: "Why have we not been able to get together as a nation to resolve our serious energy problem?" His name was Jimmy Carter—and that steamy summer of 1979 seems as familiar today as the question he raised then. In fact, our unfulfilled good intentions predate even Jimmy Carter.

President Richard Nixon, for example, declared that by 1980, "the United States will not be dependent on any other country for the energy we need." Then President Gerald Ford extended the deadline: We would achieve energy independence, he said, by 1985. And in 1985, President Ronald Reagan was promising to "ensure that our people and our economy are never again held hostage by the whim of any country or cartel." Then, almost twenty-seven years after the original energy crisis, 2006 saw another season of record gas prices, raging violence across a volatile Middle East, and renewed rhetoric of hate from a fundamentalist regime in Tehran. It was the same old problem met by the same old strategy.

Whenever we face an energy crisis, talk of energy independence briefly becomes the common currency of the American political dialogue. We have a flurry of Apollo projects and Manhattan Projects for alternative fuels; summits and conferences and energy expos. And then, as the price of oil falls or supplies increase or a war is put behind us, the sense of urgency evaporates. Too often our political leaders have turned their backs on hard realities and great possibilities. Renewables, efficiency breakthroughs, and clean technologies—necessary tools in the fight against climate change and toward energy independence—have been marginalized, often owing to the opposition of corporate special interests.

A genuine commitment to clean technology would not only have slowed the threat of global warming but could have created millions of new jobs, opened up vast new markets, improved the health of our citizens, saved the taxpayers' money, earned the respect of the world, and significantly strengthened our long-term security. Instead, we have an "energy crisis" that is with us every year and every day. Aside from the potentially catastrophic threat of global climate change, the national security risks of dependence on fossil fuels, particularly oil, are on display with each day's headlines from the Middle East. As former Central Intelligence Agency Director Jim Woolsey has written: "Improving America's oil security is the most significant near-term energy challenge the U.S. faces."

Over the past decade, U.S. oil use has increased by almost 2.7 million barrels a day—more oil than India and Pakistan together use daily. We import some 13 million barrels of oil each day—over 60 percent of our total daily consumption—at an annual cost of $300 billion. If current trends continue, America will depend on imports for 70 percent of its oil by 2025. Our dependence makes no economic sense; in terms of security, it is a huge strategic mistake.

As accessible reserves in the world's stable regions have been depleted, oil extraction has gradually shifted to more dangerous corners of the globe. Among the world's key oil producers are countries synonymous with political instability: Angola, Azerbaijan, Chad, Nigeria, Sudan, and Venezuela. What's more, about 77 percent of the world's 1.1 trillion barrel in proven oil reserves is controlled by governments that significantly restrict access to international companies, according to PFC Energy, an industry consulting firm in Washington.

Then there's the Middle East. The region contains 60 percent of the world's remaining proven oil reserves, and, according to a joint report from the Center for American Progress and Worldwatch Institute, each day nearly half of the world's oil exports travel through the Strait of Hormuz and the mouth of the Persian Gulf. Because of their geographical proximity, Europe and Asia import a larger share of their oil from the Middle East than the United States does. But this does not lessen the U.S. exposure to imported oil. For thirty years, the Middle East has been the world's marginal oil supplier, and disruptions in the flow of oil are reflected in the world price of energy and the balance of global economic power.

Global dependence on fossil fuels is projected to intensify, according to the federal government's Energy Information Agency, with global energy demand surging 71 percent between 2003 and 2030. Oil demand is expected to soar 37 percent. More than half of that increase will be due to higher demand in the United States, China, and India. Energy-related carbon dioxide emissions worldwide are set to rise a terrifying 75 percent.

The costs and risks associated with dependence on fossil fuels are not limited to oil. There's also coal, a huge factor in electricity generation, and the most intensive producer of CO_2. China is already building the equivalent of one large coal-fired power station a week. As reported in *Scientific American,* "Over their roughly sixty-year life spans, the new generating facilities in operation by 2030 could collectively introduce into the atmosphere about as much CO_2 as was released by *all* the coal burned since the dawn of the Industrial Revolution."

The United States is highly dependent on coal, and it is far too unwilling to invest in the "clean coal" technologies that could make this energy source more benign. Coal-fired power plants now account for about 50 percent of the power generated in the United States, and the

Energy Department forecasts that this will increase to 57 percent by the year 2030. Indeed, power providers in the United States are expected to build the equivalent of nearly 280 large coal-fired electricity plants between 2003 and 2030, and some 154 new coal-fired plants are already in the works. Even as dependence on fossil fuels intensifies, and the costs and risks of this dependence rise steadily, our domestic energy policies seem stuck in an earlier era.

Overall, our fuel-efficiency standards—about 21 miles per gallon—have remained essentially unchanged since 1980, when Jimmy Carter was president, our children were playing Atari games, apartheid was a way of life in South Africa, and America was tuning in to find out who shot J. R. on *Dallas*. Since then, despite a whole generation of proposals for fuel-efficiency improvements, Washington, captive to powerful interests, has stood still.

Instead of coming up with innovative solutions, American automakers during this period put most of their engineering efforts into building larger vehicles with more powerful engines. The sheer size of these vehicles offsets any potential fuel-economy gains from new technologies. By taking this approach, they have sacrificed huge profit opportunities—opportunities that overseas competitors have been happy to take advantage of. In 1997, after thirty years of intensive research, Toyota introduced the Prius, the world's first hybrid vehicle. Powered by a combination of gasoline and electricity, it gets an average of 60 miles per gallon in city driving. Two years later, Honda followed suit with the introduction of the Insight. Today, these two Japanese companies dominate the market. Toyota alone accounts for about 80 percent of U.S. hybrid sales. The first American-manufactured hybrid was not launched until 2004: the Ford Escape. I remember in the spring of 2003 meeting with a top CEO from the auto industry who had come to convince me that we did not need higher automobile fuel-efficiency standards. I asked him why, at the time, the American auto industry seemed unwilling to build more fuel-efficient cars. He was blunt—and stunningly shortsighted: "Why in the world would we change every-thing to build more fuel-efficient vehicles when no one wants them?" It turns out that he was the one who was mistaken. By 2006, market an-alysts were reporting that 57 percent of all U.S. car shoppers had con-sidered buying a hybrid, and they were willing to pay $2,500 more than for a conventional vehicle. In the beginning of 2007, Toyota an-nounced that it expected its U.S. hybrid sales to jump 50 percent in one year, to nearly 300,000 vehicles.

Japanese auto engineers are not stopping at hybrid technology. They are searching for even more environmentally friendly technolo-gies, such as fuel cells (FC), which use hydrogen for fuel. Not surpris-ingly, Honda was the first automaker in the world to market a fuel-cell-powered car. Its latest development is the FCX Concept, a next-generation vehicle that boasts a small yet highly efficient fuel-cell system. Honda has also come up with a system that can be used to produce hydrogen in the home. Toyota, meanwhile, rolled out a fuel-cell hybrid of its own in the autumn of 2005, the Fine-X. It is equipped with a tank containing highly pressurized hydrogen, the only emis-sion it produces is water vapor. Toyota is opening factories in America at a time when U.S. auto manufacturers are closing theirs. U.S. auto companies have closed plants from Atlanta to Detroit to Oklahoma City, with the loss of tens of thousands of jobs.

Washington has not only neglected to promote more efficient au-tomobiles but has also avoided making any serious commitment to al-ternative renewable fuel sources. E85, a blend of 85 percent ethanol alcohol, is a homegrown, domestic, completely renewable source of engine fuel that burns cleaner than gasoline. Today in this country, nearly 6 million vehicles can be fueled by E85, but less than 1 percent of the service stations have even a single E85 pump. We would love to drive an E85-fueled vehicle, but in Massachusetts there is only one E85 fueling station, Burke Oil in Chelsea! For less than the cost of one week of U.S. participation in the war in Iraq, the federal government could pay for the installation of alternative fuel pumps in gas stations across America.

If consumers knew they could actually locate a convenient filling station for this product, there's no question the demand would rise rapidly. The proof exists in our own hemisphere. A little more than thirty years ago, when Brazil faced an energy crisis, the government got serious about its energy policy. Its leaders set out to reduce their dependence on foreign oil—80 percent of which they imported—and their use of all fossil fuels. Just a little more than three decades later, with some additional domestic production, Brazil has stopped importing oil entirely, supported significantly by massive investments in homegrown fuels like ethanol, which they manufacture from sugar cane.

Some states in our country have embraced the opportunities to pursue alternative energy strategies, but on the federal level, energy policy during the first years of the twenty-first century has been astonishingly counterproductive. In fact, national energy policy has taken several steps backward during the George W. Bush presidency.

Although we all cheered in early 2006 when President Bush finally acknowledged that our country was "addicted" to oil, and although his administration has grudgingly gone along with some small investments in pursuing alternative energy sources, its primary energy policy thrust has been to set America on a course toward even greater addiction to oil and other fossil fuels. The administration has been operating on the bizarre assumption that we can drill our way to energy independence. Such a course will only aggravate the crises of climate change and health impacts and add to the environmental damage flowing from our fossil-fuel addiction. .

The tone was set in the administration's first and most fundamental energy policy initiative, the infamous Cheney Task Force. The task force, which was nothing more than a secret cabal of oil and gas lobbyists, released a report in May 2001 calling primarily for increased domestic fossil-fuel production on federal lands. The day after the release of the report, President Bush signed Executive Order 13212, which directed federal agencies to expedite their review of permits and take other measures as necessary to accelerate the completion of projects to boost exploitation of existing energy sources. The consequences of the administration's drill-at-all-costs policies are worth examining in detail, because they illustrate how even bad energy strategies can be made still worse, compounding the risks of fossil-fuel dependence to our national security, our economic future, our air quality, our health, and our climate, with tangible damage to our public lands and the millions of Americans who rely on them for a livelihood.

Exploring and extracting fossil fuel is a necessary part of our energy mix. We will be drilling and exploiting these resources for years to come, but we must take into account its true cost and the damage it will cause, the true cost of the investment and the alternatives available. Casualties of the drilling frenzy that ignore these costs are increasingly scattered across the American landscape. The Powder River Basin, a 14-million-acre expanse of rugged prairie in northeastern Wyoming and southeastern Montana, is a significant example. In 2003, spurred on by the vice president's policies and the president's directives, the federal Bureau of Land Management (BLM) approved a plan for natural gas development on 8 million acres of the basin, including a proposal for 51,000 new wells by 2013, making it one of the largest gas production sites in the United States.

Similar plans are popping up all across the Rocky Mountain West, even in some of the most pristine and wild places, in order to meet the goal of greater domestic production of natural gas and oil. Many environmental safeguards have been ignored or removed. In July 2005, the Government Accountability Office (GAO) reported that western offices of the BLM were so busy processing drilling permits that staff had to put compliance inspections for environmental regulations on the back burner. The Buffalo, Wyoming, office in the Powder River Basin completed about one-fourth of its environmental inspections in 2004 while striving to meet an administration goal of 3,000 permits (it issued 2,435). Seasonal restrictions on drilling to protect wildlife have been repeatedly suspended under the Bush energy plan. The Wilderness Society found that during the winter of 2002–2003, the BLM office in Pinedale, in western Wyoming, received 172 requests from energy companies for exemptions from endangered species protections. All but three were approved.

Even some of the most special protected areas are now at risk. In January 2004, the Bush administration announced plans to drill more than 1.2 million acres of Otero Mesa, located in New Mexico, for oil and gas development. The plan, which met with significant local opposition, will forever alter the diverse eco-region. This region is a critical wildlife habitat and is considered North America's largest and wildest Chihuahuan Desert grassland remaining on public lands. Energy companies are also hoping to drill inside the Valle Vidal, which covers 100,000 acres of the Carson National Forest in northern New Mexico. Also known as the "Living Valley," the Valle Vidal is an important watershed area, home to diverse wildlife and a recreational haven for countless visitors, especially hunters and anglers. The casualty list goes on. In the Rocky Mountain West, 95 percent of lands managed by the BLM are now available for oil and gas leasing.

But this drill-first, think-later approach has aroused ever-growing opposition, not just from national environmental organizations, or even from "environmentalists" locally, but from everyday citizens in the West who see firsthand the long-term, unrecoverable losses, which go far beyond damage to the land. Janine Fitzgerald, who lives outside of Bayfield, Colorado, is a good example of the newly aroused West.

THE FIGHT FOR THE HDS

Janine Fitzgerald lives near the San Juan Basin, a large depression that dips gently across the southwest corner of Colorado and south to New Mexico, located near the Four Corners area where those two states meet Utah and Arizona. Along the northern edge of the basin, just east of Bayfield, the HD Mountains rise in the distance. It's not unusual for people who love these mountains to issue shy apologies about them—pointing out that they're not quite as high, or as rugged, or as majestic as many other ranges of the southern Rockies. But the apologies are unnecessary, because the HDs are extraordinary.

Named for a nineteenth-century cattle brand used by ranchers who once grazed livestock around the foothills of the mountains, the HDs cover nearly 40,000 acres and are part of the San Juan National Forest. One of the most striking things about them is that more than half of the area—at least 28,000 acres—is completely unspoiled: No roads have been pushed through, no logging has occurred, and not even a hiking marker exists.

Entering this wilderness is like traveling back in time. Countless undamaged Ancesteral Puebloan cultural sites exist, testifying to the area's rich Native American heritage. It also once provided hunting grounds for members of the Ute, Navajo, and Apache tribes. The area contains many of the last remaining stands of ancient ponderosa pine trees—trees that have largely been lost to logging in many similar mountain regions. The Ignacio Creek, which drains the southeastern portion of the HDs, runs crystal clear, and it is an important collector for the surrounding watershed, making it critical to local water supplies.

The best way to get a sense of the majesty of the HDs is to spend an afternoon walking into them, and better yet, to walk with Janine Fitzgerald. She has lived and worked on her family's sustainable farm in the shadow of the mountains for forty-two years, and though she has a Ph.D. in sociology, a subject she teaches at Fort Lewis College in Durango, she and other old-time Bayfield residents know the mountains better than most—biologists and ecologists included.

Though people come here often to enjoy the wilderness, walking with her is not a leisurely stroll, because Janine Fitzgerald is on a mission. In shorts, a tank top, and a backpack, she pushes her way through knee-high native grasses. She stops to pull up some arnica leaves, a wild herb commonly sold as a remedy for sore muscles, and rubs a few on her calf muscles. She points out wild turkeys flying overhead, their wings pounding the air. Later, she rests her head near the massive trunk of a ponderosa pine tree and inhales deeply. The trees, many of which are at least 300 years old, smell like butterscotch.

This incredible wilderness is now in danger, about to fall victim to the drilling frenzy. In 2004, a consortium of four energy companies released a plan to drill 283 natural gas wells in the northern San Juan Basin, including 68 in the roadless area of the HDs. Buried deep within the rocks here are coal seams, which the companies are hoping to mine for coalbed methane (CBM), the latest innovation in natural gas development.

Like conventional natural gas, CBM can be used to heat our homes and businesses. In traditional coal mining, methane, a natural by-product of the coal-formation process, and bound to coal seams by water, was considered a serious hazard and was released into the atmosphere. But in 1951, engineers figured out how to capture the methane for use as natural gas by pumping water out of the coal seam. The first coalbed-methane well was drilled in the Ignacio Blanco–Fruitland gas field near Ignacio, Colorado. It took another two decades before CBM became widespread, but in recent years, and especially since the Bush-Cheney energy plan was implemented in 2001, CBM drilling has been occurring on a staggering scale.

Even assuming the administration's most optimistic estimates, there's only enough coalbed methane to supply the United States for five years. What's more, mining any nonrenewable energy source, whether it is conventional natural gas or coalbed methane, ultimately means draining resources from the earth. Even with the best practices and latest technology, this process can wreak havoc on the environment. And that's why the CBM drilling frenzy is a perfect reflection of the overall shortsightedness of current policies.

In the HDs, the trade-off between the benefits of drilling in the roadless area and what would be lost is quite stark. The HDs would largely be transformed from an unspoiled wilderness to an industrial gas field. A CBM well resembles a traditional oil well, and each would need an infrastructure to support it—including miles of roads, hundreds of miles of underground gas lines, and several large compressor stations. These changes would destroy the wilderness, interrupt the migratory path of birds, affect countless species that depend on the HDs, and contaminate and deplete water sources—the source of life in the arid West.

And what would we get from drilling in the HDs? Enough natural gas to supply the United States for just two days.

The HD Mountains are one of the last undrilled areas left in the San Juan Basin. They were largely protected in 2001, after the U.S. Forest Service adopted the Roadless Area Conservation Rule. This protection status, which prevented the building of roads, logging, and oil and gas drilling, was the result of nearly three years of research and analysis of the nation's 60 million remaining roadless acres. The Forest Service sought a wide range of opinions and hosted more than 600 public meetings nationwide, 27 of which were in Colorado. More than 28,000 Coloradans responded, and at least 90 percent supported protecting the San Juan National Forest roadless area from road building and logging. It is clear what a vast majority of Coloradans want. Irrespective of their wishes, since his first day in office President Bush has worked to undermine the roadless rule, and in May 2001, 6,000 acres of the San Juan National Forest, including a portion of the roadless area of the HDs, was opened to drilling.

In August 2006, the U.S. Forest Service released a Final Environmental Impact Statement (FEIS) of the industry proposal for the HDs. In it, the authors acknowledged that drilling would have serious environmental effects, including the destruction of many of the old-growth ponderosa pines as well as potential seepage of methane. Nonetheless, the Forest Service approved constructing 100 well pads, building 72 miles of road, including in some of the most environmentally and culturally sensitive portions of the roadless area. The Forest Service has also waived existing regulations prohibiting drilling near the Fruitland Formation outcrop, the outer rims of the "bowl" that forms the San Juan Basin, where the coal seams are quite shallow, and where many people live. In the past, drilling close to the outcrop has resulted in wells going dry, methane seeping into water sources, and home basements with contaminated water and explosive levels of gas.

The danger of uncontrolled CBM drilling in this area goes far beyond damage to trees or wildlife. Because the methane is released by de-watering the coalbed—a process that can pump as much as 17,000 gallons of water each day, at each drill pad, for many years—drilling can lead to a drop in the water table, dry up streams and wetlands, and worst of all, cause domestic water and irrigation wells to become dry. Lowering the water table may also allow methane to rise up through the rock or seep through the soil into homes. This is clearly a basic public health issue. In 2005, four homes near existing wells on the Fruitland Formation outcrop had to be abandoned and razed because of methane seepage, and a fifth burned to the ground. An untold number of homes in the Texas Creek and Pine River areas in the basin already have methane in their well water, which has to be filtered and vented at a significant cost to prevent accumulation. In 2001, gas that surged from a well outside of Durango, Colorado, contributed to a grass fire, which quickly engulfed the surrounding trees. The next year, a fire that began in a coal seam in Glenwood Springs, Colorado, sparked a massive wildfire that burned 12,000 acres, destroyed twenty-nine homes, and took one month to extinguish.

Janine Fitzgerald, and others like her, are doing everything they can to help people understand where these policies are taking the area and what is being sacrificed for two days of gas. And, in fact, their efforts to educate and organize local residents have already had a positive impact. In August 2006, the Forest Service released its final report, and it addressed some of the concerns expressed in thousands of letters citizens sent to the Forest Service. After years of collaboration with dedicated Forest Service employees, the original proposal to drill fifty-seven well pads and build 38 miles of new roads within the roadless area was reduced to thirty new wells pads and 13 miles of road. And, perhaps most importantly, the entire Ignacio Creek watershed was put off-limits to development, and, at least for the time being, so were parts of the mountaintops. In all, the latest plan reduces the impact to the roadless area from 13,000 acres to 5,000 acres.

But the battle is far from over. The August 2006 plan authorized forty-eight new wells within 1.5 miles of the Fruitland Formation outcrop. The decision was made despite concerns expressed overwhelmingly by local residents about the serious impacts of drilling near the Fruitland outcrop—and the fact that five local governments in the two surrounding counties passed unanimous resolutions calling for absolutely no drilling here.

Janine and her colleagues will continue to fight. What motivates her to keep going? "The way I look at it," she said, "is that to survive well, especially in the West, there have to be connections between low, middle, and high elevations. That's true for all of us who live here—humans, wildlife, migratory birds, all of us. We each depend on these different zones for different reasons and once you remove this middle elevation zone of the HDs, you lose that connection."

To see what could become of the HDs, one need go only as far as a few miles from the Fitzgeralds' property, where intense drilling has already occurred. The signs of the environmental damage are apparent everywhere. Roads built to access the wells snake like an interstate system through previously untouched terrain. The roads end at well pads, many of which are not fenced, and the equipment can be dangerous. A young girl who climbed onto a pump last year died instantly when she was crushed by the arm of the pump. Notices along the Animas River outside of Durango—a river known for its fishing and recreational resources—warn visitors of the existence of high levels of hydrogen sulfide, a deadly, poisonous gas that occurs naturally in the coal seam, and which can lead to eye and lung irritation and nausea and instant death in higher concentrations. Large containment ponds dug to store water dot the landscape. Get anywhere near them, and you can detect the smell. Postings often warn that the area is highly flammable.

The Fitzgerald family wants to save the HDs from looking like this. "We have to watch these guys come in with these monster trucks, and drills, and crews from all over," Janine's father, Jim Fitzgerald, said. "It just feels like it's a horror, you know? How could people let something like that happen? It takes generations to understand the land. Yet these guys just show up, making big changes. They show us their pictures of their blow holes and their cement basins, and say it's okay, no problem, your water will be fine. Well, I know better, because I pay attention. And their response is either I'm a fool or I don't know what I'm talking about."

THE RANCHERS

The current trend to drill at the expense of all other natural resources is not just affecting families like the Fitzgeralds; it's also posing a serious threat to one of the icons of the American West: the ranch. In 2004, in the New Mexico area of the San Juan Basin, there were approximately 18,000 total producing wells around Farming-ton, New Mexico, and a plan released in March 2003 by the Bureau of Land Management authorized permits for nearly 10,000 more.

Many of these wells are being drilled on land that is currently be-ing used to raise livestock by families that have been ranching here for generations. Though many ranchers feel that the rate of current drilling, and the push for more, is destroying their livelihood as well as their way of life, they cannot stop it, because they do not own the minerals beneath the surface of their land. In 1916, the federal gov-ernment retained the mineral rights under all lands granted to settlers. From that point forward, while the homesteaders owned the surface of the land, the minerals underneath were controlled by the U.S. gov-ernment, which could do what it wanted with them, including leasing the development rights to private companies. Today, of the 700 mil-lion mineral acres the U.S. government owns nationwide, 58 million of these are under privately owned lands. Under the Bush administra-tion, the push to lease drilling rights to federal minerals includes fed-eral lands used by ranchers.

This represents one of many recent threats suffered by the ranch-ing economy. Increasing land prices, threats from residential develop-ment, the growth of agribusiness, and even fears about mad cow disease among consumers have hurt the industry. Over the past two decades, more than 500,000 cattlemen have sold their stock and quit. Drilling has brought a lot of unwanted consequences, including poor air quality, a loss of grazing area, sick cows, and polluted water. But the most surprising result is something else entirely: It has trans-formed many ranchers into environmental activists. Two such ranch-ers are Tweeti Blancett and Gilbert Armenta.

The Blancett family has been ranching on 35,000 acres outside of Aztec, New Mexico, for six generations. Tweeti and her husband, Linn, evoke the traditional western values of conservatism, hard work, and a firm commitment to the ethic of live-and-let-live. A staunch Republican, she ran the Bush-Cheney campaign for her area of New Mexico in 2000. Since then, life on her ranch has changed dramatically. As Tweeti has said, "Grass and shrubs are now roads, drill pads, or scars left by pipeline paths," she said. "We once ran 600 cows on those 35,000 acres. Today, we can barely keep 100 cows because they get run over by trucks servicing wells each day, or they get poisoned when they lap up the sweet antifreeze leaking out of unfenced compressor engines."

Gilbert Armenta is a fifth-generation rancher, and his family has been living on the prairie around Aztec, New Mexico, since 1598, when the area was controlled by Spain and settled largely by the Ute and Navajo Indians. His ancestors came here originally from the Basque country of France in the Pyrenees Mountains. They raised livestock on hundreds of acres of hills and prairie land among the piñon trees. Although generations of the Armentas had a successful ranching business, in the early 1950s a drought hit the area, and the ranching industry suffered. "They started having crop failures," Gilbert recalled, sitting on the back porch of his house, dressed in jeans, boots, and a cowboy hat and sipping fruit juice. "Looking back, that drought is nothing like the one we're having now, but the amount of animals we could graze dropped to nearly zero. So, in order to support the family, my dad needed to go out and find work." Gilbert's father, Filemeno, got a job repairing pipelines for a natural gas company, and Gilbert, who was fourteen, took over the ranch. He attended a Catholic school during the day and then returned home to help with the business.

Filemeno Armenta worked in the natural gas industry until 1967, when a gas line exploded in his hands, killing him instantly. Gilbert, twenty at the time, was given the deed to the land and the responsibility of supporting his family. Like his father, he went out to look for work one day and returned home a coal miner. He held this job for the next thirty-five years, running the family business in the evenings. Five years ago, at the age of fifty-five, he retired. Though Gilbert Armenta had planned to spend his retirement farming, relaxing, and taking care of his grandchildren, it hasn't turned out that way. "I'm spending so much time, and so much money, trying to deal with this energy development," he said. "Here I am, sixty years old, and going up against these humongous companies who have just come in here and are ruining my farm and destroying my grazing land."

Thousands of coalbed-methane wells have been drilled on the federal land where Armenta—as well as dozens of other area ranchers— graze their cattle. "In the last five years, the government has allowed infill drilling, which means they can put new wells on land where wells had already existed," he explained. "Each well takes a minimum of 2 acres. You multiply that by a few thousand wells, and that's a lot of grazing land that's lost."

The development has come at a great cost to him. In the past few years, he's lost several cows, which died, he believes, from grazing on grass contaminated by the wells. He has also lost grazing areas to the roads the energy companies have built. "I've estimated the amount of money that I've lost each year because of the wells ranges from $5,000 to $10,000, which is half my yearly income," he said. But that's not the worst of it. "The greatest concern to me is that I'm always on edge, always thinking about what's happening out there on that land. I've lost my peace of mind. Part of the problem is that the Bureau of Land Management doesn't enforce its own rules or regulations. They attribute it to a lack of manpower, but I think it's just that energy companies now have free rein over our land."

Gilbert Armenta has tried to change that. With other ranchers and farmers in the area, he started an organization called the New Mexico Landowners Association. Although only six people attended their first meeting in his garage, the organization now numbers more than 100. Many who attend his meetings are employees of the energy companies—people who, because they need their jobs, cannot speak publicly about their frustrations with how the development is occurring.

Though thirty-five years is a lot of time to spend working in a mine, Gilbert looks a lot more like a cowboy than a coal miner, and even less like an environmentalist. He's not particularly comfortable with the term "environmentalist." Like other ranchers, he lives with, and tends to, the environment every day; nature and the environment are not abstract terms to him. He possesses a considerable understanding of the long history of the territory, passed down in stories from oldtimers and learned from books, and from his work as a miner he has gained a keen sense of what is happening beneath the ground. Reports from energy companies refer to the coal seams under his land in terms of cubic feet and, ultimately, dollars and cents, but he understands that the rock is organic material created through a process that began millennia ago, "back when the dinosaurs were the only things around here." "If you take something out of the earth," he said, "you have to know what you're doing. Otherwise you're going to disrupt a very important, and fragile, balance."

"Balance" is a word used by many people in communities affected by energy development; very few advocate a total halt to the development. They simply want it to be done right, and in a way that recognizes the value of all of the region's resources, not just the gas. One of Gilbert's biggest concerns is the attitude of the energy companies that manage the wells. "They come in and they treat us like trash," he said. "All I want is for them to be good neighbors, but they think we're nothing."

A tour of his property makes this obvious. The quickest way to get from his house to some of his wells is to walk straight through his alfalfa fields. Instead, he climbs into his pickup truck, partly to show the road that the company built across his land in order to access the wells, and partly to escape the July heat, with a temperature hovering just above 90 degrees. The truck bounces along a dirt road cut between the alfalfa fields and the stalls where his fifty or so head of cattle are brought when it's time for sale. He turns west along the San Juan River, which cuts a line through his property, and drives until the dirt road ends suddenly at a steep cliff, 20 or so feet above the river. The water flowing past these alfalfa fields will eventually empty into the Colorado River in Utah's Lake Powell before making its way toward the faucets of Southern California.

Because the San Juan River helps supply drinking water to so many Californians, it is shocking to see several rusted car bodies jutting out of the banks of the San Juan at intervals of about 20 feet. Gilbert explained that the car bodies—purchased at junkyards—were placed there by the energy companies that operate the wells on his land in order to help shore up the riverbanks and prevent erosion. Many of the car bodies have fallen into the river itself, and downstream a little, a car door, a tire, and parts of an engine lay half-buried in the middle of the river. "A lot of these cars put here have motors and engines and they leak oil," he explained. Gilbert Armenta is an avid fisherman, and the San Juan is a fly-fisherman's dream, but he can no longer fish the stretch of river behind his house. "If I, as an individual, was found dumping a rusted car that was leaking oil into the river, I'd pay a hefty fine for violating the Clean Water Act," he said. "But these oil companies can basically do whatever they want."

A few yards beyond where the road drops to the river, five wells stand in a cluster. Today the wells are not in use. Despite the car bodies, the riverbank recently eroded, taking part of the road with it. The operator of this particular cluster of wells, XTO oil company—a company whose 2005 profits totaled $1.15 billion last year and whose CEO was compensated $32 million—has refused to repair the road, claiming that the repair, which would cost an estimated $150,000, is the responsibility of the Armenta family. Gilbert Armenta has refused to bear these costs, and the matter has been brought to court. Since then, as the two parties await a decision, XTO has stopped operating the wells. The company has also erected fences around two other wells it operates on Gilbert's land—tall chain-link fences covered in barbed wire that Gilbert refers to as the "San Quentin fences." "I guess this is their way of saying 'screw you,' for not fixing the road. They sure seem to be going to a lot of expense to try to make me feel unwelcome on my own land."

Car bodies are not the only thing polluting this stretch of the San Juan River. It is also being polluted by toxic fluids used in the mining process. To help ease the flow of methane, drillers often force-inject a compound of sand and chemicals, like diesel fuel, called fracing (pronounced FRACK-ing) fluid, to fracture the rock and move the methane more easily. Fracing, used in most CBM well operations, was originally developed in 1949 for use in traditional oil drilling by engineers with the Halliburton Oil Well Cementing Company. Halliburton still operates a large fracing business and is involved in a substantial percentage of fracing operations in CBM wells today.

At one of the wells near the river, acid was used to fracture the rock. "They pumped 50,000 gallons of acid into the coal," Gilbert said. "They're supposed to retrieve every drop of it, but they couldn't get any of it back. We're not sure why it happened. There might be a cavity down there somewhere. Maybe the coal didn't need fracing as hard as they did it. Either way, this river is now polluted. You see all the car bodies, the tires. There's acid in there. Do the oil companies care? No, they don't."

There are other problems. Gilbert gestured toward a large pool of water on his land—water that has been pumped from the coal to release the methane. Because the produced water contains such a high concentration of dissolved salts, it cannot be used to irrigate range or croplands—an unfortunate irony for a community in a three-year drought. And then there's the odor, which can be worrisome for residents even after they've gotten used to it.

Prompted by ranchers and landowners like Gilbert Armenta and Tweeti Blancett, many states have recently begun to consider legislation that would give greater protections to surface owners, but to no great avail. In April 2006, legislators in Colorado proposed a bill that would have required energy companies to utilize best practices to minimize impacts, to negotiate with surface owners on the placement of facilities, and to fairly compensate surface owners for use and damage of the property. By the time the bill passed the Colorado House, it had become so industry-friendly that it actually left surface owners with fewer rights than before, forcing the bill's sponsors to pull it from consideration.

Gilbert Armenta and Tweeti Blancett, meanwhile, are not willing to give up their fight. The New Mexico Landowners Association is considering taking legal action against the energy companies to force them to protect the environment and compensate landowners whose livelihoods have suffered. "My goal in life was to pass on this ranch to my kids, just as it had been passed on through so many generations to me," Gilbert said. "My oldest grandson is fighting in Iraq now, and I'd love to leave this to him. But looking out at what this has become, it makes me wonder, who would even want this anymore?"

Tweeti Blancett has sometimes struggled to stay upbeat. "At times it seems hopeless. Then I hear people facing similar situations in Colorado, in Montana, Wyoming, Utah. Many are like us—conservative, Republican, pro–free enterprise people. Others are environmentalists, or just care about the land and animals. Shortly, there will be a huge natural gas explosion, but it won't be pipelines or gas wells that blow. The explosion will come from the average westerner, who is tired of being used by the oil and gas industry."

These are but two examples of the many consequences that stem from our outdated "energy policy." Unfortunately, such nightmares are being played out across our country on a daily basis. For each of these farmer- and rancher-led rebellions, there are thousands of other visionary citizens struggling against powerful economic interests to put common sense into our public policies. In community after community, whether in response to the siting of a dirty coal-fired power plant, in response to proposals to drill for oil and gas in some of our most treasured natural places—or in response to any of countless other short-term, harmful practices—more and more Americans are demanding a better future.

The drill-drill policies of the Bush administration, and the seemingly steadfast refusal of our federal government to tackle our energy problem head-on, are having one very positive effect on the national energy debate. They are forcing a real and fateful national choice about the future we are going to create. One choice, based on more of the same, is a future where the air, the water, and the land and its people have been sacrificed, even as energy imports are never reduced enough to free ourselves from foreign oil, and where the greenhouse gas emissions that feed global warming have increased, perhaps to the point of no return. It's a future where the rest of the world, and its investors and consumers, have continued to move in a very different direction, inventing their way out of the problem, and leaving us reliant on other nations' technology. In this scenario, global capital would begin to treat America as a backwater, and with good reason: We would lag way behind in developing the clean energy technologies and products dominating the global economy of the twenty-first century. U.S. employment levels, wages, and living standards would be depressed.

In this future, America's domestic prosperity, and our freedom of action in foreign policy, would remain vulnerable every single day to events and decisions in the most unstable parts of the world. Our rates of cancer and respiratory diseases would continue to spiral, disabling and killing millions of Americans and overburdening an already inadequate health-care system. Energy policics would come to dominate every other national topic, pitting region against region, and powerful interests against an aroused citizenry. For most citizens, the idea of allowing ourselves to follow this path should seem alien and even profoundly un-American, particularly since it invites the continued erosion of our influence and reputation as the world's technological and economic leader, not to mention our proud heritage as the ultimate can-do nation.

Fortunately, there is a clear alternative. As the examples in chapter seven show, this other future is already being defined by energy pioneers, virtually all of whom are working without adequate support and encouragement from the federal government. These pioneers have proven that the American qualities and strategies we've employed to meet every other big challenge in our history, including the transition from horse- to internal-combustion-powered transportation, the sudden and previously unimaginable spread of electricity and phone service, and the incredible advances brought about by computers and the Internet, will serve us just as well as we adopt an entirely new approach to our national energy policy.

To borrow from an old World War II slogan, when it comes to a sudden leap in energy technologies: "We've done it before, and we can do it again."

CHAPTER SEVEN

$$\infty$$

Prospecting for the Future

John: In 1901, the *New York Herald Tribune* gushed about a new discovery. The reporter's excitement was palpable; the new century had delivered a great new resource: "The most remarkable rush witnessed in this country for many years is at present in full blast consequent upon the discovery of petroleum in the State of Texas. The find was made at Beaumont and it is claimed that the output of the single well now spouting amounts to more than 25,000 barrels daily. This, it is proudly maintained, is far greater than that of any oil well either in Pennsylvania or Russia. The fever has affected all classes of the community. Within a few days hundreds of borings for oil have been made in all directions, and fabulous prices have been paid for land heretofore regarded as of no value."

Beaumont was the first of America's oil rushes, and clearly, the discovery was greeted with the expectation that it would be utterly transformative. On top of the general "fever" of excitement was the thrill that land previously regarded as worthless was suddenly capable of fetching such "fabulous" prices. It was viewed as nothing short of an economic miracle. At that time, encouraged by earlier discoveries in Russia, Canada, and central Europe, oil was widely considered to be a very exciting find. A century later, however, the excitement has obviously waned, as the consequences of oil—economic, geopolitical, and environmental—are better understood.

What remains compelling in the story of the discovery in Beaumont, Texas, however, is the sheer thrill of discovery: a sensation we are poised to recapture, provided we embrace the challenge of the new era of energy, the post-carbon period. Americans have always pushed the frontier of discovery. We didn't become the most powerful economy on Earth by holding back. Innovation after innovation has unfolded because the American spirit has always pushed the limits. Innovation is in the American DNA.

Any failure thus far to become more energy independent and create the technologies needed to combat the threat of climate change is certainly not a failure of American ingenuity. That ingenuity is alive and well among individuals and corporations engaged in the discovery of new and better ways to address our energy challenges. In doing so, they are proving that this new energy future is staring us in the face.

Confronted with a warning that we have but ten years to get serious about climate change, we certainly need all the inspired pioneers we can find. But most critically, the U.S. government must take immediate responsibility for our energy future, beginning with an acknowledgment that our antiquated policies are just not working for our environment—or, for that matter, for our security or our economy. As a nation, we must join—then lead—the global race for new, safer, nonpolluting sources of energy. Our future truly does depend on it.

America has many options, but the three vital first steps are: (1) excel in energy efficiency; (2) develop clean, renewable and alternative energy sources; and (3) clean up coal.

It's a huge challenge, but it's also a magnificent opportunity, in which the rewards will be worth every effort—not only because of what it means for the planet, but also because a sensible energy policy is, in fact, the best economic plan we could possibly adopt. If a "two for" is when you get two of something for the price of one, moving toward better energy efficiency and clean, renewable sources may actually be called a "five for." In addition to helping combat climate change, it will also lead to more jobs from the new technologies and products we create at home; result in greater national security based on energy independence; ensure better health due to cleaner air and water; and, not inconsequentially, provide a more healthful planet for our children and grandchildren. Few policies have the potential to produce so much public benefit. Across the country, there is evidence that this multiple win-win prospect has been embraced by shrewd corporate accountants and idealistic inventors alike. The green rush is on. We now need to ensure that it moves fast enough in the right direction.

ENERGY EFFICIENCY

In 2003, Dallas-based Texas Instruments (TI) announced plans to construct a new manufacturing plant. Texas Instruments, understandably, placed a value on staying in Texas. In order to do so, the company executives would have to meet the seemingly impossible goal of keeping the cost of building in Texas competitive with what it would cost to build abroad, in, say, China or India.

A team of TI engineers and designers went to work to see how this goal might be accomplished. Early in the process, they placed a call to Amory Lovins, co-founder of the Rocky Mountain Institute—an independent, entrepreneurial, nonprofit organization dedicated to fostering the efficient use of resources—to ask how incorporating energy efficiency into the building design and construction could help save money. Lovins, a bubbling, one-person idea factory, was eager to help. One of the most influential American advocates for greater energy efficiency, Lovins has long been aware of one very simple truth: It's a lot cheaper, easier, and faster to save energy than it is to buy or produce it.

Over the course of several days, with Amory's help, the TI team brainstormed ideas. Eventually the engineers and designers reached a broad understanding that efficiency would go a long way toward bringing costs down. An agreement was reached to reconceptualize the entire design of the factory. By March 2006, the plant had entered the final stages of construction. It showcases numerous energy-saving measures, from the grand to the simple: It's a two-story design rather than three, to save energy costs; has larger than average water pipes, with fewer elbows, to reduce friction, as well as smaller, more efficient pumps; and sports a white reflective coating on the roof to reduce the costs of cooling the inside. Architects networked controllable light fixtures with built-in motion and photo sensors for individual control and energy savings, and workers installed a 2.7-million-gallon rainwater collection pond for site irrigation. They even put in waterless urinals to save water.

The projected long-term savings are astounding. TI expects to reduce energy consumption by 20 percent and water consumption by 35 percent, which will translate to at least $750,000 of operational savings during the first year alone, and $3 million each year when the plant is fully operational. The benefit to the local economy from Texas Instruments finding a way to remain in Texas? According to an economic impact study by the Perryman Group in Waco, Texas, the plant will result in a cumulative $14.5 billion stimulus for Texas and the creation of 88,135 permanent jobs. The Texas Instruments plant exemplifies Lovins's simple truth about energy efficiency: It is generally the fastest, cheapest, safest, and surest way to reduce emissions of greenhouse gases. Whether in factory design, trucks and military vehicles, commercial buildings, or homes—even in the lightbulbs and dishwashers we choose—energy efficiency makes sense. Though we have certainly made great strides in improving energy efficiency in the last forty years, the potential for further savings is enormous. As reported in a fascinating and helpful report on this issue by the Worldwatch Institute and the Center for American Progress, U.S. energy use per dollar of gross national product is nearly double that of other industrial countries.

Significant efficiency gains are specifically required in the automobile and electricity sector. We must start with a major increase in the fuel economy of our automobiles. Building cars of the future—fuel-efficient, advanced-technology vehicles—will require automakers and their suppliers to retool their factories. The federal government has a responsibility to help them remain competitive. Tax credits will help support the necessary investments, make the new technologies cost effective, and create jobs for the workers who will build the cars of the future. Hybrid drive trains, clean-burning diesel engines, plug-in electric cars, and lightweight materials could allow vehicle fuel economies to double over the next two decades. And the $200 billion that Americans spend annually on electricity could be cut in half with cost-effective technologies already available on the market.

With only a ten-year window, energy efficiency needs to become second nature to every American, especially to our leaders in Washington; and there are clear lessons to be learned from past government policies. In 1987, for example, the government established efficiency standards for home appliances. By 1999, refrigerators were three times more efficient than the 1972 models and dishwasher efficiency more than doubled. Not only does this mean that consumers pay less in electric bills each month, it also means we cut down on the amount of fossil fuels needed to produce the electricity. In fact, more than two-thirds of the fossil fuels we consume are lost as waste heat in power plants and vehicles! Certain measures such as implementing stronger efficiency standards for air conditioners and improving energy efficiency in buildings over the next twenty years could eliminate the need to build more than 600 electric power plants, preventing as much as 200 million tons of CO_2 emissions per year.

Corporate America is demonstrating that energy efficiency can be strongly linked to profitability. By cutting energy consumption, the technology company 3M has saved more than $190 million since 1990 while preventing the release of an estimated 1.85 million metric tons of greenhouse gas emissions over the past ten years. The chemical and health-care multinational company Bayer saved $850 million and prevented the release of nearly 5 million metric tons of emissions over ten years by adopting more energy-efficient practices, all while increasing production by 22 percent. In the same sector, DuPont is yet another inspiring example of how a commitment to energy efficiency can translate into cost savings. In the mid–1990s, DuPont adopted an energy policy that included an aggressive plan to maximize energy efficiency in the areas of lighting, heating, cooling, compressed air, and cogeneration, a process that utilizes leftover heat to generate electricity. The company's manufacturing processes were changed to reduce energy use and waste. At one plant, DuPont reduced energy usage by 30 percent just by changing the way products were packaged.

DuPont's investment in energy efficiency has allowed the company to hold its energy use flat between 1990 and 2000 while increasing production 35 percent. At what cost? *A savings of $3 billion.* As John Carberry, DuPont's director of environmental technologies, explained during a 2004 congressional committee hearing: "[Our] savings continue. That is genuine business value from better energy stewardship, and it contributes to our substantial global reductions in air emissions, including greenhouse gases." DuPont is also one of a growing number of companies striving to bring more efficient products to the marketplace. Its Tyvek housewrap improves the energy efficiency of homes and buildings, with energy savings in the first year of use alone some ten to twenty times the energy required to produce the product. DuPont is manufacturing plastics that will make cars lighter and therefore more fuel efficient, and the firm's fuel-cell technologies are helping to create the next generation of high-efficiency, low-emitting power sources for applications ranging from portable CD players to cars to community power-generating stations.

We still have enormous efficiency gains waiting to be exploited. And given that we know that energy efficiency is the cheapest and fastest way to achieve reductions in energy use, there is no reason for delay. A robust national initiative to excite efficiency awareness at all levels of American enterprise should be immediately embraced.

RENEWABLES

Renewable energy sources are the next great arena of energy opportunity, and we should all be as excited about our ability to harvest energy from the wind and the sun as the residents of Beaumont, Texas, were to benefit from the discovery of oil. Today, renewables supply just 6 percent of U.S. energy needs. Fossil fuels, on the other hand, supply 85 percent. This is not because the technology does not exist to exploit renewable sources of energy, or that our nation does not have enough wind or sun, but simply because we have done little to encourage their use.

Of all renewable energy technologies, the one with the greatest potential to replace a large number of conventional power plants is wind power. Sited properly, wind power can achieve utility-scale output equal to the electricity created by coal-fired power plants. The Stateline Wind Energy Center located on the Washington-Oregon border, for example, generates 300 megawatts of electricity—enough to supply power to about 105,000 homes.

According to the Department of Energy, 6 percent of the contiguous forty-eight states is suitable for wind power development and as the Apollo Alliance, a joint project of the Institute for America's Future and the Center on Wisconsin Strategy, explains, "these regions could potentially supply more than one and a half times what the U.S. currently consumes." Despite that fact, we get only 1 percent of our nation's electricity supply from wind power today. And wind power is relatively cheap. As the American Wind Energy Association reports, with appropriate federal tax incentives, the cost to deliver wind power to American homes can be competitive with conventional sources of power. Furthermore, the economic advantages of wind power include the fact that building wind farms would create a host of new jobs, many of them in rural communities which are often well suited to accommodate them. In fact, a study by the CALPIRG Charitable Trust reports that wind power typically provides 70 percent more jobs than natural gas power plants.

Solar power also holds special promise for handling the increasing demands on America's energy infrastructure. Perhaps no one understands this better than Denis Hayes, the pivotal organizer of the first Earth Day in 1970. During the Carter administration, he directed the federal Solar Energy Research Institute (now the National Renewable Energy Laboratory). Today, Hayes is president and CEO of the Bullitt Foundation, a $100 million environmental philanthropy located in Seattle. He explains that consumer demand for energy is highest on summer afternoons, when air conditioners are running and businesses are operating, but "the intense sun of those same summer afternoons, if properly harnessed and channeled, can in turn produce enough solar power to meet these high energy demands."

As the Apollo Alliance explains in their report *Solar Energy 101*: "there are three types of solar-energy technology in commercial use: photovoltaics, concentrated solar power, and solar heating. Photovoltaics and concentrated solar power generate electricity and can be used in both residential and commercial settings. By contrast, solar heating harnesses the sun's energy for a variety of non-electrical heating applications, such as swimming pools and space heating. Additionally, new uses for solar energy are continually under development." We know that just as there is money to be saved in energy efficiency, renewable energy sources can save money and create jobs. Between five and fifteen jobs are created for every million dollars invested in solar electricity, compared to only 1.5 jobs in oil and gas exploration. Such benefits are likely one reason the solar-power industry is one of the world's fasting growing markets.

Though the domestic solar-power industry is not growing as quickly as it is in the rest of the world, it is expanding in large part, to exciting innovations by industry leaders, such as SunPower President Dick Swanson.

A former professor of electrical engineering at Stanford University, Swanson founded SunPower in 1985 to bring affordable and highly efficient photovoltaic power systems to the market. For the first several years, the company, which is based in Sunnyvale, California, had trouble finding customers. Installing solar technology was prohibitively expensive at that time for most American families, and SunPower's work was mainly for novelty demonstration projects. The company, for example, provided the solar cells used by Honda to win the 1993 World Solar Challenge. "We had people working for free," Swanson told *Stanford Magazine*. "They knew the company couldn't afford to pay them."

But that's no longer the case. The company has developed solar cells that are up to 50 percent more efficient than others on the market, helping to make SunPower a leader in today's global solar market. At this rate, customers can recoup the cost of the solar cells in as few as ten years. That's good news, not only for consumers, but also for the company. In late 2005, SunPower went public. In the initial public offering, the stock price rose 41 percent on the first day, to $25.45. In January 2007, the stock was trading at $42.07. And according to

Dick Swanson, the company will continue to grow, because the solar equipment market is projected to jump tenfold, from $1 billion in 2010 to $10 billion by 2020.

SunPower is but one of the companies that is leading the research and development of the technology that has cut the cost of solar technologies by one-eighth since the early 1990s. Imagine what we could do with serious government investments in this area.

Less well known than wind or solar energy, but also somewhat promising, is biomass energy. Biomass energy is derived from plant matter such as trees, grasses, or agricultural crops and other biological material. It can be used as a solid fuel or converted into liquid or gaseous forms for the production of electric power, heat, chemicals, or fuels.

We have used biomass energy, or "bioenergy," since people began burning wood to cook food and keep warm. Its use has the potential to not only greatly reduce greenhouse gas emissions but also reduce dependence on foreign oil, since biofuels are the only renewable liquid transportation fuels available. Overall, wood is still the largest biomass energy resource today, but certainly not the only one, or even the cleanest one. Ethanol, which can help fuel our automobile fleet, is made from starches and sugars. In the United States, ethanol, derived primarily from corn, contributes about 2 percent to the total transportation fuels mix. The U.S. Department of Energy, however, has set ambitious goals for biofuels, hoping to replace 30 percent of transportation fuels with biofuels by 2030.

The biofuels option does have limitations. Led by Jason Hill, a postdoctoral associate at the University of Minnesota, a team of five University Researchers published the first comprehensive analysis of the environmental, economic and energetic costs and benefits of ethanol and biodiesel in the pages of the proceedings of the National Academy of Sciences. According to their research, a major challenge is just getting enough of it to meet our demands without overtaxing soil and water resources. In addition, even if all the corn grown domestically were slated for ethanol conversion, the total ethanol produced from it would offset only 12 percent of the gasoline we now use. And supply issues aside, there are a number of environmental and economic concerns associated with a mad dash to biofuels. Energy crops would likely be planted in formerly uncultivated yet resource-rich lands, and an expanding global biofuels market could drive up commodity prices and impact the ability of developing countries to buy food. These challenges are not insignificant.

To address some of these concerns, scientists are developing technology to allow biomass fuels to be made from cellulose, the fibrous material that makes up the bulk of most plant matter. One of the great advantages to the cellulosic approach is that it reduces the pressure on soil and water that current practices pose. If one could cut prairie grass without disturbing the soil or needing to irrigate, we would have a far more sustainable cycle.

There are also other ways to produce biofuel: We can make it from vegetable oil, animal fat, and even recycled cooking grease. The result —called biodiesel—could be used as an additive to reduce vehicle emissions or, in its pure form, as a renewable alternative fuel for diesel engines. In fact, even the fumes from landfills (methane, a natural gas) can be captured and used as a biomass energy source.

Renewable biomass resources should be an important contributor to the development of a sustainable industrial society and effective management of greenhouse gas emissions. In the United States, bioethanol derived primarily from corn contributes about 2 percent to the total transportation fuels mix; another 0.01 percent is based on biodiesel fuel. Biomass fuels could make a real difference if they were incorporated into existing energy use. A good example is a small but important experiment with biodiesel fuel undertaken in Monroe County, Indiana.

The Apollo Alliance highlighted a particularly interesting example on the benefits of biofuels: "In 2003, Monroe County integrated progressive thinking and local interests as they shifted their school bus fleet to soy biodiesel blended fuel. In their use of biodiesel in all 107 of the district's buses, Monroe County exemplified a dedication to the local community and to the global environment. The fuel used in the Monroe County school buses is a blend of 20 percent biodiesel (B20), 80 percent traditional fuel. By changing the fleet from regular fuel to B20, the County estimates that the buses will have reduced carbon monoxide emissions by 12 percent and hydrocarbon emissions by 20 percent. This reduction in toxic pollutants creates a better environment for the children, bus drivers, and mechanics and shows a dedication to preserving the environment of Central Indiana. Furthermore, by putting B20 soybean biodiesel in school buses, Monroe County is contributing to the farming community that is so prominent in Indiana. The Indiana Soybean Board sees the local and global benefits of B20, and has been encouraging schools and municipalities all over the state to follow Monroe County's lead." This lesson should be put to use across the country.

PUTTING RENEWABLES TO WORK

In a joint report issued by the Worldwatch Institute and the Center for American Progress *American Energy: The Renewable Path to Energy Security*—we learn of the great potential of renewable energy. The report explains that, "global investment in renewable energy (excluding large hydropower),* was estimated at $38 billion in 2005—equivalent to nearly 20 percent of total annual investment in the electric-power sector. Renewable energy investments have doubled over the past three years and have increased six-fold since

---

*Hydropower, a renewable energy source, accounted for 7 percent of total U.S. electricity generation in 2004. However, hydropower poses significant environmental impacts to our nation's rivers and therefore should not be considered a major source of renewable energy for the future.

1995. . . . These dynamic growth rates are driving down costs and spurring rapid advances in technologies."

Our nation must now make a concerted commitment to renewable energy and other countries are not going to simply wait for us to make this commitment. "The prominent positions that Germany and Spain hold in wind power, for example, and that Japan and Germany enjoy in solar energy, were achieved because of strong and enduring policies adopted by their legislatures in the 1990s," the report explains. "These policies created steadily growing markets for renewable energy technologies, fueling the development of robust new manufacturing industries. By contrast, U.S. renewable energy policies over the past twenty years have been an ever-changing patchwork. Abrupt changes in direction at both the state and federal levels have deterred investors and led dozens of companies into bankruptcy. If America is to join the world leaders and achieve the nation's full potential for renewable energy, it will need focused, sustained policies based on a coordinated and consistent policy framework at the local, state, and national levels." And the potential is certainly there.

The allure of renewables is being realized even by some of our most fossil-fuel-intensive companies. In the late 1990s, General Motors, British Petroleum, and Monsanto joined with the World Resources Institute, an environmental think tank, to work toward the development of corporate markets for renewable energy. Their Safe Climate, Sound Business (SCSB) Initiative was designed to address the conflict between energy needs and the need to reduce greenhouse gas emissions. After reviewing three long-term energy scenarios, the partnership agreed that "it will be difficult to reduce CO_2 emissions without sharply increasing reliance on renewable energy sources." Based on this finding, they established the Green Power Market Development Group with the goal of developing corporate markets for 1,000 megawatts of new, cost-competitive green power by 2010. This is equivalent to the amount it would take to supply about 350,000 homes.

Today, there are thirteen corporate members of the Green Power Market Development Group—Alcoa, Delphi Corporation, Dow, DuPont, FedEx Kinko's, General Motors, IBM, Interface, Johnson and Johnson, NatureWorks, Pitney Bowes, Staples, and Starbucks—and collectively, they are the largest corporate consumers of renewable energy in the United States. Between January 2001 and December 2005, the members were collectively responsible for 360 megawatts of new green power projects and purchases, including hydrogen fuel cells, wind power, electricity from other renewables such as biomass and geothermal resources, and the direct use of landfill gas for energy.

More companies are following in their footsteps. In 2006, Whole Foods Market and Wells Fargo completed the largest green power purchases in U.S. history to date. Timberland built an impressive solar power system that will serve as the primary source of electricity at its Ontario, California, distribution center, and it is one of the top fifty largest solar installations in the world. Interface, a carpet company that has long embraced a commitment to the planet, is using the gas from decomposing organic materials at the local landfill to generate energy at its plant in LaGrange, Georgia.

These corporate advances have received little publicity. And regrettably, too many corporate leaders have yet to guide their companies on this renewable energy and energy-efficiency path. The federal government should take the lead, helping to organize an educational outreach to boardrooms across America. And boards of directors should be challenged to represent real shareholder interest by demanding transformation of their businesses' energy practices.

CLEAN COAL

Coal—the fuel that made the Industrial Revolution possible—is a particularly challenging source of energy today. It remains cheap and abundant, but those benefits are far outweighed by the true costs of coal, especially the carbon dioxide that is emitted when coal is burned. Despite the higher environmental costs, in the United States as well as in other countries with abundant coal resources, more coal is being burned now than ever before and it's unlikely this will change anytime soon. But it is important to understand that if we want to burn the plentiful stock of U.S. coal, we first have to find a way to strictly limit the amount of carbon dioxide released in the process. If we fail, we have little chance of gaining control over global warming.

Techniques have been developed—called CO_2 capture and storage (CCS) or geologic carbon sequestration—in which most of the carbon dioxide produced at power plants is not released into the atmosphere but is captured and then stored deep underground, usually in depleted oil or gas fields or in saltwater formations. As reported in *Scientific American,* all of the technological components needed for CCS at coal conversion plants are commercially ready. Implementing CCS at coal-burning plants is imperative if the carbon dioxide concentration in the atmosphere is to be kept at an acceptable level. That level, of course, is one that will enable us to avoid reaching the climate-change tipping point and the associated catastrophes. Utilities must start commercial-scale CCS projects within the next few years and expand them rapidly thereafter.

The International Panel on Climate Change estimated in 2005 that it is "highly probable that geologic media worldwide are capable of sequestering at least 2 trillion metric tons of CO_2—more than is likely to be produced by fossil-fuel-consuming plants during the 21st century." With at least 114 new coal-burning power plants currently in the building or permitting stages around the country, we have no time to waste in requiring an immediate and significant reduction in carbon emissions from coal plants.

In Texas, TXU Corporation, the state's largest power company, is planning to build eleven new coal-fired plants. Rather than acting as a responsible corporate citizen, however, TXU is rushing to build the traditional plants before any federal regulations on CO_2 can be put in place. If they succeed, the corporation's top executives could then argue that as preexisting facilities their plants must be grandfathered against regulation. As a result, Texas, already the largest single polluter among the fifty states—and by itself the tenth largest polluter of CO_2 in the world—could add about 78 million tons of CO_2 per year to the atmosphere. Given what we now know of the science of global warming, this is immoral, if not insane.

Compare that to American Electric Power (AEP)—a company that, with two dozen coal-fired power plants, burns more fossil fuels than any other U.S. company—and its plans for future operations. AEP has proposed two new power plants along the West Virginia–Ohio border that would use a new technology known as Integrated Gasification Combined Cycle (IGCC). IGCC can significantly reduce pollution and carbon dioxide emissions. Using this technology can add as much as 20 percent to the costs of building compared to traditional coal plants, but that cost is far outweighed by the long-term benefits. As Mike Mudd, the manager of new generation development at AEP, told a reporter, gasification technology "is both fiscally responsible and the right thing to do as a matter of public policy, both for AEP and Ohio." That is a viable future.

THE NUCLEAR QUESTION

The urgent need to embrace a new energy future is clear, but until renewable energy, clean coal, and huge advances in energy efficiencies combine to really set the country on the path toward energy freedom, there will be growing pressure to expand nuclear power—particularly if the ten-year window is taken as seriously as it ought to be. Nuclear energy is carbon free, and it is also available. That is the case for considering it.

If the clean energy options were properly developed and exploited, nuclear power would not be necessary. But some countries already have very significant nuclear commitments (France, for example, gets about 78 percent of its power from nuclear), and these nuclear resources are unlikely to disappear anytime soon. In the mad rush to embrace nuclear power, however, we cannot forget the three big counts against it: (1) it is more expensive than new coal- or gas-powered plants; (2) global expansion of nuclear power raises concerns that radioactive nuclear weapons ambitions may inadvertently be advanced; and (3) no one has yet resolved the issue of how to handle the radioactive nuclear waste that results from the process, which will be around for thousands of years.

Despite those drawbacks, twenty-nine nuclear power plants are being built globally. As reported in the *Washington Post,* "Well over 100 more have been written into the development plans of governments for the next three decades. India and China each are rushing to build dozens of reactors. The United States and the countries of Western Europe led by new nuclear champions are reconsidering their cooled romance with atomic power." Although it cannot be dismissed as part of the energy solution and our response to the threat of global climate change, un-til the three big hurdles are adequately addressed, nuclear energy does not offer a sound vision for the long-term future.

POSITIVE ENERGY

As we consider our way forward, it is worth remembering our history, because until recently, America has invariably met each energy challenge by inventing technologies, thereby transforming marketplaces, and literally innovating our way to a future never before imagined.

One hundred and fifty years ago in Massachusetts, in New Bedford and Nantucket, no one could have conceived of a future that didn't depend on whale oil. In the 1930s, only 10 percent of rural America had electricity. Utilities refused to wire rural counties because homes were too far apart. To bring electricity to all Americans, Congress provided more than $5 billion to finance rural electrification. By the 1950s, there was hardly a corner of America that was still dark. Across our history we've successfully moved from wood to coal, from coal to oil, and from oil to a mix of oil, gas, coal, nuclear energy, and hydro-electricity. Now, with no time to lose, we must move immediately toward greater efficiency, renewable fuels, and cleaner coal.

These are the big three of our energy future. They represent our best hope of securing our future—with regard to the economy, national security, and our environment. Some will say that we have too far to go or too much work to do to solve the problem, but that attitude is far too pessimistic for our taste. The United States—the most powerful, creative, industrial country on Earth—certainly can build on the lessons learned from industries and corporations like Texas Instruments, DuPont, and Interface. If we need confidence or examples to help us move forward, they are there. At the local level, countless communities across the country are setting out on their own to implement innovative steps to secure a sustainable energy future.

Many cities and local governments are recognizing what the federal government has refused to see: that with the right amount of political will, this problem becomes less overwhelming, and the solutions come into close reach. Under the leadership of Mayor Rocky Anderson, Salt Lake City—politically one of the reddest spots on the map and part of the congressional district that voted 77 percent for Bush in the 2004 election, his best showing anywhere—has made great strides in reducing greenhouse gas emissions. In early 2002, the city set a goal to reduce emissions in its government operations to 21 percent below 2001 levels by the year 2012. It achieved that goal in 2006, six years early. In March 2005, heeding a call by Mayor Greg Nickels of Seattle, 295 mayors from 44 states, representing a total population of more than 49.4 million citizens, signed the U.S. Mayors Climate Protection Agreement, signaling their commitment to meeting the goals set forth in the Kyoto Protocol.

California, with the combined leadership of Republican Governor Arnold Schwarzenegger, state Democratic legislators, and U.S. Senators Barbara Boxer and Dianne Feinstein, is setting the gold standard in climate policies. In 2006, the state legislature passed the California Global Warming Solutions Act, which requires a 25 percent reduction in greenhouse gas emissions by 2020. Rather than burdening the economy, the measure is expected to create 83,000 new jobs and reduce energy costs. California represents the sixth largest economy in the world, but even smaller states can make a difference.

My home state of Massachusetts—just like nineteen other states and the District of Columbia—adopted a Renewable Portfolio Standard, a state policy that requires electricity providers to obtain a minimum or greater percentage of their power from renewable energy resources by a certain date. All retail electricity providers in the state will be required to utilize renewable energy sources for at least 4 percent of their power supply by 2009. Building on all that state success, I have continuously fought in the U.S. Senate to pass a national Renewable Portfolio Standard of 20 percent by the year 2020. Unfortunately—like so many other clean energy initiatives—it was rejected by the Republican-controlled Congress of the past.

These examples did not come about because the engineers in California are more ingenious or the people of Massachusetts are more interested in renewable energy than the rest of the nation. They happened for one reason: The political will existed to make them happen. Legislative and executive leaders at the local level recognized the two most important elements at play: We have ten years to solve a very big problem, and there's money to be made in doing it. Not only *can* this happen on a national level—it *has* to. There's a wonderful example of this type of coordinated, visionary thinking, and it is taking place in Portland, Oregon.

A LOCAL ACTION PLAN ON GLOBAL WARMING

In 1993, long before climate change fully captured the American public's attention, the city of Portland became the first U.S. city to adopt a plan to reduce greenhouse gas emissions, and in 2001, it was joined in its efforts by surrounding Multnomah County. The goal of the Local Action Plan on Global Warming was that by the year 2010, the city and county together would reduce their total greenhouse gas emissions to 10 percent below 1990 levels—the benchmark year set by Kyoto. Their progress has been stunning. Despite a growth in population, Portland's emissions are already down to 1990 levels, and on a per capita basis emissions have decreased by nearly 11 percent (they are up 1 percent nationally).

The rest of us—communities, states, and nations—can learn a great deal from Portland's experiment. Two things in particular stand out about the project. One is that the city and county succeeded by undertaking a series of simple measures that not only decreased emissions but also improved residents' quality of life. The other is that, rather than damaging Portland's economy or costing the city millions of dollars, the city and county have saved money, and the economy of the area is booming.

The plan identified a variety of measures designed to reduce emissions, including getting people out of their cars, using renewable sources of energy, increasing recycling, making buildings more efficient, and continually looking for ways where emissions could be cut. Again, many of these steps were simple to carry out. Since 1996, the city has planted more than 750,000 trees and shrubs, which help to absorb carbon dioxide and generally improve the aesthetics and health of neighborhoods and rivers. Through increased efforts to promote recycling, households and businesses in the area now recycle more than 54 percent of all solid waste, which is one of the highest rates in the United States. Recycling helps to curb climate change in at least three ways: by saving energy that would otherwise be used to make and distribute new products, by lowering methane emissions from landfills, and by reducing deforestation. More than 10,000 multifamily residential units and 800 homes in the Portland area have been weatherized in the past two years, which not only saves energy but also reduces heating and cooling bills.

Green design makes good economic sense, and it's making a significant difference in Portland. In 2001, the city adopted a policy requiring all new city-owned buildings and major retrofit projects, as well as large projects that receive a certain amount of city subsidy, to achieve the "Certified" level of the Green Building Rating System of the Leadership in Energy and Environmental Design (LEED) program. In 2005, that standard was raised to LEED "Gold." The Office of Sustainable Development, which implements and manages many components of the action plan, provides technical assistance to developers who are interested in building LEED-certified private development projects. There are now more than fifty LEED-certified or registered buildings in the city, and an additional 500 are certified as green through Earth Advantage, a program established by a local electric utility.

One of the most productive methods of reducing emissions has been to focus on transportation, which accounts for over 40 percent of all greenhouse gas emissions in Multnomah County. Between 1990 and 2005, per capita transportation emissions declined 13 percent. To achieve this, Portland adopted a two-pronged strategy: The city and county made it easy for people to drive less, and they worked on increasing fuel efficiency for people who stayed on the roads. Every gallon of gasoline used—whether it comes from a monster SUV or a

Toyota Prius—emits nearly 20 pounds of carbon dioxide into the atmosphere, and therefore every gallon saved makes a difference.

Since adopting the Local Action Plan, Portland and Multnomah County have built two new light-rail lines as well as the Portland Streetcar, which travels a 6-mile loop through several neighborhoods in the city center. The new TriMet light-rail lines, which include a connection with Portland International Airport, were built on schedule and under budget, and did not require an increase in local taxes. Moreover, with less congestion on the roads, cars can travel more efficiently, fewer roads need to be built, and fewer infrastructure improvements are necessary, which not only is good news for emissions levels, but saves the city money.

The city and county didn't stop at new light-rail construction. They also adopted an aggressive plan to encourage ridership. The TravelSmart program, managed through the city's Office of Transportation, employs innovative and highly individualized approaches to getting people thinking about alternatives to driving. As part of the program, the city provides free walking maps, bike guides, and transit schedules to residents who request them. Global positioning systems are installed on buses so that people can call to find out *exactly* what time the next bus will be at their stop. By educating people about the transportation options that already exist, and making it easy for them to access those options, the Office of Transportation was able, within one year, to reduce car trips by 9 percent.

Linda Ginenthal is the education outreach program manager with the Office of Transportation. "Because car trips are the number one contributor to greenhouse gas emissions, anything we can do to get people out of cars, we want to do," she said. "Individuals can change their lightbulbs and buy more efficient appliances and insulation, but the number one thing they can do to make a difference is to drive less."

Though the environmental benefits have been great, they certainly have not been the only satisfying consequences of the Portland plan.

The light-rail system has had unexpected benefits, for example. Just seven months after the newly constructed Yellow Light Rail went on-line, more than fifty new businesses had opened along its route and real estate prices increased. New bike paths, new bus lines, and the streetcar system have created real connections between a variety of neighborhoods. And, according to Linda Ginenthal, local businesses often contact the city to report that more of their neighbors have begun to shop locally, choosing to walk to the grocery store or bakery nearby rather than getting in their cars.

A large part of Portland's success has been due to the city's willingness to think "out of the box." One of the more ambitious goals established in the Local Action Plan was that by the year 2010, 100 percent of the energy used in municipal operations would come from renewable sources. That may seem like a lofty and even unrealistic goal, but it's about to become a reality. Last year, the city asked energy developers to submit bids to supply the government's energy with renewable sources for the next twenty years. Several bids were submitted, and the city is currently negotiating with a wind-power company to build a 50-megawatt wind farm in eastern Oregon that will *fully* support the city's energy needs—which averages about $14 million worth of power each year.

The city made another very bold and innovative decision on July 12, 2006, when the Portland City Council approved a citywide renewable fuels standard, making Portland the first U.S. city to do so. By the end of 2007, all diesel fuel sold in the city must be a minimum of 5 percent biodiesel, and gasoline is required to contain at least 10 percent ethanol. Susan Anderson, the director of the Office of Sustainable Development, was instrumental in getting this law passed. "Nobody will see the difference as far as how it runs a car or how you buy it," she said. "But it will make our city cleaner while at the same time creating a larger demand for alternative fuel sources, which we hope will lead to a wider use beyond our city."

This renewable standard will reduce emissions by 1 percent a year, said Michael Armstrong, a policy analyst with the Office of Sustainable Development. "That might sound small, yet in the context of the Kyoto Protocol of reducing greenhouse emissions by 7 percent, well, this is one-seventh of that. The way we're doing this is just like that—a percentage here and a half of a percentage elsewhere. But you add those up, and it makes a significant difference."

As much as there is to learn from Portland about *how* to reduce emissions, the experiment also teaches us *why* we should. In addition to reducing its greenhouse gas emissions while its population has increased and development has flourished, the city has saved money, the local economy has boomed, and residents enjoy a higher quality of life. "The demand from communities across the U.S. and around the world for professionals who know how to build LEED buildings and who are doing cutting-edge green design work is voracious," said Armstrong. "A lot of those professionals live in Portland now, and that's been a great tool of economic development for us. We've watched this sector of the local economy just flourish with our efforts." This has, in turn, paid off handsomely for the city in terms of income taxes and fees associated with new business licenses.

The city is also able to attract and retain workers, as it is consistently recognized for its livability. It was recently designated the healthiest and most sustainable city in the nation by SustainLane, a clearinghouse for sustainable development, as well as *Reader's Digest. Money* magazine chose it as the best place to live in 2001. *Bicycling* magazine named it the best city for riding a bike; and the American Podiatric Medical Association ranked Portland among the best cities for walking. The Sierra Club named the Pearl District in Portland's downtown as one of the nation's best new developments. The list goes on.

According to Susan Anderson and Michael Armstrong, every city can do what Portland has done, and with similar economic rewards. "The more you push these efforts, the clearer the economic opportunities become," Armstrong said. "Of course, there are ways to do it that are very costly, but there are ways to do it that are great for the economy. The key is to figure out the best strategies for each city. I have a lot of confidence that what we've accomplished is possible elsewhere."

He stressed the importance of good land-use planning. "Good land-use planning is not about limiting growth but guiding how it's happening," he said. "It makes a big difference as far as driving and greenhouse gas emissions are concerned when there are stores and schools and parks and everything someone needs in close proximity to where they live, and different ways for people to get to them. Giving them the choice of walking or riding a bike, or using a streetcar or light rail, makes good sense."

Portland is at a great advantage because, back in 1979, its leaders adopted an urban growth boundary. That has made transportation planning easier and more efficient and has limited the greenhouse gas emissions that come with sprawl. But even cities without a growth boundary can still act. "The important thing is for states and local governments to find solutions that they can do today," Armstrong said. "It's like the old African adage. The best time to plant a tree was twenty years ago. The second best time to plant a tree is today."

Most of all, it's necessary to have political will. None of the efforts in Portland would have happened if it were not for Mike Lindberg, a true urban pioneer who, at the time the plan was adopted, served on the city council. He was helped in his efforts by Earl Blumenauer, who also served on the council and is now a member of Congress. "The two of them were really the political champions," said Susan Anderson, "and I was the grunt worker. We didn't have any money for this work—not an unusual story in city government—but they convinced the state to fund somebody two days a week for six months to lay the groundwork. From there, we started building partnerships, and they supported the work every step of the way.

"I think half the key is a political champion," she added. "Because this stuff is all easy, it is all cost effective. No matter what anyone says, all of this stuff makes money. Once a political champion steps up to give a community the resources it needs, then everyone will realize quickly that it is cost effective and that local businesses can absolutely make a lot of money."

The city admittedly has a way to go to meet the ultimate goal of the Local Action Plan. At 1990 levels currently, they still have to reduce emissions by 10 percent over the next four years. Will they do it? "I think we have a chance," Armstrong said. "We need to see continued strong growth in the use of renewable energy. The energy efficiency program needs to continue. We need to see people continue to take advantage of our public transportation. We're going in the right direction, we just need to see things accelerate."

On the national level, climate change, security, and economic factors are merging into a new domestic and international political reality. Political consensus is growing. Business engagement is getting stronger all the time. But we have big hurdles to overcome—and a whole host of elected officials in Washington who refuse to step over them, along with a whole cast of political consultants who will counsel their candidates not to even try.

A Saudi Arabian oil minister and a founder of OPEC once said that "the Stone Age came to an end not for a lack of stones, and the oil age will end, but not for a lack of oil." We have not run out of oil, but the idea of oil as an energy panacea has run its course. The consequences of continued dependence on oil are too great, too profound, and too dangerous. Rather than have our energy policy be the last big mistake of the twentieth century, we can and must create a policy that becomes the first great breakthrough of the twenty-first century. For the second time in our history, we must declare and win our independence—this time, not from foreign rule, but from foreign oil, and indeed, all fossil fuels.

CONCLUSION

The challenge is clear and compelling. Climate change is threatening the planet, life, and land due to human-made greenhouse gases. Fish are dying in water polluted with pesticide, chemical, and animal waste. Oceans are overfished by big industrial fishing fleets. Minority communities continue to be victimized by unwanted toxic waste dumps and dirty power plants. Roadless forests are threatened by indiscriminate fossil fuel drilling against the wishes of landowners. Industrial chemicals are seeping into all of us, from newborns to adults. New polluting, coal-fired power plants are being built with outdated technology despite overwhelming evidence of the dangers of carbon dioxide emissions.

We are paying an extraordinary price for our unwillingness to live by the precautionary principle other nations have adopted: first, do no harm. Disastrous choices have piled up, one on top of the other— creating what is certainly emerging as the greatest domestic challenge of our generation. But common sense can prevail, and Americans in every state of the union—red, blue, or purple—are finding common ground. They are making a collective statement about right and wrong: It is right to take precautions against scientifically predicted disaster; it is wrong to suffer disease and danger because polluters are allowed to call the shots. With a clarity and urgency not seen for years, these individuals are defining themselves as a new generation of environmentalists determined to take on the status quo and build a new movement.

There is both challenge and opportunity in this new environmentalism. Obviously, reading about the many threats to our planet today can be daunting—so much so that the hurdles can seem insurmountable. But a closer look confirms that the opportunities are far more inspiring than the challenges are steep: Visionary men and women working to address these problems are showing the way forward in real and tangible ways. All Americans can join in this new environmentalism.

Naysayers have argued that meeting environmental challenges is too difficult or expensive; too complicated and divisive. But those arguments ignore recent history, not to mention the stunning tradition of American achievement. In the late 1980s and early 1990s, Congress set out to renew the Clean Air Act, providing the first real opportunity to address acid rain at the national level. There was the inevitable tug-of-war between the power industry and the environmentalists. The industry fought against strict air quality standards, alleging that any regulation would cost them billions of dollars, take an unacceptably long time to accomplish, and cripple their ability to compete. They were unalterably opposed and did all they could to kill any attempt to strengthen the act. The environmental community, on the other hand, argued it would take half the time at half the cost.

Guess what? They were both wrong. After the first Bush administration signed the 1990 amendments to the Clean Air Act, it took half the time and half the money the environmentalists had predicted to achieve better air quality standards. Why? Because no one could anticipate the scale of technological advances achieved once the decision was made and goals were set. The lessons learned? Don't listen to those who counsel despair and never underestimate the ingenuity of our scientists, engineers, and entrepreneurs.

There are other lessons to be learned. If we actually move away from fossil fuels as our leading energy source, we can make dramatic progress on climate change, while also improving air and water quality. If we succeed in demanding science-based information about the chemicals used in our products, we can all begin to move from being passive consumers to active citizens empowered with the knowledge of what price we are paying for pollution. If enough people come together to demand change, even in the face of powerful interests, change will happen.

If we put an end to the era of dirty fossil fuels, we can begin an era of sustainability—environmental, economic, and political—for our nation and our world.

Still another lesson is that effective action to address our environmental challenges isn't the enemy of economic growth; it's a catalyst to create jobs and harness whole new industries. We are not going to address problems such as climate change by retreating to some sort of pre-industrial or pre-technological golden age. Entrepreneurship and technology may have contributed to our environmental problems, but they are now proving to be among the most essential tools for solving them. This is not a stale Washington debate between the environment and jobs—on the contrary, the environment *is* jobs.

A final lesson is that the new environmentalism reflects our culture, our beliefs as a people, and our best instincts as individuals. As we learn through the stories here, today's best "environmentalists" are often people who are motivated not by ideology or membership in particular organizations or causes, but by a simple sense of personal responsibility as stewards of our planet. Indeed, they feel morally compelled to take action, and their example should inspire the rest of us to live out our own beliefs as well.

Most importantly, we know that a shift of understanding is under way, particularly our understanding about the grave threat of climate change. Frankly, this topic was the most challenging to write about because new warnings are emerging on nearly a daily basis. It is therefore difficult for us—or anyone—to stay completely up-to-date on the matter. For example, at this writing, on Friday, February 2, 2007, the most recent report of the Intergovernmental Panel on Climate Change was released.

Written by more than 600 scientists and reviewed by another 600 experts and officials from 154 countries, the report is intended to be the definitive summary of climatic shifts facing the world in the coming years. As Dr. John Holdren e-mailed us the day of its release: "The new report powerfully underscores the need for a massive effort to slow the pace of global climatic disruption before intolerable consequences become inevitable. . . . In overwhelming proportions, this evidence has been in the direction of showing faster change, more danger, and greater confidence about the dominant role of carbon dioxide from fossil fuel burning and tropical deforestation in causing the changes that are being observed."

As you read this now, it's important to ask the question: What happened today? What news was reported or what did you personally witness that made it clearer yet that climate change is a serious and immediate problem? And what, in the face of so many powerful interests defending the status quo, are each of us willing to do, today and tomorrow, to force a change of course?

As much as our understanding is rapidly increasing, so is the commitment to change. The other headline news is that leaders of ten major corporations, including Duke Energy, General Electric, DuPont, Alcoa, and Lehman Brothers, have urged Congress and the Bush administration to begin to seriously address global warming by setting caps on emissions of carbon dioxide. "The science of climate warming is clear," Jim Rogers, chairman and chief executive officer of Duke Energy, said recently. "We know enough to act now. We must act now. . . . It must be mandatory so there is no doubt about our commitment to concrete action."

And the corporate community is not the only one quickly awakening to the issue; so, for example, are people of faith everywhere. In January 2007, a group of our nation's most influential religious leaders joined scientists, including James Hansen of NASA, in committing to raise awareness about environmental issues, climate change included. We are not surprised by this response from religious leaders. One thing we have long understood is that the desire to steward our natural resources is an impulse as old as the Book of Genesis: the understanding that God has created an abundant world, and placed men and women in the unique position of being able to responsibly care for it or irresponsibly damage and destroy it.

Evangelicals talk about "creation-care"—that any damage that we do to God's world is an offense against God. This is certainly not exclusively a Christian belief. It is one that appeals to all religions of the world and to anyone with a moral guidepost who embraces life as a gift to be cared for with gratitude and responsibility. None of us are exempt from this responsibility.

Each person who comes to that realization and comes away from it determined to take action—far more people than we could bring to life in this book—represents a remarkable source of renewal for the environmental movement. People around the world are finding ways to connect to each other, and in those connections are finding a shared determination to act responsibly and, above all, to take decisive and immediate action.

We both have a lot of experience with what is known in Washington as "the environmental community"—a coalition of advocacy groups. We've been proud members of this community, for a long time. But what's most exciting about the new environmentalism is that it feels an awful lot like environmentalism did before all those groups existed. What is happening now is the reconstitution of an "environmental community" bubbling up from the grassroots, from unexpected places, a movement reborn, genuinely rooted in the genius of the American people.

This moment demands a new approach. All of us must be held accountable for the environmental implications of every decision—in Congress, in state capitals, in city council and county commission sessions, and in stockholders' meetings. And above all, the public must hold itself accountable for what others do in its name.

Beyond the challenges, the specific ideas for meeting them, and the pioneers who are in this book, we also hope that something else will emerge from this journey.

We hope that in reading this book you feel more inspired to join with those who are working to solve our many problems—from the individuals like Helen Reddout and Gilbert Armenta, to the companies and religious leaders who are leading the way. We feel very happy, and indeed proud, to be part of the chorus of voices calling for change.

We have big challenges to tackle—and a whole cast of entrenched interests that for years have counseled the powerful not even to try.

That's where you come in. You can push the curve. You can shake things up. Protecting the environment is the single most urgent and exciting challenge of our era—one where every single person can leave a mark that will endure for generations.

Americans have made great issues the centerpiece of our national life before—civil rights, human rights, nuclear war. Each of these at one moment became the lens through which we looked at the world. Together we can make this moment on Earth the moment when we all decided to not just talk about the planet, but to save it.

ACKNOWLEDGMENTS

Writing a book while juggling our respective duties as Chair of the Heinz Foundations and U.S. Senator has been a challenging undertaking. We were blessed to benefit from the talent and interest of many people who believed this was a topic worth tackling.

We especially want to thank all of the people profiled in these pages. Each conversation, each story, inspired us to dig deeper and think harder about ways we might better steward our natural resources. Their individual initiative and commitment give us reason to be optimistic about our ability to meet all of the environmental challenges we face. Thank you to Bill McDonough, the leaders of Pittsburgh, Julia Brody, Ellen Parker, Cheryl Osimo, Devra Davis, Majora Carter, Deirdre Imus, Monique Harden, Nathalie Walker, Rick Dove, Helen Reddout, Dan Fagre, Jeanine Fitzgerald, Gilbert Armenta, Tweeti Blancett, Susan Anderson, Mike Armstrong, and all of the employees of the Office of Sustainable Development in Portland, Oregon.

We also relied on the knowledge of people who have made these priorities their life work. Many of them went far beyond what we might have legitimately expected or asked for, opening their schedules, their minds, and even their homes, to help bring these issues to light. For his work, we would like to extend a special thank you to Dr. John Holdren, the director of the Woods Hole Research Center and a professor at Harvard University in both the Kennedy School of Government and the Department of Earth and Planetary Sciences. We relied on him more than once to help us distill and explain the sometimes complicated science of climate change. Special thanks also to Amory Lovins, Denis Hayes, Robert Kennedy, Jr., Jane Houlihan, John Adams, Ana Soto, Ellen K. Silbergeld, Maryann Donovan, Charlie Tebbut, Joan

Mulhern, John Walke, Margaret Spring, Steve Fleischli, Jim and Terry Fitzgerald, Robin Blanchard, Josh Joswick, Gwen Lachelt, Eric and Kelly Barlow, Robert Delzell, and Darya Cowan. And also to Andre Heinz and Vanessa Kerry, who took the time to read and comment on selected portions of the manuscript. We also referred often to the research available through several organizations for which we have great respect and which have, for many years, done a wonderful job of educating the public about these issues. Special thanks to the entire staff of the Natural Resources Defense Council, the Environmental Working Group, the Apollo Alliance, the Worldwatch Institute, and the Center for American Progress.

We were also lucky to be able to draw from the interest and expertise of staff at the Senate Office and the Heinz Foundations who, amidst all their responsibilities, found time to read the manuscript and make suggestions. Thank you to David McKean, David Wade, Tricia Ferrone, Lindsay Ross, Jeffrey Lewis, Grant Oliphant, Ellen Dorsey, Maggie Caravan, Doug Root, and Jeremy Button.

Finally, a very special thank you is due to a small band of devotees of this project. First, this book would never have come to fruition without Aimee Molloy's tireless research and creative thinking about how to tell this story. She helped ensure a coherent, comprehensive text for which we are both very grateful. Heather Zichal, whose environmental knowledge and commitment is extensive, invested personally in every aspect of this project. She has our respect and gratitude for her significant contribution. So does Ed Kilgore, who helped us shape our initial concept and gave advice as we proceeded. Last, we are grateful to the team at PublicAffairs—Peter Osnos, Clive Priddle, Susan Weinberg, Robert Kimzey—for their understanding of the urgency of these issues and their willingness to publish with the public interest as their bottom line. Clive's patient editorial input was critical to keeping us on track. The full engagement of the PublicAffairs team made this a smooth, even enjoyable experience. Thank you to all.

APPENDIX A

The Energy Plan

KEEPING AMERICA'S PROMISE

America's oil dependence and contributions to global climate change are endangering our national security, our economy, and our environment. America consumes one-quarter of the world's total oil, but has less than 3 percent of its known reserves. Currently, we import about 60 percent of our oil, making us dangerously dependent on a precarious energy source that is vital to our economy and way of life. According to the Energy Information Administration, U.S. oil consumption is projected to grow significantly over the next two decades, forcing us to rely on imports for nearly 70 percent of our oil by 2025, and increasing our dependence on some of the most unstable regions in the world. America also contributes about 30 percent of the world's greenhouse gas emissions but comprises only 5 percent of the world's population.

We cannot win the war on terror and get serious about global climate change and energy security, if we do not take bold steps to actually break our oil addiction. Talk is not enough. A safer, more secure energy future is well within our reach. The imperative has never been greater to reshape the future of our energy supply and energy use. First, we must establish an oil savings goal and implement an aggressive set of policies to reach it. Second, we must immediately expand the availability of renewable fuels to run our automobiles. And third, we need to get serious about climate change and take measures to freeze and reverse our greenhouse gas emissions.

(1)
REVERSE AND STOP EMISSIONS
THAT CAUSE GLOBAL WARMING

Climate change is caused by carbon dioxide and other greenhouse gases in the atmosphere that trap the sun's heat and cause the planet to heat up. Climate change poses a growing threat to our national and economic security—and to the planet our children and grandchildren will inherit. Last year, the National Academy of Science concluded that the Northern Hemisphere was the warmest it has been in 2,000 years and that "human activities are responsible for much of the recent warming."

Science tells us that we face a grave risk of potentially devastating impacts if global temperatures increase by even more than a few degrees. Senator Olympia J. Snowe and I have introduced the most aggressive, bipartisan legislation yet put before Congress to slow, stop, and reverse greenhouse gas emissions. Our plan sets greenhouse gas emissions targets that science suggests will keep temperatures below the danger point. The level of emissions is frozen in 2010 and then gradually declines each year to 65 percent below 2000 emissions levels by 2050. The bill achieves these targets through a flexible, economy-wide cap-and-trade program for greenhouse gas emissions. It includes measures to advance technology and reduce emissions through clean, renewable energy and energy efficiency in the transportation, industrial and residential sectors.

The U.S. is the world's single largest emitter of greenhouse gases, but the U.S. alone cannot solve the challenge of global climate change. It is going to take action from other countries—both developed and developing. Our proposal includes a resolution expressing the urgent need for President Bush to re-engage in international climate negotiations.

(2)
MANDATES FOR REDUCING OIL CONSUMPTION

The United States is saddled with rising prices for gasoline, escalating uncertainty in energy markets, and increasing oil imports in the foreseeable future. These stubborn facts will not change without an aggressive policy response that promotes both radically increased energy efficiency in our vehicle fleet and a rapid shift to greater use of alternative renewable fuels. The imperative—and the opportunity—has never been greater to reshape the future of our energy supply.

SETTING OIL SAVINGS AS AN URGENT PRIORITY

The biggest flaw with the energy bill that President Bush signed into law, the Energy Policy Act of 2005, is that it does virtually nothing to reduce U.S. oil use, despite the fact that about 60 percent of oil is now imported and the percentage is projected to steadily rise.

- We must set mandatory targets for reducing U.S. oil use by 2.5 million barrels of oil a day by 2015.

A. TRANSPORTATION:
TRANSITIONING FROM OIL DEPENDENCE TO RENEWABLE FUELS

The transportation sector consumes more than two-thirds of the oil we use, accounting for 13 million barrels of oil per day, and roughly a third of our greenhouse gas emissions. We can reduce our oil dependence by transforming our transportation sector: improving the efficiency of our vehicles, making more clean and super-efficient vehicles that are affordable, and that can run on renewable fuels.

PROMOTING THE DEVELOPMENT
OF SUPER-EFFICIENT VEHICLES

Over the past 20 years, automakers have used advancements in technology to add more than 800 pounds to the average vehicle and to nearly double horsepower, while fuel economy has slipped. Today we have the technology to preserve or improve the current size, utility, performance, and safety characteristics of our vehicles, while at the same time increasing fuel economy. And over the next 20 years, hybrid technology—including hybrids that run on clean, alternative fuels—and plug-in hybrids, can deliver even greater gains in fuel economy. In the short-term, we need to take steps to ensure that there are more of all of these types of vehicles on the road.

- *Strengthen CAFE.* We must raise our federal fuel economy standards. America has already proven that such strides are possible. Fuel economy for new passenger cars nearly doubled between 1975—when standards were first adopted—and their peak in 1988, while fuel economy for new light trucks increased by 50 percent. But the rules for passenger cars haven't changed since 1985, and the average mileage of our new cars and trucks today is at its lowest level in 20 years. Increasing fuel economy standards for all vehicles to at least 35 mpg by Model Year 2019 would save oil and also bring significant reductions in global warming pollution.

- *Accelerate the Conversion of American Vehicles to Flexible Fuel Technology.*

Flexible fuel vehicles can run on higher blends of ethanol, which helps displace petroleum. I propose that by 2020, 100 percent of our vehicles should be capable of running on flex fuels.

- *Tax Credits to Convert Factories to Build the Cars of the Future.* A recent study by the University of Michigan found that unless U.S. automakers move faster to build hybrids, thousands of jobs could be lost. Producing fuel-efficient, advanced-technology vehicles will require automakers and their suppliers to retool their factories. Hybrid vehicles rely on advanced equipment such as battery packs, electric motors and generators, and electronic power controllers—components that currently come from factories in Japan and Europe. Tax credits will help manufacturers make capital investments necessary to retool their factories, increase the cost-effectiveness of advanced technologies, and stimulate job growth in the production of cleaner, more efficient vehicles. We must provide a total of $3 billion over the next five years in consumer and manufacturer tax credits to spur these changes.

- *Close the SUV Loophole.* Under current tax policy, the government grants massive tax breaks to purchasers of SUVs. The original intent of the provision was to increase capital investments by farmers and other small business owners who rely on light-trucks or vans. When this provision was added to the tax code, luxury passenger SUVs were not the market force they have become, and it appeared a good way to help small businesses. Over time, however, this provision has developed into a loophole big enough to drive a 6,000-pound SUV through. The loophole that allows the law to be misused must be eliminated.

PROMOTING BIOFUELS AND INFRASTRUCTURE

To reduce our dependence on foreign oil, we must ensure an adequate supply of advanced technology vehicles and an adequate supply of fuel to power them. Recently-passed energy legislation included a number of provisions that should be rapidly implemented and fully funded to expand investment in alternative fuels. There are more vehicles on the road that can run on biofuels. Now we must remove the barriers to ethanol and other biofuels at fueling stations across the country. And, we need to build facilities to make ethanol from switchgrass and other waste products, in addition to corn, so we can ensure that 30 percent of our fuels are biofuels by 2020.

- *Mandate Ethanol Pumps at Gas Stations.* Today, there are 6 million flex fuel vehicles on the road, but less than 1 percent of the nation's fueling stations have E85 pumps. Our plan will ensure that 18,000 gas stations owned or branded by a major oil company offer at least one ethanol pump by 2010. In addition, it provides incentives to independent and retail chain owners to install clean alternative fueling pumps.

- *Keep Ethanol Competitive with Oil.* I believe that we should take steps to ensure that there is a market for ethanol, even if the price of oil falls dramatically. To achieve that goal, we should make the Volumetric Ethanol Excise Tax credit (VEETC) variable with the price of oil to ensure that if oil prices drop, investment in ethanol does not.

- *Invest in Cellulosic Ethanol.* Cellulosic ethanol has the potential to substantially reduce our consumption of gasoline. Unlike traditional ethanol, which is made from grains such as corn, wheat or soybeans, cellulosic ethanol can be produced from a great diversity of biomass, and a technological breakthrough could lead to widespread use of cellulosic ethanol to fuel our vehicles. The federal government should increase the cellulosic ethanol production incentives to $2 billion over 10 years.

B. ENHANCING DOMESTIC ENERGY SUPPLY

PROMOTING RENEWABLE ENERGY

Twenty-one states and the District of Columbia have implemented market-based Renewable Energy Portfolio programs that require utilities to gradually increase the portion of electricity produced from renewable resources such as wind, biomass, geothermal, and solar energy. A study by the Union of Concerned Scientists found that under the Energy Information Administration's 2004 gas price forecast, a renewable standard of 20 percent by 2020 would save $26.6 billion and that commercial and industrial customers would be the biggest winners.

- *National Renewable Energy Portfolio Standard.* We must implement an aggressive federal renewable energy purchase requirement and establish a national Renewable Energy Portfolio Standard of 20 percent by 2020.

C. INCREASING ENERGY EFFICIENCY

In addition to developing new sources of energy, we must make better use of available energy. New technological advances in appliances, energy grid systems, and buildings can boost productivity, create jobs, improve the reliability and safety of the energy infrastructure, and make dramatic inroads in reducing air pollution. Energy efficiency investments are crucial for meeting both our near-term and long-term energy needs.

SETTING STRONGER EFFICIENCY STANDARDS FOR BUILDINGS AND APPLIANCES

- *Increase Federal Government Energy Efficiency.* My plan will mandate that the government decrease energy usage through efficiency and conservation measures to achieve a reduction in federal energy consumption of 25 percent by 2025.

- *New "Model" Efficiency Standards.* We must require the Department of Energy to develop national "model standards" to make new buildings at least 30 percent more energy efficient and update appliance efficiency standards and standards for manufactured homes, which account for almost one-third of new housing construction. In addition, updated standards should be reevaluated every five years for most appliances to determine whether the standards need to be strengthened.

- *National Standards for Utilities.* The Department of Energy must establish national standards requiring utilities to obtain, each year, 1 percent of their energy supplies through energy efficiency improvements at customer facilities. These savings would accumulate each year through 2025.

(3)
DEVELOPING ENERGY TECHNOLOGIES FOR THE FUTURE

- Under my plan, we will double federal government funding for energy research and development; increase incentives for private sector energy research, development, demonstration, and early deployment (ERD); expand investment in cooperative international ERD initiatives and facilitate greater coordination among relevant federal agencies.

- *Establish a new Energy Security and Conservation Trust Fund.* Reducing our dependence on oil and building a future of clean and abundant energy are urgent national priorities. Our political system, however, does not treat them that way. To assure that the nation is on a track to reduce oil dependence, I believe we must create an Energy Security and Conservation Trust Fund capitalized by rolling back tax breaks for big oil. The revenues will be dedicated to accelerating the commercialization of technologies that will reduce America's dangerous dependence on oil. The Trust Fund will allocate billions of dollors over the next decade to reduce oil dependence and create a cleaner and more reliable energy future.

What You Can Do

Given the scope of many of the problems facing our planet today, it is critical that we begin to adopt an aggressive approach to solutions at the federal level. But that is only one part of the solution. You are the other. Every day, each of us make many decisions that have a direct impact on the environment. Every time we turn on the lights or the air conditioner, or get into our cars, or board a plane, we are helping to contribute to the problem.

We don't have to become hermits or renounce technology. The answer is not to live in darkness, or to stop driving, or to refuse to fly. But there are hundreds of things that we all can do—big and small—to reduce what scientists call our "environmental footprint." Those of us in politics, traveling at times in motorcades, flying in private planes on occasion, you name it, should be the last to throw stones, but we should be the first to try and make up for what we do. When we fly, for example, we now buy carbon offsets by making a donation to an organization that specializes in carbon neutrality. We are working to improve the efficiencies of our appliances and vehicles at home. And we continue to look for new ways to do our part, knowing that while our choices may be at times imperfect, knowledge is a very powerful tool. It is in that spirit that we offer you the following information to help you consider what you can do.

RETHINKING YOUR AUTOMOBILE

In the U.S., vehicles are responsible for about 25 percent of the greenhouse gases produced. Cars and other motor vehicles are a major source of pollutants that create smog and acid rain, and release other harmful substances that exacerbate conditions such as asthma and heart disease, and damage the lungs.

WHAT YOU CAN DO:

1. Consider a more fuel-efficient vehicle. A car that gets 20 miles to the gallon will emit about 50 tons of carbon dioxide over its lifetime. Double the gas mileage and you cut the emissions by half. Consider an advanced technology vehicle like a hybrid or flex-fuel vehicle.

2. Keep your car in good condition. Get your engine tuned up regularly, change the oil, and keep your tires inflated properly—proper maintenance can increase your car's fuel efficiency by 10 percent and reduce emissions.

3. Cut driving miles. Each gallon of gas your car burns releases about 22 pounds of atmospheric-warming carbon dioxide Reducing how much you drive by just five miles each day would prevent tons of carbon dioxide from entering the air.

4. Carpool. If every car carried just one more passenger on its daily commute, 32 million gallons of gasoline (and the pollution produced by it) would be saved each day.

RETHINKING YOUR ENERGY USE AT HOME*

Twenty-one percent of energy used in the United States is used at home. There are many simple steps you can take to reduce your energy consumption at home, and most of them will save you money in the long run.

WHAT YOU CAN DO:

1. Buy energy-efficient products. When buying new appliances or electronics, shop for the highest energy-efficiency rating. Look for a yellow and black Energy Guide label on the product. It compares the energy use for that model against similar models. New energy-efficient models may cost more initially, but have a lower operating cost over their lifetimes. The most energy-efficient models carry the Energy Star label, which identifies products that use 20–40 percent less energy than standard new products. According to the EPA, the typical American household can save about $400 per year in energy bills with products that carry the Energy Star.
2. Switch to compact fluorescent bulbs. Change the three bulbs you use most in your house to compact fluorescents. Each compact fluorescent bulb will keep half a ton of carbon dioxide out of the air over its lifetime. And while compact fluorescents may be slightly more expensive than the incandescent bulbs you're used to using, they last ten times as long and can save $30 per year in electricity costs.
3. Set heating and cooling temperatures correctly. Check thermo-

---

*Recommendations from the NRDC, reprinted with permission.

stats in your home to make sure they are set at a level that doesn't waste energy. Get an electronic thermostat that will allow your furnace to heat the house to a lower temperature when you're sleeping and return it to a more comfortable temperature before you wake up. And remember that water heaters work most efficiently between 120 degrees and 140 degrees.

4. Turn off lights and other electrical appliances such as televisions and radios when you're not using them. This is a fairly simple step, but it's surprising how many times we forget. Install automatic timers for lights that people in your house frequently forget to flick off when leaving a room. Use dimmers where you can.

5. Choose renewable energy. Many consumers can now choose their energy supplier. If you have a choice, choose an electric utility that uses renewable power resources, such as solar, and wind.

REDUCING YOUR FAMILY'S EXPOSURE TO TOXINS

The list of steps that one can take to reduce one's exposure to toxins is extensive. We'll focus here on some particular issues addressed in the book. For more information on other toxins, see the resources at the end of this section.

REDUCING YOUR EXPOSURE TO TOXINS

Pollution in People Report

1. Choose PVC-free building products. Steer clear of vinyl windows and doors and choose wood instead. For flooring, choose linoleum, cork, bamboo, or wood instead of vinyl. Adhesives,

caulk, grout, and sealants may also contain phthalates. You can check for phthalate ingredients in these products using the National Institutes of Health's Household Products Database: www.householdproducts.nlm.nih.gov/ (search for "phthalate" as an ingredient). Or consult healthybuilding.net, which provides suggestions for choosing "greener" building products.

2. Choose toys carefully. A number of leading toy manufacturers have pledged to stop using PVC and phthalates. Look for toys and feeding products for babies and young children that are labeled "PVC free."

3. Look for Phthalate-free personal care products. Check ingredient lists and avoid products listing "fragrance" or phthalates. A wide variety of personal-care products may contain phthalates, including perfume, cologne, after-shave, deodorant, soap, hair and skin-care products, and makeup.

4. Buy Organic. Legitimate organically-grown food is produced without the use of toxic pesticides. Washing fruit and vegetables is always recommended and does help reduce some pesticide residues, but it is not sufficient to remove the many pesticides that are taken into the flesh of the produce.

WHERE TO GET MORE INFORMATION

AIRNOW

www.airnow.gov

The AirNOW Air Quality Index describes what the air quality index is (a composite measure of five of the criteria air pollutants) and provides current and historical air quality data for 300 U.S. cities and national parks.

AUDUBON

www.audubon.org

Audubon's mission is to conserve and restore natural ecosystems, focusing on birds, other wildlife, and their habitats for the benefit of humanity and the earth's biological diversity. Their national network of community-based nature centers and chapters, scientific and educational programs, and advocacy on behalf of areas sustaining important bird populations, engage millions of people of all ages and backgrounds in positive conservation experiences.

CLIMATECRISIS.NET

The companion Web site to *An Inconvenient Truth,* the 2006 movie about Al Gore's presentation about climate change. The site allows you to calculate your CO_2 emissions and provides recommendations for reducing them.

DEFENDERS OF WILDLIFE

www.defenders.org

Defenders of Wildlife is dedicated to the protection of all native wild animals and plants in their natural communities. They focus on what scientists consider two of the most serious environmental threats to the planet: the accelerating rate of extinction of species and the associated loss of biological diversity, and habitat alteration and destruction.

THE DEIRDRE IMUS ENVIRONMENTAL CENTER FOR PEDIATRIC ONCOLOGY

www.Dienviro.com

The Deirdre Imus Center Web site includes many tips on greening your life, including a green materials library to guide home improvement decisions; a guide for toy and home furnishing purchases; and guides for cleaning your home, maintaining you garden, as well as greening offices and schools.

EARTHJUSTICE

www.earthjustice.org

Earthjustice is a non-profit public interest law firm dedicated to protecting the magnificent places, natural resources, and wildlife of this earth and to defending the right of all people to a healthy environment. They bring about far-reaching change by enforcing and strengthening environmental laws on behalf of hundreds of organizations and communities.

THE EAT WELL GUIDE

www.eatwellguide.org

The Eat Well Guide is a directory of sustainably raised meat, poultry, dairy, and eggs from farms, stores, restaurants, inns and hotels, and online outlets in the U.S. and Canada. Visitors can enter their zip or postal code to find local outlets for organic animal products.

ENERGY STAR

www.energystar.gov

The Energy Star program helps to identify consumer appliances that use less energy. It also identifies steps you can take to improve the energy efficiency of your home, prevent drafts, excess humidity and other common problems. The Energy Star website has numerous tools for researching these issues and to determine what's right for you and your family. For example, according to Energy Star, if your refrigerator was made before 1993, it's probably time for a new one, both for cost savings and for the environment. You can enter specific information about your refrigerator and energy use to find out for sure.

ENVIRONMENTAL DEFENSE

www.environmentaldefense.org

Environmental Defense brings together experts in science, law and economics to tackle complex environmental issues that affect our oceans, our air, our natural resources, the livability of our man-made environment, and the species with whom we share our world. Whether you are a policymaker, businessperson, journalist or consumer, you will find information that can help you change the way you do business, save money and protect the planet.

ENVIRONMENTAL WORKING GROUP

www.ewg.org

The EWG uses science to educate the public and advocate for change on many environmental issues related to toxins, human health, and the environment. Their web site has extensive information, reports, and resources related to the toxic chemicals discussed in this book along with many other important issues.

FRIENDS OF THE EARTH

www.foe.org

Friends of the Earth defends the planet and champions a healthy and just world. Active in 70 countries, Friends of the Earth has the world's largest network of environmental groups.

GREEN CHOICES

www.greenerchoices.org

The Consumers Union's online shopping guide is packed with tips, recommendations and rating charts to help you make environmentally friendly purchases.

THE GREEN GUIDE

www.thegreenguide.com

This website provides news and advice about product choices and daily practices that are better for health and the environment.

THE HEALTHY BUILDING NETWORK

www.healthybuilding.net

The web site of the Healthy Building Network provides information on making purchasing decisions, especially related to PVC building materials, plastic lumber, pressure-treated wood, and formaldehyde.

LEAGUE OF CONSERVATION VOTERS

www.lcv.org

The League of Conservation Voters (LCV) is the independent political voice for the environment. To learn more about sound environmental policies and to elect pro-environmental candidates who will adopt and implement such policies, we recommend this website.

NATIONAL ENVIRONMENTAL TRUST

www.net.org

The National Environmental Trust is a non-profit, non-partisan organization established in 1994 to inform citizens about environmental problems and how they affect our health and quality of life. Check out their campaigns and special reports to learn about the issues on which they are currently focused.

NATIONAL WILDLIFE FEDERATION

www.nwf.org

National Wildlife Federation inspires Americans to protect wildlife for our children's future. Visit their website to learn what you can do to keep our country's wildlife legacy alive.

NATURAL RESOURCES DEFENSE COUNCIL

www.nrdc.org

The NRDC is an environmental action organization focused on preserving the nation's natural resources and ensuring a safe and healthy environment for all living things. Many of the environment-saving tips above—along with numerous others—are available on the NRDC web site.

POLLUTION IN PEOPLE

www.pollutioninpeople.org

Pollution in People is a study of ten Washingtonians that was organized by the Toxic Free Legacy Coalition of Washington. The web site describes the study results and also includes recommendations of safer alternatives to toxic chemicals we encounter in everyday life.

SAVE THE HD MOUNTAINS

www.savehdmountains.org

The website of citizens working to protect and preserve the HD Mountains in Southwest Colorado.

SIERRA CLUB

www.sierraclub.org

The Sierra Club's members are more than 750,000 of your friends and neighbors. Inspired by nature, they work together to protect our communities and the planet. The Club is America's oldest grassroots environmental organization.

STOP GLOBAL WARMING

www.stopglobalwarming.org

Stop Global Warming has a list of easy things you can do to reduce your CO_2 emissions, along with estimates of the amount of CO_2 emissions you can reduce (and cost savings) of each of these things. Also available via this website is Laurie David's book, *Stop Global Warming: The Solution is You.*

THE U.S. ENVIRONMENTAL PROTECTION AGENCY

The website of the U.S. EPA provides extensive information on environmental issues, water quality, air quality, monitoring and testing, chemicals, and environmental regulations. Due to the volume of information, the site can be a bit difficult to navigate. Some of our recommendations of the EPA's best online resources:

http://www.epa.gov/tri/
Toxic Release Inventory—You enter your zip code, and the EPA web site tells you about reported toxic releases in the area.

http://es.epa.gov/techinfo/facts/safe-fs.html
The EPA's Fact Sheet on NonToxic Household Products. Describes the toxic properties of many common household products (especially cleaning products) and describes non-toxic alternatives.

http://www.epa.gov/owow/nps/dosdont.html
EPA recommendations of steps you can take to help improve water quality.

WATERKEEPER ALLIANCE

www.waterkeeper.org
Waterkeeper Alliance connects and supports local Waterkeeper programs to provide a voice for waterways and their communities worldwide. To champion clean water and strong communities, Waterkeeper Alliance supports and empowers member Waterkeeper organizations to protect communities, ecosystems and water quality.

WASHINGTON TOXICS COALITION

www.watoxics.org
This web site includes tips for reducing the use of toxic chemicals in your home and garden, and for working with your local municipality to eliminate toxins in schools, government buildings, and parks.

NOTES

CHAPTER ONE: THE ART OF THE POSSIBLE

4   **Her book *Silent Spring*, released in 1962, documented the extent to which DDT wreaked havoc on the environment**: See Rachel Carson, *Silent Spring*, introduction by Linda Lear and afterword by E. O. Wilson (Boston: Houghton, 2002).

5   **"The major claims of Miss Rachel Carson . . ."**: "Rachel Carson Dies of Cancer; 'Silent Spring' Author Was 56," obituary, *New York Times*, April 15, 1964, available at http://www.rachelcarson.org/index.cfm?fuseaction= obituary.

5   **"It is the public that is being asked to assume the risks . . ."**: Ibid.

6   **DDT was eventually banned**: See EPA Web site, at http://www.epa.gov/ history/; see also www.who.int/malaria/docs/TreatmentGuidelines2006. pdf.

7   **Many of the world's ecosystems are headed for collapse**: See *Millennium Ecosystem Assessment: Living Beyond Our Means—Natural Assets and Human Well-Being*, Statement from the Board, at http://www.wri.org/biodiv/pubs _description.cfm?PubID=4115.

7   **"Today's technology and knowledge can reduce considerably the human impact ecosystems"**: Ibid.

8   **A few years later . . . her invention was selling at Saks Fifth Avenue**: One source that was particularly helpful in our research about Marion Donovan's Boater invention was http://americanhistory.si.edu/archives/d8721. htm.

9   Statistics on disposable diapers are drawn from Donella Meadows, "The Great Disposable Diaper Debate," Sustainability Institute, at http://www. sustainer.org/dhm_archive/index.php?display_article=vn321diapersed.

9   **Diapers are now the third-largest single contributor to solid waste at landfills**: See http://www.gdiapers.com/began.

12   **McDonough and Braungart have developed a Cradle-to-Cradle certification process**: For more information on McDonough and Braungart's work and the Cradle-to-Cradle design philosophy, go to http://mbdc.com/.

12   *Cradle to Cradle: Remaking the Way we Make Things* (North Point Press, 2002) is a valuable and inspiring resource for anyone interested in learning more about the Cradle to Cradle philosophy. More information is available at http://www.mcdonough.com/cradle_to_cradle.htm.

13   **gDiapers are made with no chlorine**: See http://www.gdiapers.com/.

14 For quotes about Pittsburgh, see Dan Fitzpatrick, "What Is Pittsburgh?" *Pittsburgh Quarterly,* Winter 2006, at http://pittsburghquarterly.com/pages /winter2006/030what_is_pgh.htm.

16 **The first green office-design project in Pittsburgh was, in fact, Bill McDonough's redesign of the Heinz Family Offices**: For more information on this project, see http://www.mcdonoughpartners.com/projects/heinz/ default.asp?projID=heinz.

16 For description of the Pittsburgh Convention Center, see http://www. pittsburghcc.com/html/greenbuilding.htm.

18 *The Economist* **ranked Pittsburgh the most livable city in the United States**: See http://store.eiu.com/index.asp?layout=pr_story&press_id=660001866 &ref=pr_list.

CHAPTER TWO: A BODY OF EVIDENCE

21 **the World Health Organization (WHO) tried to end a malaria epidemic in Borneo by using DDT**: Rachel Wynberg and Christine Jardine, *Biotechnology and Biodiversity: Key Policy Issues for South Africa,* 2000.

22 **WHO was forced to parachute in 14,000 new cats**: Ibid.

23 **"Five hundred new chemicals to which the bodies of men and animals are required somehow to adapt<el>"**: Rachel Carson, *Silent Spring,* introduction by Linda Lear and afterword by E. O. Wilson (Boston: Houghton Mifflin, 2002).

23 **pesticide use alone has increased by 50 percent over the past thirty-six years**: U.S. EPA, *Pesticide Industry Sales and Usage: 1994 and 1995 Market Estimates,* August 1997, Table 10, page 26, at http://www.epa.gov/oppbead1 /pestsales/95pestsales/market_estimates1995.pdf

23 **there are now *more than 80,000 chemicals* in widespread use in commerce**: Statistics at EPA's Web site vary from 75, 000 to 100,000. See EPA, "Persistent Bioaccumulative and Toxic (PBT) Chemical Program," at http:// www.epa.gov/pbt/tools/toolbox.htm. See also EPA, "What Is the TSCA Chemical Substance Inventory?" at www.epa.gov/opptintr/newchems/ pubs/invntory.htm

23 **This year we will manufacture or import more than 1 million pounds each of about 3,000 of these chemicals**: See EPA's "Chemical Hazard Data Availability Study," at http://www.epa.gov/chemrtk/pubs/general/hazchem. htm.

23 **the chemicals used to manufacture many of the products we use . . . are never tested**: Ibid.

23 **new chemicals . . . tested for toxicity *only* if . . . grounds for believing they could prove to be harmful**: See EPA, "TSCA Statute, Regulation, and Enforcement," at http://www.epa.gov/compliance/civil/tsca/tscaenfstatreq. html. See also Office of Management of Budget's assessment of the EPA's

chemical testing program, atwww.whitehouse.gov/omb/expectmore/detail.10000232.2005.html.

24   **EPA has banned or limited the use of five existing chemicals or groups of chemicals**: GAO, "Actions Are Needed to Improve the Effectiveness of EPA's Chemical Review Program," at http://www.gao.gov/highlights/d06 1032thigh.pdf.

24   **every one of us . . . is carrying almost 200 different synthetic or toxic chemicals**: See Monique Harden, "Body Burden Research," at http://urbanhabitat.org/node/171.

24   **All of the chemicals tested . . . were found in at least some of the participants**: "Executive Summary," Third National Report on Human Exposure to Environmental Chemicals, 2005, Centers for Disease Control, at www.cdc.gov/exposurereport/3rd/pdf/thirdreport_summary.pdf.

24   **Similar results were found through biomonitoring tests conducted by the Environmental Working Group**: "Body Burden: The Pollution in People," Environmental Working Group, at http://www.ewg.org/reports/bodyburden1/index.php.

25   Statistics on women's health are drawn from the American Cancer Society, at http://www.cancer.org/downloads/STT/CancerFacts&Figures20 02TM.pdf; the National Mental Health Information Center, at http://mentalhealth.samhsa.gov/publications/allpubs/fastfact6/default.asp; the American Fertility Association, at http://www.theafa.org/faqs/afa_infertilityriskassessment.html; and the Global Alliance for Women's Health, at http://www.gawh.org/programs/03_02_00/summary.htm.

25   **According to the Breast Cancer Fund and Breast Cancer Action**: "The Facts and Nothing but the Facts," Breast Cancer Action, at http://www.bcaction.org/Pages/GetInformed/Facts.html.

26   **Women on Cape Cod were being diagnosed with breast cancer at a significantly higher rate**: Robin Lord, "Toxic Chemicals Abundant in Homes," *Cape Cod Times,* September 15, 2003, http://www.capecodonline.com/cc-times/toxicchemicals15.htm.

26   For more information on the Massachusetts Breast Cancer Coalition (MBCC), go to their Web site, at http://www.mbcc.org.

28   To find out more about the Silent Spring Institute, go to http://www.silentspring.org/.

28   **Silent Spring Institute was awarded $3 million from the Massachusetts Department of Public Health**: See *Silent Spring Review 2004,* at http://library.silentspring.org/publications/pdfs/SSIreview2004.pdf.

29   **Ana M. Soto and Carlos Sonnenschein, had been working . . . to better understand how estrogen . . . could induce cancer-cell growth**: Caroline M. Markey, Enrique H. Luque, Monica Munoz de Toro, Carlos Sonnenschein, and Ana M. Soto, "In Utero Exposure to Bisphenol A Alters the Development and Tissue Organization of the Mouse Mammary Gland," *Biological*

Reproduction 65 (2001):1215-1223, at http://www.biolreprod.org/collected /toxicology.dtl.

29 **Dr. Devra Davis . . . developed and tested the hypothesis that some commonly used pesticides and toxic chemicals could act like estrogens**: For a review of Dr. Davis's book *When Smoke Ran Like Water,* go to the Web site of the Women's Environmental Network, at http://www.wen.org.uk/general _pages/BookReviews/br_Smoke&Silent.htm.

29 **Mary Wolff, at New York's Mount Sinai School of Medicine, found an association between organochlorine pesticides . . . and breast-cancer risk**: Mary S. Wolff et al., "Blood Levels of Organochlorine Residues and Risk of Breast Cancer," *Journal of the National Cancer Institute* 85, no. 8 (April 21, 1993):648–652, at http://jnci.oxfordjournals.org/cgi/content/abstract/ 85/8/648.

32 **researchers . . . have found growing evidence of estrogen-mimicking chemicals in surface waters**: USGS, "Investigations of Endocrine Disruption in Aquatic Systems Associated with the National Water Quality Assessment (NAWQA) Program," at http://pubs.usgs.gov/fs/FS-081-98/.

32 **male smallmouth bass in the Potomac . . . were found to be producing a female egg-yolk protein**: David Fahrenthold, "Male Bass Across Region Found to Be Bearing Eggs," *Washington Post,* September 6, 2006.

33 **the dust contained twenty-six different hormone-altering compounds, and the air contained nineteen**: See *Silent Spring Review 2004,* at http:// library.silentspring.org/publications/pdfs/SSIreview2004.pdf.

33 **researchers from the University of Rochester published a truly groundbreaking study**: K. Marsee, T. J. Woodruff, D. A. Axelrad, A. M. Calafat, and S. H. Swan, "Estimated Daily Phthalate Exposures in a Population of Mothers of Male Infants Exhibiting Reduced Anogenital Distance," *Environmental Health Perspectives,* August 2006, reviewed at http://www.ourstolenfuture .org/NewScience/oncompounds/phthalates/2006/2006-0205marseeetal. htm.

35 **Spengler has shown that exposure to indoor pollution can be even more harmful . . . than outdoor exposure**: To learn more about the research of John Spengler, go to http://www.hsph.harvard.edu/facres/spnglr.html.

36 For more on the Institute for Green Oxidation Chemistry, go to http:// www.chem.cmu.edu/groups/Collins/.

36 To learn more about the Center for Environmental Oncology, go to http: //www.environmentaloncology.org/.

37 To learn more about the philosophy of the Imus Ranch, go to http:// www.msnbc.msn.com/id/3359675/.

38 **exposure to environmental toxins has also been linked to childhood cancers**: National Cancer Institute Research on Childhood Cancers: Factsheet, at http://www.cancer.gov/cancertopics/factsheet/NCI-childhood-cancers research.

39   **a University of Washington study found that children who ate a diet of organic food a level of pesticides in their bodies six times lower**: Cynthia L.
Curl, Richard A. Fenske, Kai Elgethun, "Organophosphorus Pesticide Exposure of Urban and Suburban Preschool Children with Organic and
Conventional Diets," *Environmental Health Perspectives* 111, no. 3 (March
2003):377–382.

39   **Polyvinyl chloride . . . is still used in the manufacture of many children's
toys**: Pamela Lundquist and Aisha Ikramuddin, "PVC: The Most Toxic
Plastic," Children's Health Environmental Coalition, at http://www.chec
net.org/HealtheHouse/education/articles-detail.asp?Main_ID=185.

39   **At birth, each child carried an average body burden of *200 chemicals***:
"Body Burden: The Pollution in Newborns," Environmental Working
Group, at http://www.ewg.org/reports/bodyburden2/execsumm.php.

39   **tested the breast milk**: "Mothers' Milk: Record Levels of Toxic Fire Retardants Found in American Mothers' Breast Milk," Environmental Working
Group, at http://www.ewg.org/reports/mothersmilk/es.php.

40   **"Exposure to DEHP has produced a range of adverse effects . . ."**: "FDA
Public Health Notification: PVC Devices Containing the Plasticizer
DEHP," Food and Drug Administration, at http://www.fda.gov/cdrh/
safety/dehp.html.

41   To learn more about Greening the Cleaning, go to http://www.imus
ranchfoods.com/index1.aspx?BD=18129.

41   **the governor [George Pataki] issued an Executive Order**: "Pataki Signs
Executive Order Mandating Procurement of 'Green Products,'" Legislative and Regulatory Update, January/February 2005, at http://dvnews
maker.digivis.com/issa/index.jsp?pageType=3&layoutType=1&id=1492&a
rticleObjectName=com.issa.article.Article.

42   **Governor Richard J. Codey of New Jersey signed Executive Order No. 76**:
"Codey Signs Green Cleaning Executive Order," press release, January 12,
2006, at http://www.nj.gov/cgi-bin/governor/njnewsline/view_article.pl?
id=2883.

42   **Connecticut Governor M. Jodi Rell signed Executive Order 14**: at http://
www.ct.gov/governorrell/cwp/view.asp?A=1719&Q=312904.

43   **In July 2006, the EU imposed a ban on . . . electronic equipment containing . . . deca-BDE**: "The EU Ban on Hazardous Substances in Electrical and
Electronic Products," The EU in the United Kingdom, July 6, 2006, at http:
//ec.europa.eu/unitedkingdom/about_us/office_in_northern_ireland/
euweekly/repeu06/0625_en.htm.

43   **a major new legislative initiative will govern the way the EU treats chemicals**: To learn more about the EU's new regulatory framework, go to http:
//ec.europa.eu/environment/chemicals/reach/reach_intro.htm.

43   **The Toxic Substances Control Act (TSCA), passed in 1976, was intended
to provide complete evaluations of existing chemicals**: See EPA, "TSCA

Statutes, Regulation, and Enforcement," at http://www.epa.gov/compli-ance/civil/tsca/tscaenfstatreq.html.

43 **In 1998, the federal government and the chemical industry established a voluntary program . . . to test chemicals**: For a report on the effectiveness of the voluntary testing program initiated in 1998, see Michael McLaugh-lin, "Commercial Chemicals' Safety Unknown," UPI, August 9, 2006, posted on the Web site of the Environmental Working Group, at http://www.ewg.org/news/story.php?id=5436.

44 **a team . . . studied the effects of phthalate exposure in rats**: Milena Du-rando, Laura Kass, Julio Piva, Carlos Sonnenschein, Ana M. Soto, Enrique H. Luque, and Mónica Muñoz-de-Toro, "Prenatal Bisphenol A Exposure Induces Preneoplastic Lesions in the Mammary Gland in Wistar Rats," *Environmental Health Perspectives* 115, no. 1 (January 2007):80–86.

44 **"Phthalates have established a very strong safety profile . . .":** Read the health claims on the industry Web site, Phthalates Information Center, at http://www.phthalates.org/yourhealth/index.asp.

45 **drop in breast cancer . . . could be due to the fact women stopped using synthetic HRT**: "Breast Cancer Drop Linked to HRT," BBC News, Decem-ber 15, 2006, at http://www.phthalates.org/yourhealth/index.asp.

45 **The CPSC denied the petition in 2003**: *Trouble in Toyland, 20th Annual Toy Safety Review,* November 2005, NJPIRG Law and Policy Center, page 20, at http://www.njpirg.org/reports/troubleintoyland2005.pdf.

45 **A bill banning the use of phthalates in toys was recently introduced in the California State Assembly**: "Bill Banning Use of Phthalates in Toys Is De-feated in California: Toy Industry Association Provides Key Testimony at January 10th Hearing," press release, Toy Industry Association, January 19, 2006, http://www.toy-tia.org/Content/NavigationMenu/Press Room/Press_Releases1/01_19_06/01_19_06.htm.

46 **Scientific studies have found that atrazine is a reproductive toxin and can cause cancer**: Jennifer A. Rusiecki et al., "Cancer Incidence Among Pesti-cide Applicators Exposed to Atrazine in the Agricultural Health Study," *Journal of National Cancer Institute* 96, no. 18 (September 15, 2004): 1375–1382, at http://jnci.oxfordjournals.org/cgi/reprint/jnci%3b96/18/1375.pdf.

46 **the incidence of ovarian cancer in women with high exposures to atrazine was two to four times higher**: Gina Soloman, "Ovarian Cancer," posted on the Web site of Collaborative on Health and the Environment, February 17, 2004, at http://www.healthandenvironment.org/ovarian_cancer/peer_reviewed.

46 **researcher Tyrone Hayes . . . found that the pesticide caused deformities in frogs**: Goldie Blumenstyk, "The Price of Research," *Chronicle of Higher Education,* October 31, 2003, at http://chronicle.com/free/v50/i10/10a 02601.htm.

46 **the EPA ruled that atrazine could remain on the market**: EPA, "Atrazine Interim Reregistration Eligibility Decision (IRED) Addendum Q&A's, October 2003," http://www.epa.gov/pesticides/factsheets/atrazine_addendum.htm.

46 **The European Union . . . moved to ban atrazine**: "Atrazine and Simazine Banned in the EU but 'Essential Uses' Remain in the UK," Pesticide Action Network, UK, December 2003, at http://www.pan-uk.org/pestnews/Issue/pn62/pn62p19a.htm.

46 **EPA secretly met . . . with lobbyists from Syngenta during the evaluation process**: J. R. Pegg, "EPA Sued for Backroom Deals with Pesticide Makers," Environmental News Service, February 21, 2005, at http://www.ensnewswire.com/ens/feb2005/2005-02-21-10.asp.

47 **EPA canceled the CHEERS study after a number of organizations . . . expressed outrage**: See EPA announcement, at http://www.epa.gov/cheers/.

47 **the agency proposed a study to test the effects of pesticide use on children's health**: "Agency Information Collection Activities; Submission to OMB for Review and Approval; Comment Request; Longitudinal Study of Young Children's Exposures in Their Homes to Selected Pesticides, Phthalates, Brominated Flame Retardants, and Perfluorinated Chemicals (A Children's Environmental Exposure Research Study—CHEERS), EPA ICR Number 2126.01," Federal Register Environmental Documents, at http://www.epa.gov/fedrgstr/EPA-GENERAL/2004/March/Day03/g4704.htm.

48 **In December 2006, the European Union formally adopted REACH regulations**: REACH, European Commission, athttp://ec.europa.eu/environment/chemicals/reach/reach_intro.htm.

CHAPTER THREE: ABUSE OF POWER

53 **one in six infants . . . has a blood mercury level above what the agency considers safe**: "What You Need to Know About Mercury in Fish and Shellfish," Center for Food Safety and Applied Nutrition, U.S. Food and Drug, March 2004, at http://www.cfsan.fda.gov/~dms/admehg3.html.

54 **Florida . . . was able to achieve sharp reductions in mercury pollution**: National Resources Defense Council, "New EPA 'Do-Nothing' Mercury Pollution Rules Dangerous to Public Health," press release, March 24, 2005, at http://72.32.110.154/media/pressreleases/050324.asp.

54 **mercury was the most dangerous toxin in our environment**: "EPA to Regulate Mercury and Other Toxics Emissions from Coal- and Oil-fired Power Plants," Factsheet, Air Toxics, U.S.E.P.A., December 14, 2000, at http://www.epa.gov/ttn/atw/combust/utiltox/hgfs1212.html.

54 **In 2001, EPA acknowledged that mercury pollution from utilities could be reduced by nearly 90 percent by 2008**: http://www.epa.gov/oig/reports/2005/20050203-2005-P-00003.pdf.

54 **An EPA analysis noted that this revision to the act allowed . . . power plants to actually *increase* mercury emissions**: Government Accountability Office, "Clean Air Act: Observations on EPA's Cost Benefit Analysis of Its Mercury Control Options," GAO-05-252, February 2005, at http://www.gao.gov/new.items/d05252.pdf. See also National Resources Defense Council, at http://www.nrdc.org/air/pollution/fclearsk.asp.

54 **In all, more than 100,000 of our nation's lakes and 846,000 miles of our rivers were under fish advisories in 2003**: Traci Watson, "States Look Harder for Mercury," *USA Today*, August 24, 2004, at http://www.usatoday.com/news/nation/2004-08-24-states-mercury_x.htm.

55 **Since 1999, the thirty biggest utility companies . . . have contributed $6.6 million to President Bush and the Republican National Committee**: Public Citizen, "Study: Top U.S. Air Polluters Are Closely Tied to Bush Fundraising, Pollution Policymaking Process," May 5, 2004, at http://www.citizen.org/pressroom/release.cfm?ID=1706.

56 **The Clean Air Act achieved some stunning results**: Janea Scott et al., *The Clean Air Act at 35: Preventing Death and Disease from Particulate Pollution*, Environmental Defense, 2005, at http://www.environmentaldefense.org/documents/4936_caa35.pdf.

56 **more than 152 million Americans . . . are being exposed to unhealthy levels of air pollution**: American Lung Association, "State of the Air: 2005 Report Calls on Congress to Stop Siding with Corporate Polluters," April 28, 2005, at http://www.lungusa.org/site/pp.asp?c=dvLUK9O0E&b=564421.

58 **the pollution . . . has shortened the lives of as many as 9,000 people**: Clean Air Task Force, "Power to Kill: Death and Disease from Power Plants Charged with Violating the Clean Air Act," July 2001, at http://www.catf.us/publications/view/10.

58 **The changes adopted a series of loopholes:** For more information, visit the National Resources Defense Council at http://www.nrdc.org/air/pollution/pnsr.asp.

59 **people of color were 79 percent more likely than whites to reside in communities where pollution posed the highest health risks**: See David Pace, "AP: More Blacks Live with Pollution," Associated Press, December 14, 2005, http://hosted.ap.org/specials/interactives/archive/pollution/part1.html. To find out how the health risk from industrial air pollution in your neighborhood compares to other neighborhoods across the country, you can enter your address at the AP Web site http://hosted.ap.org/dynamic/external/onlinenews.ap.org/pollution/test_searchY.html?SITE=AP&SECTION=HOME.

60 Information on the Afton, North Carolina, Superfund site is drawn from Robert D. Bullard, *Dumping in Dixie: Race, Class, and Environmental Justice* (Boulder: Westview Press, 1990).

63 **Several similar investigations followed, the most significant conducted in**

1987 **by the United Church of Christ**: Commission for Racial Justice, *Toxic Wastes and Race in the United States* (New York: United Church of Christ, 1987).

63   **Another study . . . found significant discrepancies in how federal environmental protection laws were enforced in poor communities**: Marianne Lavelle and Marcia Coyle, "Unequal Protection," *National Law Journal*, September 21, 1992, S1–S2.

63   **President Bill Clinton . . . signed Executive Order 12898, requiring the federal government to abide by environmental justice principles**: See Executive Order 12898, at http://www.epa.gov/fedrgstr/eo/eo12898.pdf.

64   **Today, more than two-thirds of all African Americans . . . live within 30 miles of a coal-fired power plant**: Clear the Air/Physicians for Social Responsibility, *Children at Risk: How Air Pollution from Power Plants Threatens the Health of America's Children*, May 2002, at http://www.environet.policy.net/relatives/4121.pdf.

64   Statistics on pollution levels during the 1996 Summer Olympics are drawn from Environmental Working Group, "Autos and Asthma," at http://www.ewg.org/sites/asthmaindex/about/.

64   **Asthma, one of the leading health problems among all Americans**: American Lung Association, "Asthma in Adults Factsheet," http://www.lungusa.org/site/pp.asp?c=dvLUK9O0E&b=22596.

65   **families with annual incomes below $10,000 suffer more than twice the rate of asthma**: Rachel Massey, MSc, MPA, and Frank Ackerman, PhD, *Costs of Preventable Childhood Illness: The Price We Pay for Pollution*, Global Development and Environment Institute Working Paper No. 03-09, page 18, at http://ase.tufts.edu/gdae/Pubs/rp/03-09ChildhoodIllness.PDF.

65   **In Boston, for example, the Roxbury Environmental Empowerment Program (REEP) is helping to develop the next generation of leaders**: See http://www.ace-ej.org/reep.

66   **The Bucket Brigade is a program that is having tremendous results in Louisiana**: We are particularly grateful to the members of the Louisiana Bucket Brigade for allowing us to narrate the history available at http://www.labucketbrigade.org/.

77   **In September 2006, the Office of Inspector General issued another critical . . . report**: Office of Inspector General, EPA Needs to Conduct Environmental Justice Reviews of Its Programs, Policies, and Activities, Report No. 2006-P-00034, at http://www.epa.gov/oig/reports/2006/20060918-2006-P-00034.pdf.

CHAPTER FOUR: THE WATER OF LIFE

81   **one-third of our river and stream miles, and almost half of all lake acres, do not meet water-quality standards**: "Executive Summary," *Liquid Assets 2000*, U.S. Environmental Protection Agency, at http://www.epa.gov/water/liquidassets/execsumm.html.

83   **the largest-ever fish kill to date occurred in Lake Thonotosassa, Florida**: "A Brief History of the Clean Water Act," *NOW,* Public Broadcasting System, December 20, 2002.

84   Information on the history of Riverkeeper is drawn from interview with staff and its Web site; see http://riverkeeper.org/ourstory_40Anniversary. php.

88   **Nixon announced the creation of the Environmental Protection Agency**: See EPA Web site, at http://www.epa.gov/history/.

90   **The Clean Water Act helped to prevent . . . pollution from flowing into our rivers**: See EPA Web site, at http://www.epa.gov/history/topics/fwpca/05. htm.

90   **Most water pollution today can be directly linked to agricultural practices**: "Nonpoint Source Pollution: The Nation's Largest Water Quality Problem," EPA841-F-96-004A, at http://www.epa.gov/nps/facts/point1.htm.

91   **there are approximately 18,800 factory farms in operation**: See EPA Web site, at http://www.epa.gov/npdes/regulations/cafo_revisedrule_factsheet pdf.

93   **the Neuse River suffered the largest fish kill ever recorded in the state's history**: See Web site of the Neuse River Foundation, at http://www.neuse river.org/abouttheneuse/historyofwaterqualityproblems.

93   **The problem . . . was found to be *Pfiesteria piscicida:*** See Web site of the Neuse River Foundation, at http://www.neuseriver.org/abouttheneuse/ pfiesteria.

109   **In 2003, the EPA established rules requiring industrial dairy operators to adopt a Nutrient Management Plan**: See EPA Web site, at http://www.epa. gov/nps/MMGI/Chapter2/ch2-2c.html.

110   **the river drains . . . 41 percent of the 48 contiguous states**: Environmental Working Group, "Dead in the Water," at http://www.ewg.org/reports/ deadzone/part2.php.

110   **The Mississippi Basin supports a diverse agricultural economy**: See the Web site of the Mississippi National River and Recreation Area, at http:// www.nps.gov/archive/miss/features/factoids/.

111   **today the river . . . carries roughly fifteen times more nitrate load from agricultural runoff**: "Nitrogen in the Mississippi Basin: Estimating Sources and Predicting Flux to the Gulf of Mexico," USGS Fact Sheet 135-00, at http://ks.water.usgs.gov/Kansas/pubs/fact-sheets/fs.135-00.html.

111   **This gulf "dead zone" covers an average of 5,000 square miles**: Environmental Working Group, "Dead in the Water," at http://www.ewg.org/re-ports/deadzone/part2.php.

111   **dead zones . . . number approximately 150 worldwide each year**: See Environmental Working Group, "Dead in the Water," at http://www.ewg.org/ reports/deadzone/world.php.

111   **ocean degradation is "rapidly passing the point of no return"**: UNEP/

IUCN, *Ecosystems and Biodiversity in Deep Waters and High Seas,* UNEP Regional Seas Reports and Studies No. 178 (Geneva, Switzerland: UNEP, 2006), at http://www.unep.org/pdf/EcosystemBiodiversity_DeepWaters_20060616.pdf.

112 **Last year, the National Oceanic and Atmospheric Administration categorized nearly a third of the federally managed fisheries as "overfished"**: See NOAA press release at http://www.publicaffairs.noaa.gov/releases 2006/jun06/noaa06-061A.html.

112 **about one-third of all fishing stocks worldwide have collapsed**: Boris Worm et al., "Impacts of Biodiversity Loss on Ocean Ecosystem Services," *Science* 314 (November 3, 2006):787–790.

113 **new techniques threaten the long-term sustainability of global fish stocks**: UNEP/IUCN, *Ecosystems and Biodiversity in Deep Waters and High Seas,* UNEP Regional Seas Reports and Studies No. 178 (Geneva, Switzerland: UNEP, 2006), at http://www.unep.org/pdf/EcosystemBiodiversity_Deep Waters_20060616.pdf.

117 **"the root cause of this crisis is a failure of both perspective and governance"**: "Executive Summary," *America's Living Oceans: Charting a Course for Sea Change,* Pew Oceans Commission, Leon E. Panetta, Chair, page vii, at http://www.pewtrusts.org/pdf/env_pew_oceans_final_report_summary.pdf.

CHAPTER FIVE: GLOBAL CLIMATE CHANGE

119 **"all of them want us to believe the science is settled and it's not"**: "Inhofe: Don't Worry About Global Warming Because 'God's Still Up There," Think Progress, at http://thinkprogress.org/2006/11/17/inhofe-hoax/.

119 **the climate skeptics have trotted out the author of *Jurassic Park***: David Sandalow, "Michael Crichton and Global Warming," Brookings Institution, January 28, 2005, at http://www.brookings.edu/views/op-ed/fellows/sandalow20050128.htm.

119 **Oil companies have given money to advocacy organizations that deny the science**: "Put a Tiger in Your Think Tank," *Mother Jones,* May/June 2005, at http://www.brookings.edu/views/op-ed/fellows/sandalow20050128.htm.

121 **global temperatures have increased an average of 1.08 degrees**: United Nations Intergovernmental Panel on Climate Change (IPCC), "Summary for Policymakers," *Climate Change 2001: Synthesis Report,* at http://www.ipcc.ch/pub/un/syreng/spm.pdf.

120 **The Earth is very probably hotter today than at any time in at least the past thousand years**: IPCC, "Summary for Policymakers," *Climate Change 2001: Synthesis Report,* at http://www.ipcc.ch/pub/un/syreng/spm.pdf.

120 **The years 2005, 1998, 2002, 2003, 2006, and 2004 were, respectively, the**

six warmest: "2005 Warmest Year in over a Century," NASA, January 24, 2006, at http://www.nasa.gov/vision/earth/environment/2005_warmest. html; "Climate of 2006: Annual Report," National Climatic Data Center, NOAA, January 11, 2007, at http://www.ncdc.noaa.gov/oa/climate/re search/2006/ann/global.html#Gtemp.

120 **all but one of the twenty hottest years on record have occurred since 1980**: IPCC, "Summary for Policymakers," *Climate Change 2001: Scientific Basis. Contribution of Working Group I to the Third Assessment Report of the Intergovernmental Panel on Climate Change,* Figure 1(a), page 3, at http:// www.ipcc.ch/pub/spm22-01.pdf.

120 *Science* **magazine analyzed 928 peer-reviewed scientific papers**: Naomi Oreskes, "Beyond the Ivory Tower: The Scientific Consensus on Climate Change," *Science* 306, no. 5702 (December 3, 2004):1686.

121 **an increase of over 35 percent in the atmospheric concentration of carbon dioxide**: "Reining in Carbon Dioxide Levels Imperative but Possible," Earth Institute News, at http://www.earthinstitute.columbia.edu/news/ 2006/story03 07 06.php.

121 **carbon dioxide is now at its highest level in at least 650,000 years**: "New Research in *Science* Shows CO_2 Highest in 650,000 Years," AAAS, at http:// www.aaas.org/news/releases/2005/1128ice.shtml.

121 **other greenhouse gases . . . are together exerting a further warming effect**: "Global Warming Facts and Our Future," Marian Koshland Science Museum of the National Academy of Sciences, at http://www.koshland-science-museum.org/exhibitgcc/causes02.jsp.

123 **EPA published a report stating, "There is general agreement that the observed warming is real . . ."**: U.S.E.P.A., *U.S. Climate Action Report,* Appendix D, "Climate Change Science: An Analysis of Some Key Questions," at http://yosemite.epa.gov/oar/globalwarming.nsf/UniqueKeyLookup/SH SU5BNJ9A/$File/appD.pdf.

123 **According to the National Climatic Data Center, average temperatures in the U.S. in 2006 were 2.2 degrees Fahrenheit above the twentieth-century mean.** Source is http://www.ncdc.noaa.gov/oa/climate/research/2006/ ann/us-summary.html.

123 **In 2006, the hottest year ever recorded in the contiguous United States**: Ibid.

124 **Lake Champlain . . . did not freeze at all**: "Potential Climate Indicator," at http://www.uvm.edu/~empact/climate/freeze_data.html.

125 **in New York City . . . they now occur an average of five times a year**: Cameron Wake, "Climate Change in the Northeast: Past, Present, and Future," slide presentation at Hudson Valley Climate Change Conference, Poughkeepsie, New York, December 4, 2006, at http://www.dec.state. ny.us/website/hudson/hvcc1000cpw.pdf.

126 **Many coastal regions of the northeastern United States are experiencing**

twice as many extreme precipitation events today as in the 1950s: Cameron Wake, "Climate Change in the Northeast: Past, Present, and Future," slide presentation at Hudson Valley Climate Change Conference, Poughkeepsie, New York, December 4, 2006, at http://www.dec.state.ny.us/website/hudson/hvcc1000cpw.pdf.

126 **The number of Category 4 and 5 hurricanes globally has nearly doubled since the 1970s**: "Number of Category 4 and 5 Hurricanes Has Doubled over the Past 35 Years," National Science Foundation, Press Release 05-162, September 15, 2005, at http://www.nsf.gov/news/news_summ.jsp?cntn_id=104428.

126 **Signs of climate change are evident the world over**: *Beyond Scarcity: Power, Poverty, and the Global Water Crisis, Human Development Report 2006,* United Nations Development Programme, at http://hdr.undp.org/hdr2006/.

126 **Even plant and animal species are feeling the effects**: "Global Fingerprints of Greenhouse Warming: A Summary of Recent Scientific Research," Pew Center on Global Climate Change, http://www.pewclimate.org/docUploads/Pew%20Center_Global%20Fingerprints_3.06.pdf.

127 **People everywhere are noticing the changes**: Derrick, Z. Jackson, "A Duck Hunt for Global Warming," *Boston Globe,* December 2, 2006, at http://www.pewclimate.org/docUploads/Pew%20Center_Global%20Fingerprints_3.06.pdf.

128 **half of all carbon dioxide released . . . has been absorbed by the oceans**: Elizabeth Kolbert, "The Darkening Sea: What Carbon Emissions Are Doing to the Ocean," *New Yorker,* November 20, 2006, at http://www.newyorker.com/fact/content/articles/061120fa_fact3.

128 **Such significant alterations in the ocean's chemistry**: Kathy Tedesco et al., "Impacts of Anthropogenic CO_2 on Ocean Chemistry and Biology," at http://www.research.noaa.gov/spotlite/spot_gcc.html.

129 **Over the past century, the sea level has risen some 4 to 8 inches**: IPCC, "Summary for Policymakers," *Climate Change 2001: Scientific Basis. Contribution of Working Group I to the Third Assessment Report of the Intergovernmental Panel on Climate Change,* page 4, at http://www.ipcc.ch/pub/spm22-01.pdf.

131 **Over the past century, the average local temperature within the park has increased**: Daniel B. Fagre, "Global Environmental Effects on the Mountain Ecosystem at Glacier National Park," *Natural Resource Year in Review–2002,* National Park Service, at http://www2.nature.nps.gov/yearinreview/yir2002/03_C.html.

134 **even if we were able . . . to completely stop emitting greenhouse gases**: IPCC, "Technical Summary," *Climate Change 2001: Scientific Basis. A Report of Working Group I of the Intergovernmental Panel on Climate Change,* pages 75–76 and Figure 25, at http://www.grida.no/climate/ipcc_tar/wg1/pdf/WG1_TAR-FRONT.PDF.

135 **At the current rate . . . carbon dioxide levels would double . . . by around**

the middle of the century: Elizabeth Kolbert, "The Darkening Sea: What Carbon Emissions Are Doing to the Ocean," *New Yorker*, November 20, 2006, at http://www.newyorker.com/fact/content/articles/061120fa_fact 3.

135 quite possibly reaching a tripling of the pre-industrial level by 2100: "Climate Change Post-2100: What Are the Implications of Continued Greenhouse Gas Buildup?" Congressional Briefing Session, Spring 2005, Environmental and Energy Study Institute, at http://www.eesi.org/publications/Briefing%20Summaries/9.21.04%20Post-2100%20Climate.pdf.

137 an increase of 3.6 degrees Fahrenheit is flirting with disaster: Frank Ackerman and Elizabeth Stanton, *Climate Change: Costs of Inaction*, Report to Friends of the Earth, October 2006, at http://www.foe.co.uk/resource/reports/econ_costs_cc.pdf.

137 More recent data about the melting rate of the Greenland and Antarctic ice sheet: "Satellite Gravity Measurements Confirm Accelerating Melting of Greenland Ice Sheet," *Science* 313 (September 29, 2006):1958–1960.

138 The disappearance of the West Antarctic Ice Sheet would mean: Frank Ackerman and Elizabeth Stanton, *Climate Change: Costs of Inaction*, Report to Friends of the Earth, October 2006, at http://www.foe.co.uk/resource/reports/econ_costs_cc.pdf.

138 "NASA Sees Rapid Changes in Arctic Sea Ice," NASA News Archive, September 13, 2006, at http://earthobservatory.nasa.gov/Newsroom/Nasa News/2006/2006091323081.htm.

138 Michael McCarthy and David Usborne, "Massive Surge in Disappearance of Sea Ice Sparks Global Warning," *The Independent*, September 15, 2006, at http://news.independent.co.uk/environment/article1603667.ece.

140 the United States ranked fifty-third in taking steps to address global warming: Elizabeth A. Kennedy, "Sweden Tops Climate Change List," Associated Press, November 13, 2006, at http://www.washingtonpost.com/wp-dyn/content/article/2006/11/13/AR2006111300700_pf.html.

140 The Kyoto Protocol can be viewed online, at http://unfccc.int/resource/docs/convkp/kpeng.html.

142 To read the Byrd-Hagel Resolution, go to http://www.nationalcenter.org/KyotoSenate.html.

CHAPTER SIX: DRILL, THEN DRILL SOME MORE

146 Energy-related carbon dioxide emissions . . . represent 82 percent of the total human-derived greenhouse gas emissions: "Greenhouse Gases, Climate Change, and Energy," Energy Information Administration, U.S. Department of Energy, at http://www.eia.doe.gov/oiaf/1605/ggccebro/chapter1.html.

147 we produce about 25 percent of the carbon dioxide emitted globally:

"Greenhouse Gases, Climate Change, and Energy," Energy Information Administration, U.S. Department of Energy, at http://www.eia.doe.gov/oiaf/1605/ggccebro/chapter1.html.

147 **President Richard Nixon . . . declared that by 1980, "the United States will not be dependent on any other country for the energy we need"**: Richard Nixon, State of the Union Address, January 30, 1974, at http://www.presidency.ucsb.edu/sou.php.

147 **President Gerald Ford extended the deadline**: Gerald Ford, State of the Union Address, January 15, 1975, at http://www.ford.utexas.edu/LIBRARY/SPEECHES/750028.htm.

147 **President Ronald Reagan was promising to "ensure that our people and our economy are never again held hostage<el>"**: Ronald Reagan, Remarks on the Opening of the International Energy Exposition, May 1, 1982, at http://www.reagan.utexas.edu/archives/speeches/1982/50182d.htm.

148 **"Improving America's oil security is the most significant near-term energy challenge the U.S. faces"**: R. James Woolsey, "Energy, U.S. National Security, and the Middle East," Media Monitors Network, May 7, 2005, at http://usa.mediamonitors.net/content/view/full/14737/.

148 For information on annual U.S. energy consumption, see reports by the Energy Information Administration, U.S. Department of Energy, at http://www.eia.doe.gov.

149 **About 77 percent of the world's 1.1 trillion barrels in proven oil reserves is controlled by governments that significantly restrict access**: Justin Blum, "National Oil Firms Take Bigger Role; Governments Hold Most of World's Reserves," API, August 3, 2005, at http://www.api.org/aboutoilgas/security/blumnatoilfirms.cfm.

149 **Middle East . . . contains a remarkable 60 percent of the world's oil reserves**: Energy Information Administration, U.S. Department of Energy, at http://www.eia.doe.gov/oiaf/ieo/pdf/oil.pdf.

149 **Global dependence on fossil fuels is projected to intensify**: Energy Information Administration, U.S. Department of Energy, *International Energy Outlook 2006*, Chapter 1, at http://www.eia.doe.gov/oiaf/aeo/pdf/table1.pdf.

149 **Energy-related carbon dioxide emissions worldwide are set to rise . . . 75 percent**: Energy Information Administration, U.S. Department of Energy, *International Energy Outlook 2006*, Chapter 7, at http://www.eia.doe.gov/oiaf/ieo/pdf/emissions.pdf.

149 **China is already building the equivalent of one large coal-fired power station a week**: Keith Bradsher and David Barboza, "Pollution from Chinese Coal Casts a Global Shadow," *New York Times*, June 11, 2006.

149 **new generating facilities in operation by 2030 could collectively introduce . . . as much CO_2**: David G. Hawkins, Daniel A. Lashof, and Robert H. Williams, "What to Do About Coal," *Scientific American*, September 2006.

149 **Coal-fired power plants now account for about 50 percent of the power generated in the United States and . . . this will increase to 57 percent by 2030**: Energy Information Administration, U.S. Department of Energy, *International Energy Outlook 2006,* Chapter 6, at http://www.eia.doe.gov/oiaf/ieo/electricity.html.

150 **power providers . . . are expected to build the equivalent of nearly 280 large coal-fired electricity plants between 2003 and 2030**: David G. Hawkins, Daniel A. Lashof and Robert H. Williams, "What to Do About Coal," *Scientific American,* September 2006.

150 **fuel efficiency standards . . . have remained essentially unchanged since 1980**: Alliance to Save Energy, "Closing CAFE Standard Loopholes," at http://www.ase.org/images/lib/policy/cafeloopholes2.pdf#search=%22%22Closing%20CAF%C3%89%20Standard%20Loopholes%22%22.

150 **it gets an average of 60 miles per gallon in city driving**: James R. Healey, "New-Car Miles Per-Gallon Estimates to Drop Next Year," *USA Today*, December 11, 2006.

150 **two Japanese companies dominate the market**: http://www.forbesautos.com/news/features/2006/phevs/plug-in-hybrids_4.html.

150 **The first American-manufactured hybrid was not launched until 2004**: "History of Hybrid Vehicles," at http://www.hybridcars.com/history/history-of-hybrid-vehicles.html.

151 **By 2006, market analysts were reporting that 57 percent of all U.S. car shoppers had considered buying a hybrid**: J. D. Power and Associates, "Honda, Toyota, Ford, and Volkswagen Land the Most Vehicles at the Top of the Inaugural Automotive Environmental Index," August 31, 2006, at http://www.jdpower.com/global/pressreleases/pressrelease.asp?StudyID=1171.

151 For more on Honda's FCX Concept, see http://world.honda.com/Tokyo2005/fcx/. For more on Toyota's Fine-X, see http://www.carbodydesign.com/concept-cars/2005/10-14-toyota-fine-x-concept/toyota-fine-x-concept.php.

151 **nearly 6 million vehicles can be fueled by E85, but less than 1 percent of the service stations have even a single E85 pump**: "Automakers Want More Ethanol Pumps," at http://www.consumeraffairs.com/news04/2006/03/ethanol_congress.html; see also "E85 and Flex Fuel Vehicles," at http://www.epa.gov/smartway/growandgo/documents/factsheet-e85.htm

152 **Brazil has stopped importing oil entirely**: Adam Lashinsky and Nelson D. Schwartz, "How to Beat the High Cost of Gasoline Forever!" *Money,* January 24, 2006, http://money.cnn.com/magazines/fortune/fortune_archive/2006/02/06/8367959/index.htm.

153 **President Bush signed Executive Order 13212, which directed federal agencies to expedite their review of permits**: See Executive Order 13212, athttp://www.whitehouse.gov/news/releases/2003/05/20030516-4.html.

153 **BLM approved a plan for natural gas development on 8 million acres of the basin**: Environmental Working Group, "Who Owns the West? Oil and Gas Leases," at http://www.ewg.org/oil_and_gas/part9.php.

153 **BLM were so busy processing drilling permits that staff had to put compliance inspections . . . on the back burner**: Government Accountability Office, *Oil and Gas Development: Increased Permitting Activity Has Lessened BLM's Ability to Meet Its Environmental Protection Responsibilities*, GAO-05-418, at http://www.gao.gov/new.items/d05418.pdf.

154 **BLM . . . received 172 requests from energy companies for exemptions from endangered species protections**: Wilderness Society, "New Information Documents Bush Administration's Land-Management Shift," at http://www.wilderness.org/NewsRoom/Release/20040526.cfm.

154 **Bush administration announced plans to drill more than 1.2 million acres of Otero Mesa**: Wilderness Society, "Too Wild to Drill: Otero Mesa, New Mexico," at http://www.wilderness.org/WhereWeWork/NewMexico/TWTD-Otero.cfm.

154 **Energy companies are also hoping to drill inside the Valle Vidal**: John Arnold, "Valle Vidal Drilling Banned," *Albuquerque Journal,* December 14, 2006, at http://www.abqjournal.com/north/520770north_news12-14-06.htm.

154 **In the Rocky Mountain West, 95 percent of lands managed by the BLM are now available for oil and gas leasing**: "Access to Public Lands," in *Energy and Western Wildlands: A GIS Analysis of Economically Recoverable Oil and Gas,* page 5, at http://www.wilderness.org/Library/Documents/upload/Western-Wildlands-GIS-Analysis-Access-West-Lands.pdf.

155 Information on the HD Mountains and the proposed gas drilling can be found at the Web site of the San Juan Citizens Alliance, at http://www.sanjuancitizens.org/hd_mtns/hd_mtns.shtml and at http://www.savehdmountains.org.

156 **The first coalbed-methane well was drilled in the Ignacio Blanco–Fruitland gas field**: "History of Coalbed Methane Gas Well Spacing," at http://www.oil-gas.state.co.us/Library/sanjuanbasin/blm/Background/cbch4ws.htm.

157 **there's only enough coalbed methane to supply the United States for five years**: U.S. Geological Survey, "Coalbed Methane Activities in the Energy Resources Program," at http://energy.cr.usgs.gov/oilgas/cbmethane/.

157 **Enough natural gas to supply the United States for just two days**: Jim Greenhill, "Study: Resources Not Worth Drilling in the HDs," *Durango Herald,* December 5, 2002, at http://www.durangoherald.com/asp-bin/article_generation.asp?article_type=out&article_path=/outdoors/out021205.htm.

157 For information on the Roadless Area Conservation Rule, see updates at http://roadless.fs.fed.us/.

158   To read the Final Environmental Impact Statement, go to link at http://
      www.fs.fed.us/r2/sanjuan/news/2006/nsjb.shtml. See also the Web site of
      local advocacy group Save the HD Mountains, at http://www.savehdmoun-
      tains.org/.

158   **In 2005, four homes near existing wells on the Fruitland Formation out-
      crop had to be abandoned**: For a discussion of the hazards associated with
      drilling on the Fruitland outcrop, see "Likely Consequences of Drilling
      on the Outcrop," at http://www.savehdmountains.org/outcrop.htm.

160   **A young girl who climbed onto a pump last year died instantly**: Valerie
      Gritton, "Girl, 12, Dies Playing on Pump Jack," *Farmington Daily Times,*
      April 5, 2005, at http://www.pbpa.info/archives/newsletters/05_05.html.

160   For information on the impacts of drilling for coalbed methane gas, see
      Oil and Gas Accountability Project, *Oil and Gas at Your Door? A Landowner's
      Guide to Oil and Gas Development,* 2nd ed. (Durango: OGAP, 2005), available
      at http://www.earthworksaction.org/LOguidechapters.cfm#CHAPTERS.

160   **In 2004 . . . there were approximately 18,000 total producing wells around
      Farmington, New Mexico, and a plan . . . for nearly 10,000 more**: "Broad
      Coalition Sends Message to BLM: Do Oil and Gas Right," press release,
      Natural Resources Defense Council, at https://www.nrdc.org/media/
      pressreleases/040204.asp.

161   **In 1916, the federal government retained the mineral rights under all
      lands granted to settlers**: Environmental Working Group, *Who Owns the
      West?* Executive Summary, at http://www.ewg.org/oil_and_gas/printer
      friendly.php.

161   Interviews and see Tweeti Blancett, "Why I Fight: The Coming Gas Explo-
      sion in the West," May 5, 2003, at http://www.hcn.org/serlets/hcn.Article?
      article_id-13965.

161   **Today, of the 700 million mineral acres the U.S. government owns nation-
      wide, 58 million of these are under privately owned lands**: "BLM to Hold
      Listening Session in Washington on Split Estate Issues," BLM press release,
      at http://www.blm.gov/nhp/news/releases/pages/2006/pr060302_se.
      htm.

161   **Over the past two decades, more than 500,000 cattlemen have sold their
      stock and quit**: See Paul Hawken, "On Corporate Responsibility," at
      http://www.commondreams.org/views02/0602-01.htm.

165   **XTO oil company . . . whose 2005 profits totaled $1.15 billion and whose
      CEO was compensated $32 million**: See XTO Energy annual report
      at http://phx.corporate-ir.net/phoenix.zhtml?c=97780&p=irol-reports
      Annual.

166   **Fracing, used in most CBM well operations, was originally developed in
      1949 . . . by Halliburton**: "Halliburton Celebrates 50-Year Anniversary of
      Process That 'Energized' Oil and Gas Industry," press release, June 21,
      1999, at http://www.halliburton.com/news/archive/1999/hesnws_0621
      99.jsp.

CHAPTER SEVEN: PROSPECTING FOR THE FUTURE

170   **In 1901, the *New York Herald Tribune*.** See news article at http://www.iht. com/articles/2001/01/17/edold.t_34.php.

173   For more information on TI's green building, go to http://www.ti.com/ corp/docs/rennerroadfab/sitefeatures.shtml.

174   **U.S. energy use per dollar of gross national:** Worldwatch Institute and Center for American Progress, American Energy: The Renewable Path to Energy Security (Washington, D.C.: Worldwatch Institute, 2006).

174   **the government established efficiency standards:** Ibid.

175   **stronger efficiency standards for air conditioners:** Bill Prindle, "How Energy Efficiency Can Turn 1300 New Power Plants into 170," Alliance to Save Energy, May 2, 2001, at http://www.crest.org/articles/static/1/9913 45218_982762890.html.

175   **energy efficiency can be strongly linked to profitability:** The Climate Group, "Low Carbon Leaders of the Decade," http://www.theclimate-group.org/assets/Low%20Carbon%20Leaders.%20Final%20List.12-1-05. doc.

175   **"DuPont's investment in energy efficiency:** DuPont, "An Expanded Commitment," at http://www2.dupont.com/Sustainability/en_US/Newsroom /speeches/coh_101006.html.

176   **renewable sources supply just over 6 percent of total:** Worldwatch Institute and Center for American Progress, *American Energy: The Renewable Path to Energy Security* (Washington, D.C.: Worldwatch Institute, 2006), page 6.

176   **The Stateline Wind Energy Center:** "About the Stateline Wind Energy Center," PPM Energy, at http://www.ppmenergy.com/stateline.html.

177   **6 percent . . . is suitable for wind power:** Apollo Alliance, "Wind Energy 101," at http://www.apolloalliance.org/strategy_center/reports_and_ resources/clean_energy_101/wind101.cfm.

177   **we get only 1 percent of our nation's electricity supply from wind:** American Wind Energy Association, at http://www.awea.org/pubs/factsheets/ WindEnergyAnUntappedResource01-13-04.pdf.

177   **study by the CALPIRG Charitable Trust:** "Renewables Work: Job Growth from Renewable Energy Development in California," at http://www.cal pirg.org/reports/renewableswork.pdf.

177   **As the Apollo Alliance explains:** Apollo Alliance, "Solar Energy 101," at http://www.apolloalliance.org/strategy_center/reports_and_resources/ clean_energy_101/solar101.cfm.

178   **Swanson founded SunPower in 1985:** "Sunny Side Up," *Stanford Magazine,* January/February 2007, at http://www.stanfordalumni.org/news/ magazine/2007/janfeb/dept/sunpower.html.

179   **SunPower is but one of the companies:** Apollo Alliance, "Solar Energy

101," at http://www.apolloalliance.org/strategy_center/reports_and_resources/clean_energy_101/solar101.cfm.

179 **We have used biomass energy**: Apollo Alliance, "Biomass Energy 101," at http://www.apolloalliance.org/strategy_center/reports_and_resources/clean_energy_101/biomass101.cfm#_ftn13.

179 **30 percent of transportation fuels with biofuels by 2030**: "Factsheet: The President's Biofuels Initiative to Reduce Foreign Oil Dependence," at http://www1.eere.energy.gov/biomass/initiative_sheet.pdf.

179 **Led by Jason Hill**: "Ethanol Fuel Presents a Corn-undrum," *UMN News,* July 18, 2006, at http://www1.umn.edu/umnnews/Feature_Stories/Ethanol_fuel_presents_a_cornundrum.html.

180 **bioethanol derived primarily from corn contributes**: "Building a Sustainable Biofuel Production System," *News Journal,* College of Chemistry, UC–Berkeley, at http://chemistry.berkeley.edu/Publications/journal/volume14/no1/content/global_warming_p4.html.

181 **to follow Monroe County's lead**: Apollo Alliance, "Biomass Energy 101," at http://www.apolloalliance.org/strategy_center/reports_and_resources/clean_energy_101/biomass101.cfm#_ftn13.

182 **These dynamic growth rates**: Worldwatch Institute and Center for American Progress, *American Energy: The Renewable Path to Energy Security* (Washington, D.C.: Worldwatch Institute, 2006).

182 **The prominent positions that Germany**: Ibid.

183 **360 megawatts of new green power projects**: See the Group's report at http://www.thegreenpowergroup.org/groupevents.cfm?loc=us.

183 **the largest green power purchases**: "Large Purchasers of Green Power," Department of Energy, Energy Efficiency and Renewable Energy, at http://www.eere.energy.gov/greenpower/buying/customers.shtml?page=1&companyid=113&print.

183 **Timberland built an impressive solar power system**: "Timberland Affirms Commitment to the Environment," press release April 17, 2006, at http://www.socialfunds.com/news/release.cgi/5414.html.

183 **Interface . . . is using the gas from decomposing organic materials**: "Landfill Gas Emissions to Power Interface Flooring Systems Plant," at http://www.interfacesustainability.com/landfill.html.

184 **more coal is being burned now than ever before**: "Annual Coal Report (2005)," Energy Information Administration, Department of Energy, at http://www.eia.doe.gov/cneaf/coal/page/acr/acr_sum.html.

184 **Techniques have been developed—called CO_2 capture and storage (CCS)**: David G. Hawkins, Daniel A. Lashof, and Robert H. Williams, "What to Do About Coal," *Scientific American,* September 2006, page 70.

184 **geologic media worldwide are capable of sequestering . . . CO_2**: Ibid.

184 **In Texas, sixteen new coal-fired plants are proposed**: Randy Lee Loftis, "Texas Cool to Confront Global Warming," *Dallas Morning News,* Septem-

ber 3, 2006, at http://www.dallasnews.com/sharedcontent/dws/dn/latest news/stories/090306dnproglobal.3350a24.html.

185   **AEP has proposed two new power plants**: Craig Canine, "How to Clean Coal," Natural Resources Defense Council, at http://www.nrdc.org/on earth/05fal/coal.pdf.

186   **twenty-nine nuclear power plants are being built globally**: "The Latest News Related to PRIS and the Status on Nuclear Power Plants," at http://www.iaea.org/programmes/a2/.

186   **In the 1930s, only 10 percent of rural America had electricity**: "Electric Market Restructuring: Issues for Rural America," at http://www.ers.usda.gov/publications/ruralamerica/ra171/ra171a.pdf.

187   **Mayor Rocky Anderson, Salt Lake City . . . has made great strides**: Doug Smeat, "Rocky Notes Salt Lake's Progress in His State of City Address," *Deseret News,* January 17, 2007, at http://deseretnews.com/dn/view/0,1249, 650223613,00.html.

187   Read the U.S. Mayors Climate Protection Agreement and the list of signatories, at http://www.seattle.gov/mayor/climate/#media.

188   For more information on the California Global Warming Solutions Act, including a copy of the legislation, go to http://www.pewclimate.org/what_s_being_done/in_the_states/ab32/index.cfm.

188   **California represents the sixth largest economy in the world**: See "Cal Facts 2004," at http://www.lao.ca.gov/2004/cal_facts/2004_calfacts_econ.htm.

188   **Massachusetts . . . adopted a Renewable Portfolio Standard**: See "Renewable Portfolio Standard," at http://masstech.org/cleanenergy/policy/rps.htm.

189   Read Portland's Local Action Plan on Global Warming, at http://www.portlandonline.com/shared/cfm/image.cfm?id=112118.

191   **Every gallon of gasoline . . . emits nearly 20 pounds of carbon dioxide**: "How can a gallon of gasoline produce 20 pounds of carbon dioxide?" at http://www.fueleconomy.gov/feg/co2.shtml.

192   **100 percent of the energy used in municipal operations**: "OSD Strategic Plan," City of Portland, Office of Sustainable Development, at http://www.portlandonline.com/shared/cfm/image.cfm?id=130417.

193   **all diesel fuel sold in the city**: "Clean Energy Economic Development," City of Portland, Office of Sustainable Development, at http://www.portlandonline.com/osd/index.cfm?c=ecied.

INDEX

PUBLICAFFAIRS is a publishing house founded in 1997. It is a tribute to the standards, values, and flair of three persons who have served as mentors to countless reporters, writers, editors, and book people of all kinds, including me.

I. F. STONE, proprietor of *I. F. Stone's Weekly,* combined a commitment to the First Amendment with entrepreneurial zeal and reporting skill and became one of the great independent journalists in American history. At the age of eighty, Izzy published *The Trial of Socrates,* which was a national bestseller. He wrote the book after he taught himself ancient Greek.

BENJAMIN C. BRADLEE was for nearly thirty years the charismatic editorial leader of *The Washington Post.* It was Ben who gave the *Post* the range and courage to pursue such historic issues as Watergate. He supported his reporters with a tenacity that made them fearless, and it is no accident that so many became authors of influential, best-selling books.

ROBERT L. BERNSTEIN, the chief executive of Random House for more than a quarter century, guided one of the nation's premier publishing houses. Bob was personally responsible for many books of political dissent and argument that challenged tyranny around the globe. He is also the founder and was the longtime chair of Human Rights Watch, one of the most respected human rights organizations in the world.

For fifty years, the banner of Public Affairs Press was carried by its owner Morris B. Schnapper, who published Gandhi, Nasser, Toynbee, Truman, and about 1,500 other authors. In 1983 Schnapper was described by *The Washington Post* as "a redoubtable gadfly." His legacy will endure in the books to come.

Peter Osnos, *Founder and Editor-at-Large*